How to Build BIG-INCH CHEVY SMALL-BLOCKS

Graham Hansen

CarTech®

CarTech®

CarTech®, Inc.
838 Lake Street South
Forest Lake, MN 55025
Phone: 651-277-1200 or 800-551-4754
Fax: 651-277-1203
www.cartechbooks.com

© 2011 by Graham Hansen

All rights reserved. No part of this publication may be reproduced or utilized in any form or by any means, electronic or mechanical, including photocopying, recording, or by any information storage and retrieval system, without prior permission from the Publisher. All text, photographs, and artwork are the property of the Author unless otherwise noted or credited.

The information in this work is true and complete to the best of our knowledge. However, all information is presented without any guarantee on the part of the Author or Publisher, who also disclaim any liability incurred in connection with the use of the information and any implied warranties of merchantability or fitness for a particular purpose. Readers are responsible for taking suitable and appropriate safety measures when performing any of the operations or activities described in this work.

All trademarks, trade names, model names and numbers, and other product designations referred to herein are the property of their respective owners and are used solely for identification purposes. This work is a publication of CarTech, Inc., and has not been licensed, approved, sponsored, or endorsed by any other person or entity. The Publisher is not associated with any product, service, or vendor mentioned in this book, and does not endorse the products or services of any vendor mentioned in this book.

Edit by Travis Thompson

ISBN 978-1-61325-325-0
Item No. SA87P

Library of Congress Cataloging-in-Publication Data

Hansen, Graham.
  How to build big-inch Chevy small-blocks / by Graham Hansen.
     p. cm.
  ISBN 978-1-934709-66-5
  1. Chevrolet automobile--Motors--Maintenance and repair--Handbooks, manuals, etc. 2. Chevrolet automobile--Motors--Modification--Handbooks, manuals, etc. 3. Chevrolet automobile--Motors--Cylinder blocks--Handbooks, manuals, etc. I. Title.
  TL215.C5H36 2011
  629.25'2--dc22

2010036412

Written, edited, and designed in the U.S.A.
Printed in the U.S.A.
15 14 13 12 11 10 9

Title Page:
The cool thing about a big-inch small-block is that you can build a seemingly tame looking engine with cast aluminum intake, a single four-barrel carb, and typical production headers and make over 600 hp and 55 ft-lbs of torque. Those are low 11-second quarter-mile times for a 3,400 pound street car.

Back Cover Photos

Top Left:
Does this engine look like a 454? The beauty of a standard-deck small-block is that it takes a well-trained eye to tell when you're packing lots of inches. An internally balanced engine with 23-degree heads can hide 420 to 454 ci from all but the savviest onlooker.

Top Right:
The easiest way to increase displacement is with stroke. With a long stroke crank and big bore, it's possible to create a 454-ci engine out of the same engine envelope that was creates originally as a tiny 265-ci mouse motor.

Middle Left:
The easiest way to tell a forged crank from a casting is by gently hitting a non-machined part of the crank with a small hammer. The forging will ring while a casting will have a dull thump to it. You can also tell a forged crank by its wide forging mark at the crank centerline (right).

Middle Right:
For engine builders using free-floating wrist pins, Spirolocks are the best way to secure them. However, Spirolocks require some skill to install and a special tool to help remove them.

Bottom Left:
Spring seats do more than just protect an aluminum head from damage from the spring. Both o.d. and i.d. spring seats locate the spring to prevent it from moving around at engine speed.

Bottom Right:
It's easy to be deceived by glamorous dyno tests that achieve big horsepower numbers. But for a street car, the key is to balance good horsepower with a decent power curve and excellent torque. This makes for a much more enjoyable street engine.

TABLE OF CONTENTS

Chapter 1: Introduction 4	**Chapter 9: Cylinder Heads** 76
	Iron vs. Aluminum 76
Chapter 2: Stroker Theory 8	Angle of Attack 76
Efficiency Factor 9	Ports o' Call 77
The Torque Curve 10	Evaluating Flow 80
Comparisons 12	Iron Heads 81
The Siren Song of RPM 13	Aluminum Heads 83
	Conclusion 87
Chapter 3: Cylinder Blocks 14	
Early Blocks 14	**Chapter 10: Exhaust Systems** 88
1986 and Later Blocks 16	Exhaust Opening 88
Bow Tie Blocks 17	Primary Pipe Diameter 89
Dart Blocks 19	Primary Pipe Length 90
World Products 20	Collector Effects 91
The Cost of Power 23	Header Variables 93
	H and X-Pipes 94
Chapter 4: Crankshafts 24	Making Everything Fit 95
Crank Basics 24	
Cast Cranks 25	**Chapter 11: Induction Systems** 96
Forged Cranks 27	Induction Theory 96
Stroke 29	Port Length 97
Torsional Dampers 32	Port Size 98
Conclusion 32	Dual-Plane Intakes 98
	Single-Plane Intakes 99
Chapter 5: Connecting Rods 34	Carburetors 101
Stock Rods 34	EFI 104
Material 35	
Stroker Rods 36	**Chapter 12: Lubrication System** ... 108
Fasteners 37	Oil Pumps 109
I-Beam, H-Beam 41	Oil Pans 111
	Synthetics 112
Chapter 6: Pistons and Rings 42	Oil Coolers 113
Materials and Processes 42	Conclusion 113
Dished or Domed? 44	
Compression Height 46	**Chapter 13: Building and Blueprinting** 114
Weight 49	Measuring Tools 120
Rings 49	Assembly Tools 125
Chapter 7: Camshafts 54	**Chapter 14: Power Packages** 126
Flat and Roller 54	Favorites 126
Eccentric Info 56	Test One: 406ci Torque Monster ... 130
Intake Centerline 57	Test Two: 383ci Street Motor ... 131
Lobe Separation Angle 57	Test Three: 415ci Street/Strip ... 132
	Test Four: 383ci Cruise Night Special ... 133
Chapter 8: Valvetrains 64	Test Five: 406ci High Horsepower ... 134
Lifters 64	Test Six: 454ci Monster mouse ... 135
Pushrods and Guideplates 67	Test Seven: 383ci Quarter Pounder ... 136
Retainers 69	
Valvesprings 71	**Appendix A: Source Guide** 137
Rocker Arms 72	
Miscellaneous Components 74	**Engine Build Sheet** 140

How To Build Big-Inch Chevy Small-Blocks

Chapter 1

Introduction

If you subscribe to the notion that too much power is just enough, then we have a book for you. Every day, engine builders are pushing the limits of making power with large displacement small blocks. What was once the realm of exotic race engines has now become fair game for street enthusiasts and those looking for what the late road racer and engineer Mark Donohue called "The Unfair Advantage."

This book will deal strictly with street small-block engine combinations that are based on the first generation small-block Chevy. We will investigate all the different bore and stroke combinations, look at a few of the better parts combinations, and we'll even run through a few power tests to show you what kind of power you can expect from your next small-block adventure. Every small-block part and engine combination

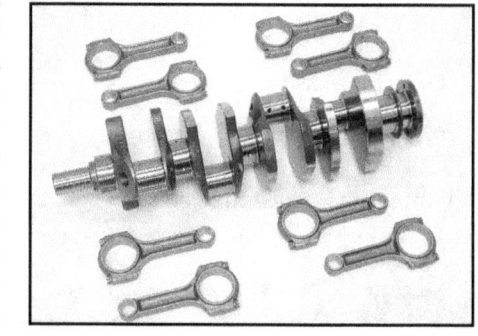

The easiest way to increase displacement is with stroke. With a long stroke crank and a big bore, it's possible to create a 454ci engine out of the same engine envelope that was created originally as a tiny 265ci mouse motor.

will be aimed at street operation. Some combinations will be more adventuresome than others, but we hope to point you in the right direction and give you some ideas about which cylinder heads, camshafts, and induction systems we have found work best in these large displacement applications.

Perhaps the biggest question is not whether to build a stroker small block but rather what style of engine to build. For any single displacement, you could build that engine two or three dozen different ways, ranging from an extremely mild combination that makes excellent off-idle torque, all the way up to an ultra-exotic engine with all the latest race technology for limited street use. The key then becomes defining exactly

Building any small block, regardless of its displacement requires attention to detail and careful assembly procedures. But the result of all that work is a powerful engine that is also incredibly durable.

How To Build Big-Inch Chevy Small-Blocks

Introduction

The key to any engine's power potential is found in the cylinder heads. Careful attention to selecting the best cylinder head, regardless of displacement, will reward you with excellent power. The beauty of a big-inch small block is that it's hard to choose a head thats too big.

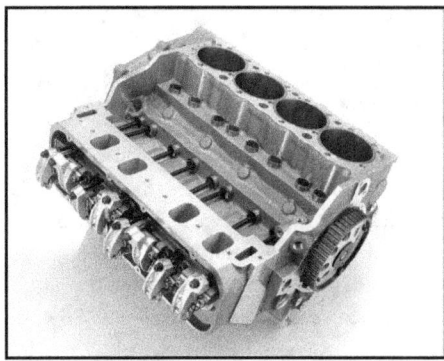

Most of the popular cylinder head manufacturers now offer 14-, 15-, and 18-degree heads for the small-block Chevy that promise incredible power, but are also significantly more expensive. These heads also require expensive valvetrain components. This is a Dart aluminum block with 18-degree heads that sport 2.18/1.625-inch valves.

A big-inch small block doesn't have to be a 454 or 440ci motor. Perhaps the most popular small-block street engine is the 383 that can be built with nothing more than a 4.030-inch bore and an inexpensive cast 3.75-inch stroke crank. This is GM Performance Parts' HT 383 short-block, that is an excellent steel crank starting point for a stroker small block.

how you plan to use this engine. If your next engine is intended to climb mountains all day pulling a horse trailer or a race car, it will be drastically different from a 434ci small block for the drag strip or road course that can push the RPM band way up. There are also various street engine combinations that fall somewhere in between these two ends of the performance spectrum. Being honest about your plans and expectations will go a long way toward achieving your goals. Keep in mind that being conservative and compromising on some of the more radical expectations will probably get your farther in the long run.

Go Big

The edge that the big-inch small block enjoys is the subterfuge factor. Savvy street guys know there are certain production 400ci blocks with only two freeze plugs per side. Add an internally balanced stroker crank, and you could construct a 420ci small block that appears to all the world like a 350. Even with a lumpy cam, no one would expect a 350 to run like a big block, but 500 hp and gobs of torque are easy goals to attain when you start with a bunch more cubic inches.

The only limitation to going big is the depth of your wallet. Even a very conservative 1.2 hp per cubic inch (ci) factor will deliver 520 hp from a 434ci engine compared to only 426 hp from a 355. But beyond the horsepower is the torque that is generated by large displacement engines.

Displacement generates torque. That's why earthmovers and big trucks employ huge displacement engines that spin very slowly. They don't make much in the way of horsepower, but they do make loads of torque. The beauty of this concept is that you can build a rather mild, larger displacement small block that can generate exceptional torque and still have an engine with an almost-stock idle quality. This engine could be capable of quick e.t.s and production-like part-throttle operation with lightning-quick throttle response.

This book will address any small block larger than 355ci as a large displacement engine. The most popular upgrade is the 383, which is the easiest stroker small block you can build. Take one production 350 block, bore it 0.030-inch oversize, add a 3.75-inch stroke crank from a 400 small block, and that will give you a 383. In the early days of this swap, the 400 crank's main journals had to be ground down to the smaller 350 diameter. This displacement upgrade has become so popular that you don't even have to bother looking for a used crank,

Chapter 1

Hidden Horsepower

One of the great things about a big-inch small block is the fact that it is extremely difficult to tell the displacement of an engine by its external appearance. This means you can build a large displacement small block, like a 420-434-454ci mouse, and tell the world it's a 355 or 383. There are only a few giveaways, and generally you can hide these as well.

If you are using a production 400ci block, most of these use three freeze plugs along the side of the block. But there were a few two-freeze-plug blocks that look like a 350 block. The other obvious giveaway is a production iron harmonic damper with an offset weight, because 400ci small blocks are externally balanced. We'll get into what this means in the crankshaft chapter, but suffice to say for now that it is relatively easy to hide this kind of balancer, or better yet, have the engine internally balanced so that this detail never shows up at all. The only other external clue is if you are using an aftermarket block, like one from GM Performance Parts, Dart, or World Products. These blocks are easily spotted by the more knowledgeable hot rodders, but even this can be accounted for by telling them that you're sporting a 383.

So why would you want to hide the fact that you're packing more inches? On the street scene, streetlight acceleration contests are commonplace. The key if and when you're faced with one of these is much like playing poker: don't show your hand to anyone. If they ask (and they will), you tell them as little as possible. How far you want to go in hiding displacement is up to you. Keep in mind that a big-inch motor will hide a relatively big camshaft with a decent idle. Tuning the engine so that the idle isn't too lumpy is also in your favor. However, one aspect that is hard to cover up is the sound your engine makes. Big cubic-inch small blocks have an unmistakable exhaust note that sounds all the word like a rat motor because of the large displacement. The savvy street runners will be attuned to that sound and figure out your game soon enough. But perhaps you can make a few of them tumble before they get wise. It's all in how you play the game!

Compression helps make power, but if you stay below 9.5:1 with iron and 10.5:1 with aluminum heads, most street engines can stay out of detonation. This is no small deal when the cost of even 100-octane unleaded is $3 to $4 per gallon.

since companies like Eagle, Scat, Crower, Callies, and many others now offer drop-in 3.75-inch stroke cranks in numerous configurations and materials. We'll get into more detail in the chapter on crankshafts. The point is that these engines are incredibly easy to build, the parts are available, and the milder versions of some of these stroker motors can cost only slightly more than a stock small-block rebuild. When you have an opportunity like that, it's hard to pass it up.

Of course, for each displacement, you have literally hundreds of options. For truck towing or off-road, rock-crawling applications, a 383, 406, or larger small block with small heads and a mild cam can offer big-block torque capability without the weight or cost penalties. Take those same displacement engines, add slightly larger heads, a more aggressive cam, and a good dual-plane intake manifold, and you the opportunity to make impressive torque and horsepower without sacrificing mid-range power. For example, you could build a 383 using mid-sized heads like a set of Airflow Research 195cc heads or the excellent castings from Canfield or TFS and create a stormin' small block that could easily generate in excess of 500 ft-lb of torque and 450-plus horsepower. This would be a slightly more expensive engine since it would

The beauty of a standard deck small-block is that it takes a well-trained eye to tell when you're packin' lots of inches. An internally balanced engine with 23-degree heads can hide 420 to 454ci from all but the savviest onlooker.

Introduction

Exotic induction systems are not really necessary for a stout naturally aspirated small block. 600 to 650 hp is possible with a single 850 cfm carb and a single-plane manifold.

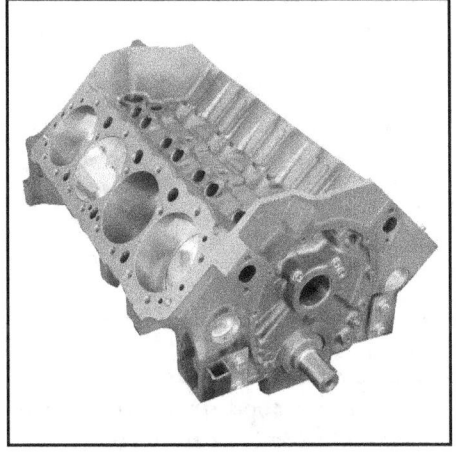

You don't have to know all the details about building engines to play in this arena. There are literally dozens of companies that will build either a short block or the entire engine for you if you desire.

A big-inch small block also has to be able to breathe on the exhaust side as well. Properly sized headers and a high-flowing exhaust system are crucial to making good horsepower and torque.

employ a hydraulic roller camshaft, but it could still be affordable (well below $7,000 from carburetor to oil pan).

Of course, there's also the big-inch, max-output engines that everybody dreams of building. We like to call these efforts "bottom of the page" engines because these guys just go straight to the bottom of the catalog page for the biggest heads, the biggest cam, and the tallest intake manifold to construct a monster engine that will make killer power. The scary part about this plan is that it is so easy to do. Most of the exotic parts are available right off the shelf. Dart builds 23-degree CNC-machined heads that push into the 230cc intake port range! That's only slightly smaller than an oval port big-block cylinder head. If you really want to get exotic, you could also step up to the race-oriented 15-degree, 18-degree, and SB-2-style heads that stand the valves more vertical for even better flow.

We're not even talking about custom, one-off castings, but about parts that are currently sitting on the shelf. You can also expect to get into some serious coin when you start shopping on the NHRA drag racing and Winston Cup shelves, but you can believe that a set of SB2.2 heads on a 454ci small-block with 10.5:1 compression and a single 4-barrel carburetor (or a state of the art EFI package) could easily be worth over 700 hp and in excess of 600 ft-lb of torque.

So where does all this lead us? Right back to parts catalogs and the question of what kind of engine you want to build. We will look at what's available, where to find the parts, and their cost. We'll also identify the best parts and pencil out a few engine combinations to help you assemble a small block that you'd love to thrash. Along the way, you'll also get an idea of the importance of the proper combination of parts. One goal for this book is to introduce the concept of the systems approach to engine designing. We use that word because that's what you're doing. Assembling an engine is just screwing it together. The important part is designing each part to work with the next to create a system that makes the most power for the least investment. Assemble the right collection of parts, and you can end up with a solid small block that will run like a rat, impress all your friends, and cost much less than the price of a new car.

CHAPTER 2

STROKER THEORY

This book is dedicated to a singular purpose — to investigate the opportunities that exist to build a large displacement small-block Chevy. Horsepower and torque depend on several situations that exist within an internal combustion engine, but one crucial component is displacement. Compute the volume of a cylinder based on the diameter of the bore and the length of the piston's stroke and you have a displacement in cubic inches. Multiply that by its number of cylinders, and you have size of your engine (see the "Calculating Displacement" sidebar). We're going to investigate how to stretch the conservative boundaries of that original 265ci small-block Chevy and see how many extra inches we can squeeze into that small-block case.

Let's start with a few basic parameters that determine how big an engine we can build. Bore spacing is a term used to describe the distance between the centerline of each cylinder. A small-block Chevy has a bore spacing of 4.40-inches, which means there is a finite amount of room to make the cylinders larger in diameter. The original 1955 265ci small block had a very small 3.75-inch bore that had grown to 4.125-inches by 1970. As you can guess, this leaves very little room to make the cylinders much larger. All original small blocks utilized cooling water jackets that surrounded each cylinder. The exception to this is the 400ci small-block case that employs siamesed cylinders that connect the common cylinder walls to enhance structural rigidity. This removes cooling water from between the cylinders, which created all kinds of early rumors of cooling problems with the original 400ci small block that history has proved unfounded.

As you can see, unless we stretch the bore spacing of our original small block, it will be difficult to increase the bore much beyond about 4.155-inches (0.030-inch overbore on a stock 4.125-inch bore) for most production blocks. The reason for this is the cylinder walls become much too thin to remain stable at high horsepower and torque output.

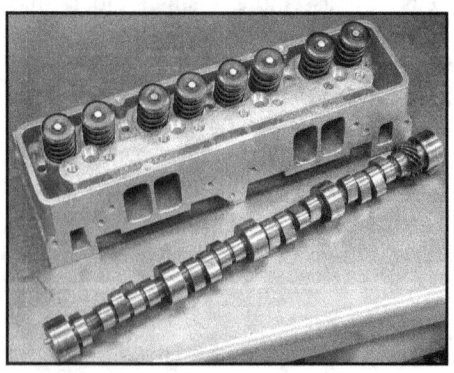

Building an engine is more than just assembling the parts. You want to think about the entire system and how each of these components will work together to make good power.

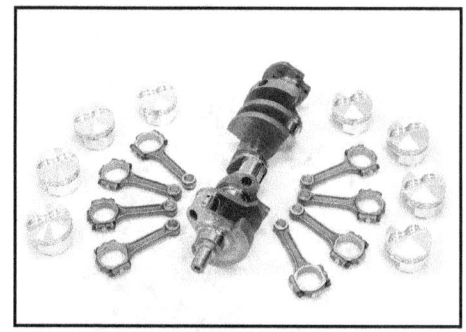

Displacement is all about bore and stroke. With a good steel stroker crank and quality big-bore pistons, you can assemble anywhere from a 406 to 440ci small block for around $2,000.

When the cylinder walls begin to move around, we lose ring seal and power will fall off. However, both GM and the aftermarket has come up with several subsequent versions of the small-block Chevy that allow slightly larger bores to increase displacement while retaining the small-block's standard 4.40-inch bore spacing. We will get into those details in the chapter on cylinder blocks, but it's possible to expand the bore size out to an amazing 4.250-inches, while still using the small block 4.40-inch bore spacing.

If we are limited in bore diameter, then the next place to look to increase displacement is with stroke. Here, we have a little more room to move around. The original 265ci small block used a very short 3.00-inch stroke and the block was designed with plenty of clearance in the crankcase area for a larger stroke. Again by 1970, GM engineers had stretched that stroke out to 3.75-inches to create the 400. Increasing stroke means you must also increase the size of the crankshaft counterweights in order to offset the weight of the piston and rod swinging through a larger arc. This means there must be room inside the crankcase to accommodate these larger counterweights. Where this clearance usually becomes critical is at the bottom of the cylinder bores and the oil pan mounting rails. Larger strokes will require additional clearance to prevent interference as the engine spins over.

Another area often overlooked when increasing stroke is the clearance between one or two connecting rods and the camshaft. The increased stroke pushes the large end of the rods closer to the camshaft and often requires custom stroker connecting rods and/or a camshaft with a small base circle to create the required clearance. Of course, you can also opt for a tall-deck block with taller cylinders that also raises the camshaft centerline relative to the crankshaft to allow more clearance. This move also requires other custom components that drive up the price of the engine, but that's something you must factor in when considering which displacement is right for your wallet and your power requirements. We'll get into the specifics of how big we can build a small block in later chapters, but it is possible to build a small-block Chevy up to a 454ci, and even larger, if you are willing to spend the big bucks.

Efficiency Factor

The reason for building a larger displacement engine is to make more power. But it's important to understand where this power will be produced within the power curve. It is an accepted fact of internal combustion engines that power per cubic inch is not a linear function. In other words, horsepower per cubic inch (hp/ci) decreases as displacement increases. All other factors being equal, small displacement engines

If you're going to build a thumper engine, the smart move is to invest in a high-quality aftermarket cylinder block. The price is between $1,700 and $2,200, but the durability is invaluable.

generally make more hp/ci than larger displacement engines. This is due to several factors, including increased friction created by greater piston travel due to longer stroke, larger bearing diameters that create more friction, and the inherent power absorption from larger, heavier components that require power to accelerate their greater mass. Despite these limitations, the larger displacement still makes serious power, which is why everyone is so intrigued with increasingly larger engines.

Let's take a look at each of the two functions of power — torque and horsepower. When cylinder pressure is created on top of the piston, this forces the piston down. Pushing against the crankshaft. The length of the crankshaft arm, or throw, from the crankshaft centerline is leverage that multiplies the piston force and spins the crankshaft. Torque is defined as the twisting motion created by the crankshaft. Without getting into a complex discussion of how dynamometers work, let's shorten the learning curve by describing the typical dyno as using a water brake with a strain gauge

It's easy to be deceived by glamorous dyno tests that achieve big horsepower numbers. But for a street car, the key is to balance good horsepower with a decent power curve and excellent torque. This makes for a much more enjoyable street engine.

to measure the amount of torque the engine creates at any given RPM. This torque can be described as a given amount of twist measured in pounds of force delivered over a given lever length — usually a foot. This creates a force measured in pounds per foot. For example, if we create a force equivalent to placing a one-pound weight on the end of a one-foot long lever, then we've

Chapter 2

One place where you can get away with a big single-plane intake and a big carburetor is with a large displacement small block. With engines of 420ci and larger, those big 850 and 900 cfm 4150-style carburetors can actually be very streetable.

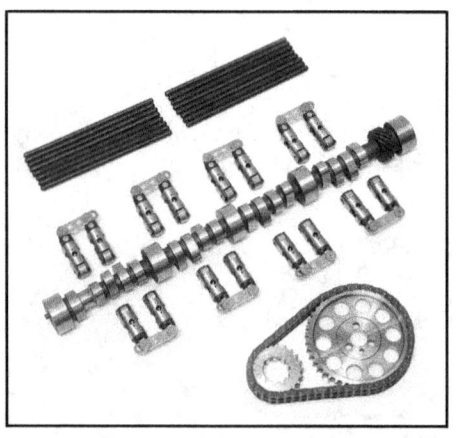

Once you've chosen the cylinder heads, then you can pick a camshaft that will optimize the heads based on their flow potential. While flat-tappet cams do a great job, roller cams will always deliver a little more power.

created one foot-pound of torque. Since engineers like to apply a shorthand to their descriptions to save time, this has been shortened to torque in ft-lbs. So if a given engine generates 400 ft-lb of torque, this could be described as 400 pounds of force exerted over a lever measuring 1 foot in length or in various other equal configurations. This twisting motion tends to be a static function and does not describe work being done since time is not included in this measurement. Work over time is the definition of horsepower.

James Watt (1736-1819) was a Scottish engineer who needed to come up with a way to equate power from his newly developed steam engine to a power level that people could easily understand. Through observation and measurement, Watt developed an estimate that the average draft horse could produce 33,000 ft-lb of work in one minute. This can be shortened in the following equation to the now-standard horsepower equation:

HP = (Torque x 2 x Pi x RPM) / 33,000
HP = TQ x RPM / 5252

As an example, let's say that our 400ci small block makes 450 ft-lb of torque at 4,400 rpm. Given this power output, what is the horsepower?

HP = 450 ft-lb x 4400 rpm/ 5252
HP = 376.99

This formula can also be inverted and used to calculate torque based on horsepower:

TQ = HP x 5252 / RPM

For example, let's say our small block is making 500 hp at 5,000 rpm:

TQ = 500 x 5252/5,000
TQ = 525.2 ft-lb of torque at 5,000 rpm

Now that we have a basic understanding of how torque and horsepower are calculated, we need to know a little more about these power measurements. As we stated earlier, small displacement engines tend to be more efficient due to their shorter stroke, which reduces the piston travel distance, and frictional losses from ring drag. The friction created by cylinder pressure that pushes the rings against the cylinder walls helps to seal the rings, but it also creates massive frictional loads. This friction is power that is lost to heat and represents a little less than 50 percent of the total power lost to heat, friction, and pumping losses. Given this, increasing stroke causes the piston and ring package to travel a greater distance for the same RPM, which means the frictional losses from a

Cylinder heads are a big part of any engine-building plan. In fact, once you have the intended usage and displacement defined, the next thing to decide upon would be the cylinder heads. Here is one place where spending the money will pay off in power.

long-stroke, large-displacement engine will be far greater than an engine with a shorter stroke and smaller displacement. This is the trade-off to building a larger displacement engine.

So if larger displacement engines suffer from all this lost power, why build them? Despite these inherent inefficiencies, adding displacement is still the easiest way to make outstanding power. A good rule of thumb for street type performance engines is 1.1 hp/ci. This means that if you have a 406ci small block, then 406 x 1.1 = 446 hp. Not all street engines will achieve this level of performance. Some may dip down as low a 0.8 hp/ci, while others can push the envelope up as high as 1.25 to 1.30 hp/ci and higher.

While horsepower has always been the most popular measurement, torque is also a big-time player and should not be overlooked. The problem with placing too much emphasis on horsepower is falling into the trap of creating an engine that relies on RPM to create the horsepower while sacrificing low and mid-range torque. For a street engine, this can result in a sluggish engine that requires deep gears and lots of RPM to perform well. Let's take a look at the relationship between torque and horsepower and where the power curve falls.

THE TORQUE CURVE

The advantage that large displacement engines offer is that wonderful kick in the seat of your pants that torque delivers. That long stroke delivered by a

Keep in mind that all the power in the world is of little help if you can't hook it up. Big torque numbers demand excellent traction in order to put all that power to the job of accelerating the car.

larger engine creates displacement that makes torque at extremely low RPM levels. It's this torque that accelerates the vehicle forward. Frictional losses that long-stroke engines must sacrifice occur at all engine speeds. However, at higher RPM the piston must travel that greater distance at the same RPM as a shorter-stroke engine and the friction generated begins to really take its toll on horsepower. However, the added leverage combined with a large piston area really generates some serious torque. It's not unusual for 400ci street engines to create 480 to 530 ft-lb torque output at relatively low engine speeds of 3800 to 4500 rpm. These are power levels more often reserved for big-block engines displacing 454 cubic inches or more. Add in the weight advantage of an aluminum-headed small block weighing as much as 100 to 200 pounds less than an iron-headed big block making the same torque, and it doesn't take much to realize that you have built a much quicker and faster car. This is the advantage of a large displacement small-block Chevy.

When looking at power numbers from an engine dyno, most enthusiasts head straight for the peak horsepower number. The more astute readers will also look at the peak torque and the RPM where each of these power levels are attained. But the truly sharp power connoisseur will closely evaluate not only the peak power levels but also the entire power curve from the lowest RPM test point to how radically the engine falls off its horsepower peak. All of these functions determine how well this engine will perform in a particular vehicle. One of the most important considerations when building a performance engine is to spend time deciding exactly how the engine will be used and in what vehicle it will be used in. These parameters help determine the kind of engine that should be built. Too often, enthusiasts will build an engine based on unrealistic goals or power levels and then place it in a car or other vehicle that is entirely unsuited for it. The result is a car that never performs up to expectations because it was built all wrong in the first place. This is an important point worth

One definite advantage to a big-inch small block is engine weight. An aluminum-headed small block can weigh 100 to 125 pounds less than iron-headed big block. That reduces front-end and overall weight and changes the weight distribution closer to 50/50, which will improve traction.

Calculating Displacement

If you were paying attention in geometry class in high school, then you might remember that the volume of a cylinder is calculated by multiplying pi (3.1417) times the radius of the diameter squared times the length of the cylinder. If we have a bore of 4 inches, then the radius is half of the diameter, or one half of 4, which is 2. With a given stroke of 3.75 inches, we can calculate the volume of this cylinder as 3.1417 x 2 x 2 x 3.75 = 47.1255 cubic inches. We now have one cylinder at 47.1255 times 8 cylinders, that creates 377ci.

We can create a shortcut for this operation by combining one of the earlier steps. If we substitute 0.7854 for the pi times radius squared operation, we can compute displacement by multiplying bore x bore x stroke x 0.7854 x number of cylinders. This is our short formula for computing displacement. For example, with a bore of 4.155 and a stroke of 3.75, we have: 4.155 x 4.155 x 3.75 x 0.7854 x 8 = 406.77ci.

Chapter 2

emphasizing. Engine dynos are great tools for measuring engine power. But ultimately — we race cars, not dynos.

COMPARISONS

Let's look at a 377ci small block that initially looks impressive. Using a 4.155-inch bore 400 block and a steel 3.48-inch stroke crank, this small block used a set of Edelbrock Victor Jr. aluminum heads combined with a rather long duration Isky mechanical roller cam that's spec'd out at 264/272 degrees of duration at 0.050-inch tappet lift. The induction system consists of a Victor Jr. intake and a Barry Grant 750 cfm annular discharge carburetor. The engine created impressive peak numbers with 589 horsepower at 6,500 rpm while peak torque came in at 516 ft-lb of torque at 5,200-5,400 rpm.

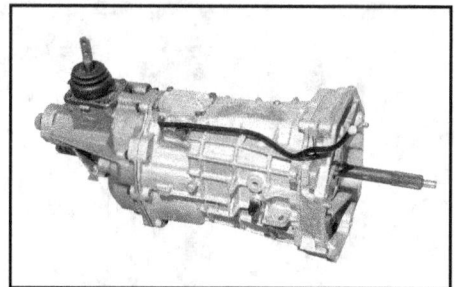

One thing to keep in mind is the type of transmission you will be using. Automatics demand a broader torque band with more mid-range torque. A manual trans, like this T-56 6-speed, with its 2.66:1 first gear ratio and relatively close gear spread, allows the flexibility to build a slightly more aggressive engine with less low-speed torque.

shift point for this engine right at 7,000 rpm, which is serious RPM for a street engine. The torque is also excellent with a 1.37 ft-lb/ci rating but it occurs at a rather high 5,200 rpm. Looking at the low end of the curve, the engine builder decided not to test the engine below 4,200 rpm although the engine did make 434 ft-lb of torque at that point. It's possible that if he had tested the engine at a lower RPM, then engine still would have made at least 400 ft-lb of torque at around 3,800 rpm. Another interesting point is the RPM spread between peak horsepower and peak torque. In this application, there is a relatively narrow 1,200 rpm spread between the two peaks, which means that this engine would work best with a 4 or 5-speed manual transmission to keep it within its power band either in a drag race or road race application.

First, let's acknowledge that this is a serious small block making almost 600 hp! But for a street engine, the long duration camshaft would offer poor idle quality and would be sluggish below 3,000 rpm due to the excessive camshaft overlap. This engine would be better suited with a manual transmission but if an automatic were chosen, it would require at least a 4,000 rpm stall speed converter in order to put the engine closer to the strong part of its torque curve. Ideally, this engine would demand almost a 5,000 rpm converter in order to put it at its torque peak for a drag race application. Again, this is easily accomplished, but it seriously detracts from its street manners.

Now let's investigate a second engine, a 420ci small block using a 4.155-inch bore, a 3.875-inch stroke and a 236/244 degree at 0.050-inch tappet lift mechanical roller Comp Cams camshaft. The induction system consists of mildly ported 195cc Airflow Research heads, a Victor Jr. intake, and a Holley 750-cfm HP series carburetor. The headers used in this test were a set of 1 7/8-inch street headers complete with a 2 1/2-inch exhaust system and Flowmaster mufflers. This engine was intended to be driven on the street with a goal of at least 500 hp in a relatively heavy street car with an automatic.

377ci Small Block POWER CURVE

RPM	TQ	HP
4200	434	347
4400	454	380
4600	490	429
4800	508	464
5000	514	489
5200	516 *	510
5400	516	530
5600	514	548
5800	508	561
6000	501	573
6200	494	583
6400	483	589 *
6600	467	587
6800	452	585
7000	432	576

Peak HP 589 @ 6,400
Peak TQ 516 @ 5,200

420ci Small Block POWER CURVE

RPM	TQ	HP
2000	410	156
2500	455	216
3000	471	269
3500	501	334
4000	510	388
4500	519 *	444
5000	507	482
5500	490	513
6000	459	524 *
6250	428	510

Peak HP 524 @ 6000
Peak TQ 519 @ 4500

The first thing we want to look at is the horsepower per cubic inch. This short-stroke, big-bore engine makes an outstanding 1.56 hp/ci. Let's take a look at where this occurs. Peak horsepower comes in at 6,400 rpm and falls off only slightly, losing only 13 off the peak all the way up at 7,000 rpm. This makes the

Peak horsepower occurs at a reasonable 6,000 rpm while the torque peaks at a much lower 4,500 rpm giving us a power band of 1,500 rpm from 4,500 to 6,000 rpm. Let's compare these two engines' strong and weak points. Unquestionably, the 377ci engine makes a ton more horsepower, with 589 versus the larger engine's 524, an advantage for the 377 of 65 hp. But looking at the torque curves, the larger 420 makes much more torque, out producing the 377 by 45 ft-lb at 4,500 rpm and per-

Stroker Theory

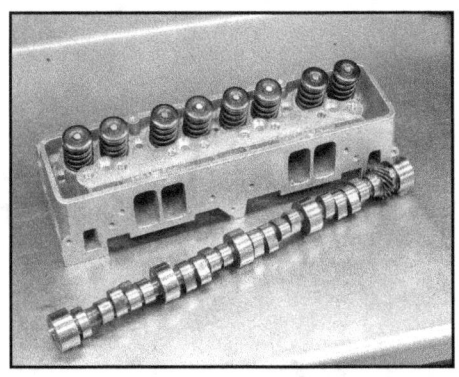

If there is a crucial match-up, it is probably between the cylinder heads and the cam. Create a mutually beneficial relationship between these components and you will make big power across the entire RPM band.

haps as much as 100 ft-lb at 4000 rpm. By 5,000 rpm, the 377 has assumed command, delivering more horsepower from this point on up. If each engine were optimized for drag racing, the more powerful 377 would easily out-accelerate the larger 420. But compromise the gear ratio and transmission selection for street car use and the stronger torque curve of the larger 420 would create a much better acceleration rate given a less-than-optimal rear gear ratio.

It's this stronger torque curve created by the larger displacement engine that helps acceleration and makes horsepower — without resorting to long duration camshafts and higher compression ratios. If you look at the basic horsepower equation, maintaining the torque curve at high-RPM levels will deliver very impressive horsepower numbers. Unfortunately, this comes at the price of a very peaky engine that only runs strong above 5,000 rpm. That's why it is so important when evaluating horsepower numbers to always ask to see the power curve or at least ask at what RPM the engine achieved its peak horsepower number. It's not that difficult to build a naturally aspirated 700 hp 302ci small block if you use big heads, a big cam, a large carburetor, headers, and a large plenum intake manifold. Of course, you'll have to spin this engine to over 8,000 rpm to make this kind of power; the power band will be narrow, perhaps as confined between 6,800 to 7,800 rpm.

Even worse for a street engine, it will be a stone below 4,000 rpm.

This is why big cubic-inch street engines are becoming increasingly popular. Using our previous example, the 420 makes a respectable 1.24 hp/ci with a similar 1.23 ft-lb /ci at a very low 4,500 rpm. The beauty of all this torque is that you can put a very streetable 3.50 gear behind this engine and the car will still run high 11's in a properly set up 3,500-pound street car. Combine that with an overdrive transmission like a TH700-R4 automatic or the popular late model T-56 6-speed that's used in the fourth generation Camaros and Firebirds and you'd have a strong street engine that would easily handle loafing down the freeway in overdrive at 70 mph at just above an idle.

THE SIREN SONG OF RPM

Another good reason to build a large displacement small block that builds torque rather than horsepower is the evil stuff that can and does occur at high RPM. There is something to be said for an ultra-powerful 400-plus cubic inch small block that spins to 7,000 rpm and makes gobs of horsepower. But the price you pay for that luxury is expensive valvetrain parts. The first item to consider when contemplating a high-RPM engine is valvetrain durability. To control a mechanical roller cam (which is the only real cam to use in this situation), requires high spring pressure, which tends to abuse the valvetrain even when things are going they way they're supposed to. Even mechanical roller cams designed for the street will abuse roller tappets. Also, spring pressures of over 500 pounds on the nose will require a dedicated inspection plan to prevent internal damage. This could mean inspection of the roller tappets as often as every 5,000 miles if you intend to put lots of street miles on an engine of this kind.

As you can see, there's a ton of information to know if you are going to build a big-inch small block, more than we can cover in this short overview. Much of this information involves engine building common sense and

Bore and Stroke Combinations

Bore (inches)	Stroke (inches)	Displacement (cubic inches)
4.125	3.480	372
4.000	3.750	377
4.155	3.480	377
4.030	3.750	383
4.155	3.530	383
4.060	3.750	388
4.125	3.750	400
4.155	3.750	406
4.165	3.750	409
4.155	3.800	412
4.125	3.875	415
4.155	3.850	418
4.155	3.875	420
4.165	3.875	422
4.185	3.850	423
4.125	4.000	428
4.155	4.000	434
4.165	4.000	436
4.185	4.000	440
4.125	4.125	441
4.155	4.125	447
4.155	4.250	454
4.250	4.000	454
4.165	4.250	463
4.185	4.250	468
4.250	4.125	468
4.250	4.250	482

attention to detail. Constructing a 600 hp naturally aspirated small block that makes all its power below 6,500 rpm is easily accomplished and can be used as a specialty street engine with very little concern for durability. The key to this is the proper selection of parts combined to create the proper torque and horsepower curve to suit your application. After careful parts selection and assembly, all that's left to do is go out and enjoy all your newfound power. Don't be surprised if traction becomes a serious issue. But that's a good problem to have.

Chapter 3

Cylinder Blocks

If you were building a house, you'd want to ensure that the foundation is a solid as possible before you built the rest of that multi-story dream home. The same is true with engines, and that the foundation is the cylinder block. This chapter will deal mainly with the first-generation small-block Chevy that includes the post-1986 modifications for the one-piece rear-main seal and hydraulic roller camshafts. We will not deal with the LT1 or LS1 engines in this book. There's still plenty to talk about when it comes to blocks since GM Performance Parts alone offers 16 different iron and aluminum mouse-motor blocks. Add the castings from Brodix, Dart, World Products, and others, and there are dozens of variations to choose from in the world of cylinder blocks.

Let's start with the most basic information for the small-block Chevy production blocks. Chevy produced several blocks prior to the 350, but since these blocks do not offer much in the way of large cubic inch potential, we would refer you to one of the many other books that deal with the older small-block configurations. We will concentrate on the 4.000, and 4.125-inch bore blocks that make up the bulk of small-block Chevy production blocks.

Early Blocks

The original small-block Chevy block was designed with 4.40-inch bore spacing and a deck height of 9.025-inches. This means that the block deck is 9.025-inches from the crankshaft centerline. These two dimensions deter-

Serviceable production 400 blocks are becoming increasingly difficult to find. Most 400 blocks use three freeze plugs, making them easy to spot. But certain blocks like the highly prized 509 castings came with only two freeze plugs, which make them look like a 350 from the outside.

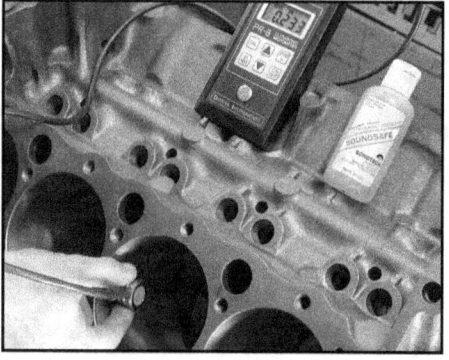

If you want big inches, you need a big bore. Most 4.125-inch cylinders get very thin when subjected to overbores of more than 0.030 to 0.040-inch. If you are planning on making big power, consider having the block sonic checked. The critical areas are the thrust surfaces, where the piston pushes against the cylinder wall, located on the inboard wall on the driver side and the outboard wall on the passenger side of the block. Minimum thrust surface thickness should be 0.200 to 0.250-inch for a performance block like one from Dart or Bow Tie. Production 400 blocks are often much thinner than this. Non-thrust walls can be thinner at 0.090 to 0.110-inch.

The GM Performance Parts Sportsman Bow Tie block offers the most advantages for a decent price. The Bow Tie offers increased strength and durability over any production block and can be easily identified by the cast-in bow tie on its flanks.

Cylinder Blocks

All aftermarket blocks include priority oiling, with a separate main oil galley located alongside the camshaft bore. This supplies oil directly to the mains, as opposed to a more tortured journey used in production blocks. This cutaway of a GM aluminum Bow Tie block illustrates this point well.

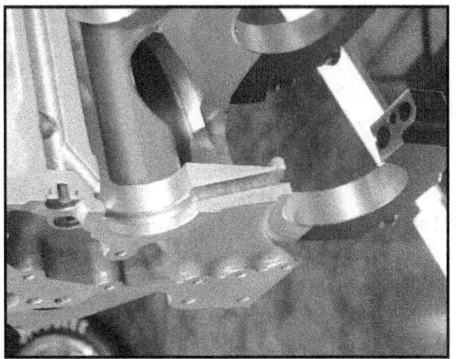

Like all aftermarket blocks, the Dart Little M scallops the water jackets to allow increased coolant flow and thicker cylinder walls. The Little M is available in both 4.00 and 4.125-inch bores with either 350 or 400-sized mains using either nodular iron or steel main caps.

mine the overall configuration of the small-block Chevy. Starting in 1968, Chevy changed its crankshaft main journal diameter from 2.30-inches to 2.45-inches to increase crankshaft strength and to accommodate the larger displacement 350ci engine first built in 1967. The 350 offered this medium size journal diameter along with a 4.00-inch bore and a 3.48-inch stroke. This is by far the most populous of all the pre-1986 small blocks. These Chevy blocks were produced in both two and four-bolt main caps. These blocks can be used for performance applications of up to about 450 hp, but be forewarned that as these blocks age, they are susceptible to cracking in the lifter valley and underneath the main webs. This is especially true of the 4-bolt main blocks since the majority of these blocks were used in trucks and performance applications that saw especially rough duty. The smart move is to always have any used block cleaned and Magnaflux tested for cracks before any machine work is performed.

In 1970, Chevrolet introduced a third revision to the standard small block with the 400 block. This block featured a large 4.125-inch bore that required siamesing the cylinder wall liners at the mid point, which also increased structural rigidity. This means that the outside diameters of the cylinder walls were actually joined, eliminating the coolant passage around the area between the cylinders. These blocks retained their bore spacing and external dimensions but internally the main journal diameter increased again, this time from 2.45 to 2.65 inches to support the additional load of the longer 3.75-inch stroke. These 400 blocks were built for several years, but their popularity has led to a rapid decline in the number of serviceable blocks available for performance use. 400s came in both 2-bolt and 4-bolt configurations, but ironically, in the main cap web area, the 2-bolt main versions are the stronger of the two. The 4-bolt main caps cannot be interchanged with the two-bolt main blocks. The 2-bolt main blocks offer more material in the area directly above the main webbing that was deleted for weight considerations when the 4-bolt blocks were cast.

The ideal performance configuration for a production 400 block would be to convert to a set of aftermarket steel 4-bolt main caps and drill and tap the outer two bolt holes for each additional cap. This will also require align boring the main caps to establish the proper housing bore diameter and also demands a specific two-piece rear-main seal that is offered by Fel-Pro. All of this incurs significant machine work and cost. Even if you find a standard bore 400 block that passes the crack test, you might want to seriously consider the price difference between investing considerable money into a stock production block of dubious lineage compared to the cost of a

The World Products Motown block offers similar features to other aftermarket blocks including thicker deck surfaces, blind head-bolt holes, and nodular-iron main caps. You can also get a Motown race block that offers splayed billet main caps and additional material in the standard deck height only.

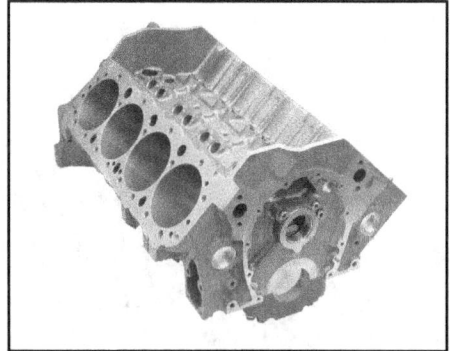

Deck height is the distance between the crankshaft centerline and the cylinder head deck surface. The standard small-block deck height is 9.025-inch, but Dart, GM Performance Parts, and others offer tall-deck versions that include heights of 9.325 and 9.500 inches. A taller deck height requires either a custom intake manifold or intake spacers.

Chapter 3

If you intend to use an oil pump stud like this ARP fastener in place of the bolt, be sure to use it when checking bearing clearance. The stud will change the way the cap deflects and could affect bearing clearance. Always check the number 5 main bearing clearance with the oil pump torqued in place.

new aftermarket block. This is especially important if the engine will be intended for power levels exceeding 550 hp. For example, it's possible to invest well in excess of $1000 in machine work alone when you consider the cost of cleaning, Magnafluxing, boring, torque plate honing, adding 4-bolt main caps, align boring, and decking the block. Conversely, you could invest in a GM Performance Parts Sportsman block that offers exceptional strength requires very little machine work to be up and running. However, this offers several advantages over a used block. The initial cost of the new block is certainly higher (around $1,800 or more), but the net result is a much stronger foundation that allows you to increase power without worrying about reliability.

1986 AND LATER BLOCKS

By 1986, Chevrolet engineers decided to address some of the small block's inherent shortcomings that included problems associated with long-term rear-main seal integrity. In other words, that troublesome 2-piece rear-main seal had to go. In its place, GM created a round, one-piece, rear-main seal design that required a new rear crankshaft flange. This constituted the first major change in the small-block Chevy block

Most production blocks use simple press-in plugs in the front oil galleys. For performance applications, it's a good idea to tap these three holes for 1/4-inch pipe plugs. The middle galley should be tapped shallow to prevent overlapping and restricting oil flow to the front main oil galley.

since 1955, creating two distinctly different blocks. One-piece rear-main seal cranks cannot be used in blocks designed for use with two-piece rear-main seals. However, several aftermarket companies as well as GM Performance Parts offer a rear-main seal adapter that will allow you to use a two-piece rear-main seal style crankshaft in a one-piece rear-main seal block.

Initially, all performance engine buildups used the two-piece rear-main seal construction since all performance crankshafts followed the two-piece design. Recently, however, the aftermarket performance world has begun to recognize the leak-free benefits of the one-piece rear-main seal style block and crank. One advantage to the one-piece configuration occurred the next year in 1987 when most Chevy small-block production blocks (excluding trucks) were converted to hydraulic roller tappets. Again, it took time for the aftermarket to embrace this modification, but now there are many advantages to building a mild performance small block using hydraulic roller tappets and a one-piece rear-main seal. As an example, you can now easily build a 383ci small block using a cast-iron, one-piece rear-main seal stroker crank along with a performance hydraulic roller camshaft while retaining the stock hydraulic roller tappets and the factory retainers. This not only offers a displacement increase over a standard

Several aftermarket blocks are available with steel main caps. You can also add aftermarket 4-bolt steel main caps to a stock production block, but this is an expensive machining operation that can thin your wallet by more than $500.

Cylinder Blocks

Many engine builders swear by studs instead of bolts. Studs offer increased clamping loads with reduced block and bore distortion. Be sure to decide which fastener to use before final honing. If converting from main bolts to studs, you must have the block align honed or bored since the studs will change the bore distortion, which will change the housing bore diameter.

This shot illustrates grinding necessary on a production block inside the pan rail to clear the rods on a 3.75-inch stroke crank with a 350 block. This requires finesse because if you grind too far, you can hit a water jacket and ruin the block. Aftermarket blocks fill the pan rails, which adds more material for grinding.

Before 1986, all small-block Chevys used a two-piece rear-main seal (left). But beginning in '86, this changed to a one-piece seal (right) that required a new crank, oil pan, and oil pan gasket. Most performance aftermarket blocks still use the original two-piece design because the crank flange is larger and somewhat stronger.

355, but also reduces the cost of converting to a hydraulic roller cam. We'll get into more details on camshafts in Chapters 7 and 8 on cams and valvetrains.

Bow Tie Blocks

The days of worrying if your engine would stay glued together because you are forced to use a production block are now long gone. Between the aftermarket and GM Performance Parts, there are literally dozens of iron blocks available in virtually any configuration you can imagine. The original high performance iron cylinder block from the Chevrolet was called the Bow Tie and exists today in several variations. For big cubic-inch applications, GM Performance Parts offers five different standard deck or tall-deck, iron blocks that will accommodate 4.125 to 4.155-inch bore diameter.

A good deal among the large-bore Bow Tie blocks is the Sportsman block that comes in a standard 9.025-inch deck height, nodular iron 4-bolt main caps, and either a 3.986-inch or a 4.117-inch bore size that can safely be bored out to 4.155-inch for large displacement motors.

The Sportsman block differs from older production blocks since it is intended to be used with a one-piece rear-main seal style crank, rather than the more traditional two-piece-seal crank. One place where these blocks also save a little money is that they are assembled using nodular iron main caps instead of the more traditional steel caps. According to GM tech sources, these blocks will accommodate up to a 3.75-inch stroke crank, but with some minor grinding, a 3.875-inch stroke can be fitted. One advantage for all Bow Tie blocks is that the area just above the pan rail is solid cast iron, which allows grinding room for clearance in this area. Production blocks extend the water jackets into this area, drastically limiting the amount of room available for stroker cranks. Many production blocks have been ruined when the engine builder hit a thin wall casting when grinding clearance for a stroker crank.

The Sportsman block will certainly increase in popularity now that there are several companies building stroker cast and forged one-piece rear-main seal crankshafts. We will get into more detail about those options in Chapter 4 on crankshafts. Among the several different GM Performance Parts blocks available, there is also a 9.325-inch, tall-deck, cast-iron block. This tall-deck block increases the deck height over the stock 9.025-inch spec to allow the use of longer stroke crankshafts and longer connecting rods. This tall-deck block is the GM Performance Parts Rocket block. It features a 0.390-inch higher camshaft location that creates more clearance for the use of a longer stroke. According to Chevy, this block can fit up to a massive 4.125-inch stroke crankshaft without the need for a small-diam-

Chapter 3

A long-stroke crank can also require clearancing at the bottom of the cylinder to clear the connecting rod.

Big displacement requires a long-arm crank. If there's a 4-inch stroke in your future, you might consider an aftermarket block like the Dart Iron Eagle or the GM Rocket block, which feature a 0.391-inch raised camshaft bore. This offers more clearance for a long-stroke crank. Just for the record, it is possible to stuff a 4-inch stroke in a block with standard cam location, but it's tight.

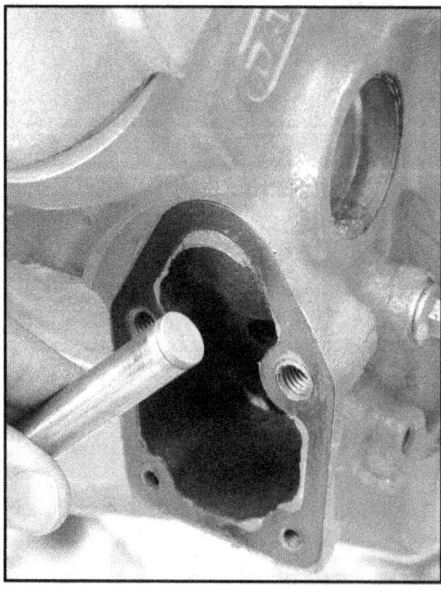

Late model blocks with a one-piece rear-main seal delete the mechanical fuel-pump boss. Most aftermarket blocks offer this feature, but often require a 0.200-inch longer fuel-pump pushrod, which also happens to be the length of a big-block pushrod.

eter base circle cam. The camshaft also uses big-block cam bearing diameters, which means that the cam would have to be specially ground with small-block specs on big-block journals. The oil pan rails are also spread 0.800-inch (0.400-inch per side) to clear the longer stroke crank. Other features include a priority main lubrication path, dual starter locations, and a mechanical fuel pump boss.

Like most of the other CNC-machined Bow Tie blocks, this block would require minimal machining after establishing the final bore size and deck plate honing the piston-to-wall clearance. The advantage of this CNC-machining is that GM can do quality, high-volume machining on these blocks for a far better price than if you were to have the block machined at a private machine shop. GM originally created this program to meet the demand from the factory-backed Winston Cup racers. Even so, you can expect a tall-deck block like this to require significant custom machine work in order to properly fit all the more exotic pieces that would be required to complete this type of engine. Given its race-oriented nature, you would expect this block to be very expensive, yet our latest price check through Scoggin-Dickey Performance Center put this casting at $2,600, which is reasonable given its race heritage and low volume. It's also important to note that this tall-deck block is no lightweight. While a production iron block weighs in around 180 pounds, this Rocket block tips the scales at a hefty 202 pounds. That's the price you pay for all that extra height.

If weight is an issue, GM Performance Parts makes that a priority with three different aluminum blocks. There are two standard deck height blocks that will accommodate 4.155-inch bores with either 350 or 400-style main bearings. There's also a monster 9.525-inch tall-deck version with 350-style mains and 8620 steel main caps. Since all three of these blocks are intended for competition use, they are configured for dry sump style oiling, which means the rear-main cap does not offer a boss to mount a wet-sump style oil pump. At 89 pounds, the stock deck height aluminum block is about as light as you can get.

Cylinder Blocks

If you are researching different aftermarket blocks for street use, make sure the number 5 main cap is equipped with a wet-sump main cap. Many aftermarket blocks like this Rocket Block are offered with dry-sump options that eliminate the wet-sump oil-pump boss.

Dart Blocks

GM isn't the only game in town for high performance small-block cases. Dick Maskin's Dart Machinery has slowly become known as one place to look for performance castings. Maskin's decades of Pro Stock experience have taught him the value of starting with a strong, high-quality block. The result is a plethora of performance pieces that you can choose from to create your own big-inch small block. Dart offers virtually everything a street enthusiast could ask for in a big-inch case with the Little M series of iron blocks.

The Little M iron blocks are where all but the most affluent engines builders will play. Iron blocks offer the advantage of incorporating all production-based small-block parts such as camshaft, oil pump, timing chain, oil filter, motor mounts, and clutch linkage, so you don't have to be concerned with searching out expensive, one-off, specialty parts. The most popular Little M block is the standard deck height, 4.125-inch bore, stock oil-pan rail width block, which uses either 350 or 400-style main journal sizes. You can also order your block with steel 4-bolt main caps, if that's your preference. These blocks also offer dual starter locations so the starter can be moved to the driver side of the block for extra oil pan clearance. You can also order a Dart block with a raised cam location that still comes with a standard deck height. Despite their race nature,

This is a factory-included pan rail clearance slot in the World Products Motown block to clear a 3.875-inch stroke crank. Most aftermarket blocks will accommodate a 4-inch stroke crank with the right connecting rods and modest clearancing.

these Dart blocks also come with a mechanical, standard, small-block boss but requires the use of a 0.200-inch longer big-block pushrod. All of these blocks are also machined for 2-piece rear-main seals to fit standard performance cranks. You even have the option of using a chain, belt, or gear drives that are configured for the taller raised camshaft location. Dart's specs specify an excellent 0.275-inch cylinder wall thickness minimum at a bore diameter of 4.185-inch.

Dart also offers a second line in the iron block department called the Iron Eagle block. This block incorporates many of the features found in its aluminum blocks in a more race-oriented version. All these blocks come with steel, 4-bolt main caps, as opposed to nodular-iron caps. They also feature spread oil-pan rails and a raised camshaft location with your choice of either small-block or big-block cam journal diameters. In the Iron Eagle line, options include a taller 9.325-inch deck height, a 0.391-inch raised cam location, an optional big-block cam bore size, and spread oil pan rails. You also have the option of either 350 or 400-style main journal diameters and either wet or dry-sump configurations.

If weight is a prime concern and you don't mind lightening your wallet, Dart also offers an aluminum small-block casting in both standard and two different raised-deck configurations with 9.325 and 9.500-inch deck heights. The taller deck heights make it much easier to squeeze in

This is Dart's aluminum small-block casting. You can pare close to 100 pounds off the heft of an iron casting, but it will come at twice the price of an iron block. The Dart is also offered in a massive 9.500-inch deck height for those monster-sized mouse motors.

How To Build Big-Inch Chevy Small-Blocks

Chapter 3

This is a cutaway of a World Products block that illustrates the thicker cylinder walls that can accommodate up to a 4.250-inch bore. Even with this big bore, the block still offers more than 0.200-inch of wall thickness on the thrust surfaces.

One way to ensure the lifter bores are true to the cam centerline is to have them machined and then bushed. This might also be a good time to step up to a larger lifter diameter.

a 3.875 or 4.00-inch crank while retaining a decent rod length. The alloy blocks employ high-strength ductile iron cylinder sleeves while offering two main bearing bore choices. Steel, four-bolt main bearing caps are standard and the block offers all the same options as the iron pieces for dual starter locations, mechanical fuel pump boss, and stock motor mount bosses. The aluminum block also comes standard with a 0.391-inch raised camshaft location and requires the use of big-block cam bearings to increase camshaft strength and reduce torsion twist. Maskin also makes a point to emphasize that Dart uses only virgin aluminum in all of its castings, which means that aluminum contaminated with sand and other impurities are not included in his aluminum blocks and heads. This feature makes the aluminum castings much easier to weld and repair, without increasing their price. It's just another step in Dart's quality-assurance program.

The aluminum block shaves roughly 100 pounds off the heft of a comparable iron block, and according to Maskin, there is very little loss in power for this weight savings. Generally, aluminum blocks sacrifice a small amount of power over an iron block due to a combination of increased heat transfer away from the cylinders as well as a significant amount of cylinder wall movement that inhibits piston ring seal. Maskin claims that his aluminum blocks don't suffer those cylinder wall migration problems. The big hurtle is the price. Dart's retail sticker on an aluminum Dart block is $4280, which puts it at roughly twice the price of its iron versions.

WORLD PRODUCTS

World Products is a major player when it comes to iron performance castings. World offers two similar castings: The Motown and Motown Race blocks. These are World's latest effort using a stock deck height and camshaft location. The beauty of the Motown block is that even with a standard bore center to allow use of stock bolt pattern heads, Motown claims there is sufficient wall thickness to push the bore out to 4.250-inch! Combine this with a 4.00-inch stroke, and

Cylinder Blocks

Aftermarket Blocks

All blocks in these charts offer 4-bolt main caps except for block PN 10051183 (*).
** Indicate dry sump aluminum blocks

GM Performance Parts Blocks

Part Number	10051183*	10185047	24502501	24502503	24502525
Deck Height	9.025	9.025	9.025	9.025	9.150
Max Bore	4.090	4.090	4.030	4.155	4.155
Crank Journal	2.45	2.45	2.45	2.45	2.45
Crank Seal	1 piece	1 piece	2 piece	2 piece	2 piece
Material	Iron	Iron	Iron	Iron	Iron
Weight	187	182	183	183	183
Part Number	12480174	12480175	22551790	10185075**	24502495
Deck Height	9.025	9.025	9.325	9.025	9.525
Max Bore	4.150	4.155	4.190	4.155	4.125
Crank Journal	2.45	2.45	2.65	2.65	2.65
Crank Seal	1 piece	1 piece	2 piece	2 piece	2 piece
Material	Iron	Iron	Iron	Aluminum	Aluminum
Weight (lbs.)	182	182	202	90	101

Dart Blocks

We have only listed the more popular or interesting part numbers here. Dart offers numerous options, each with its own part number. Contact Dart for the entire part lumber listing.

Part Number	31121111	31121211	31122211	31121221	3112221
Deck Height	9.025	9.025	9.025	9.325	9.325
Bore Dia.	4.000	4.125	4.125	4.125	4.125
Crank Journal	2.45	2.45	2.65	2.45	2.65
Crank Seal	2 piece	2 piece	2 piece	2 piece	2 piece
Material	Iron Eagle	Iron Eagle	Iron Eagle	Iron Eagle	Iron Eagle
Weight (lbs.)	205	205	205	210	210
Part Number	31111112	31111212	31111232		
Deck Height	9.025	9.325	9.500		
Bore Dia.	4.000	4.125	4.125		
Crank Journal	2.45	2.45	2.45		
Crank Seal	2 piece	2 piece	2 piece		
Material	Aluminum	Aluminum	Aluminum		
Weight (lbs.)	95	100	100		

World Products Blocks

Part Number	084020	084030	084120*	084130*
Deck Height	9.025	9.025	9.025	9.025
Bore Dia.	4.115	4.115	4.115	4.115
Crank Journal	2.45	2.65	2.45	2.65
Crank Seal	2 piece	2 piece	2 piece	2 piece
Material	Iron	Iron	Iron	Iron
Weight (lbs.)	190	190	195	195

* Motown Race Block with steel splayed main caps

---

you have a 454ci standard deck height small block. Obviously, this is the largest bore and stroke you could squeeze into a standard deck height, and the operant word here is "squeeze." Several factors affect the durability of this combination, but the fact remains that it is possible now that Fel-Pro offers a 4.250-inch head gasket for this combination. Keep in mind that this large of a bore allows no freedom to enlarge the cylinder at a later date to compensate for wear. We'll get into this combination with more specifics in later chapters, but the fact remains that you can build a monster small-block Chevy displacing big-block cubic-inches that externally looks no different than a 350ci mouse motor.

Investigating a slightly more conservative version, you could easily create a 4.155-inch bore and 3.875-inch stroke combination that will literally bolt into place with few modifications to the block to allow you to create a 420ci "little" block. If you want to push the envelope a little, you can certainly run this block out to a 4.200-inch bore and a 4-inch stroke and create a 443ci mouse, which is plenty big. Plus, there are all kinds of combinations in between. With inches like these, it is difficult not to achieve enormous torque at relatively low engine speeds, which makes street driving downright fun.

Getting back to the Motown block specifics, the cylinder walls have been substantially increased in thickness order to create a 0.250-inch wall thickness with a bore size of 4.200 on the thrust surfaces. With a 4.250-inch bore, this leaves only 0.150-inch in between the cylinders. While this is not the thrust side of the cylinder, it does contribute to cylinder wall integrity and stiffness. Just for the record, the lifter side of the left bank and the outboard side of the right bank are the thrust surfaces on any standard rotation small block. Another serious consideration is the minimal amount of material you need to create adequate head-gasket sealing. This question is probably best answered with a realistic look at the power output. With a nitrous or supercharged application, heavy cylinder pressure loads will probably create problems. However, a naturally

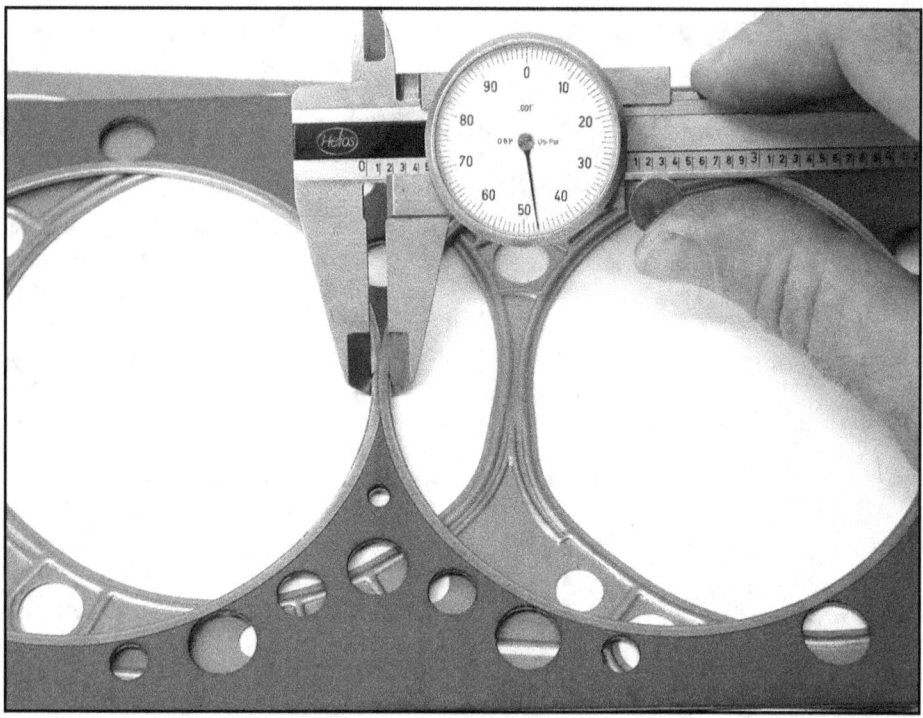

Fel-Pro makes a custom 4.250-inch small-block gasket for those adventuresome engine builders willing to stretch the small block out to this big-block bore size. The key to making this work is sealing the thin siamesed area between cylinders.

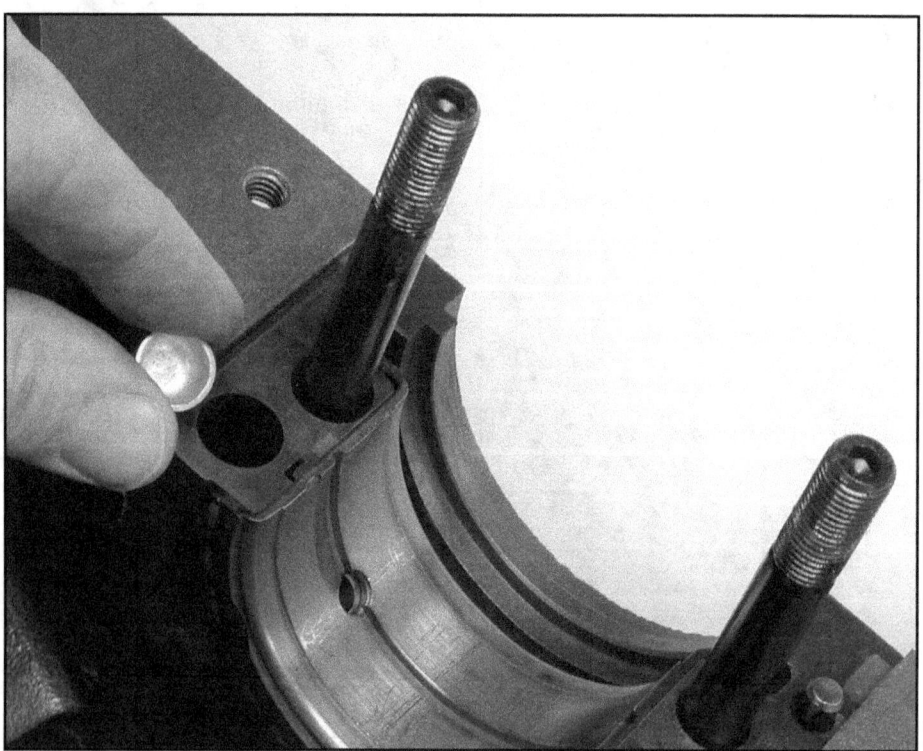

When building any small block, make sure to include the press-in plug below the number 5 main cap. Bow Tie blocks are shipped without this plug and machine shops will often pull this plug when cleaning the block. If it is left out, oil from the pump is allowed to bypass the oil filter, which is never a good idea.

aspirated combination at 600 hp or less should work. The real answers will come with time and experience but for now it appears to be a successful move.

Like all the other aftermarket blocks, the Motown also features filled oil pan rails and thicker bulkheads at the front and back of the block to help support the front and rear-mains. The Motown comes with nodular-iron main caps with 7/16-inch bolts, which include register pins to ensure the caps are properly located on the block. As with other performance blocks, the Motown also includes blind head-bolt holes, which means they are not tapped down into the coolant jackets. This eliminates the hassle of sealing head-bolt threads to prevent seepage past the bolts. In addition, the Motown block offers a minimum of 0.600-inch deck thickness for increased deck integrity, which is especially important at high-horsepower output. Of course, all this strength also adds weight, contributing to the Motown coming in at a not-so-svelte, 190 pounds.

World also offers a Motown Race block upgrade that is reinforced with splayed bolts and billet-steel main caps that use 1/2-inch inboard bolts and 7/16-inch studs on the outboard. Splaying or angling the main cap bolts tends to distribute the load over a greater area, which offers additional strength.

The GM Rocket block offers a 9.325-inch deck height with a raised cam location that will allow up to a 4.125-inch stroke crankshaft without clearance problems. While this is by far the largest crank, the block is limited to a 4.155-inch bore, which, if combined with the long stroke, will create a 447ci small block.

Cylinder Blocks

Lube Lines

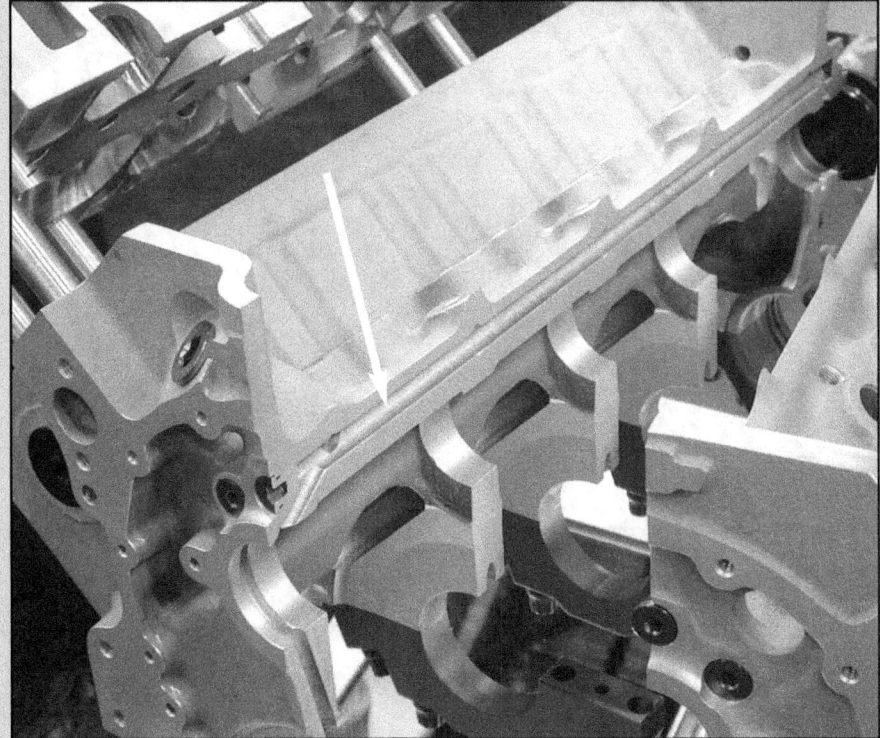

One change to the original Chevrolet block design that is employed in all aftermarket blocks is what is called a priority main oiling system. The original small-block Chevy employed a very efficient lubrication system, which is one reason for its immense durability under high-RPM conditions. If the small block has a lubrication Achilles heel, it is the path the oil must take in order to make it to the main and rod journals. The production lubrication system pushes oil from the oil pump, up through the oil filter, and then straight up the back lifter valley wall of the block. It then travels through an angled passage comes down through the driver's side deck and intersects the main oil galley atop the cam journals. If you look at a production block with the cam bearings removed, you can see a 360-degree slot cut into the cam journals. This slot channels the oil from the main oil gallery, around the cam bearings, and down each main web to the main bearings. Once at the main, the oil is directed to each of the rod journals through passages drilled in the crankshaft.

While this system has worked well in production blocks for almost 50 years, when it came time to build a new performance block, the engineers decided to reduce the circuitous oil routing. This was accomplished by creating a dedicated oil passage (arrow, above) that directs oil from the central part of the block directly to the main bearings without forcing it to travel around the cam journals. This may seem like a small point, but it's an advantage of every aftermarket block that just makes life a little easier for the main and rod bearings under the stress of 600-plus horsepower. Most aftermarket blocks also offer a front oil inlet that is drilled and tapped to allow you to plumb oil directly to the front of the engine from an external oil filter/cooler combination rather than extending plumbing back to rear of the engine.

Additional features in the race block include reinforced main web and bulkheads. The race blocks are also available with basic machining or as fully race-prepped castings complete with torque-plate honed cylinder walls. The additional strength adds another 5 pounds, taking the race block casting up to a bare weight of 195 pounds. The World Products catalog states that the block will accommodate up to a 3.875-inch stroke crank, but judicious whittling can create enough clearance to accept one of those monstrous 4-inch strokers.

The Cost of Power

We've spent a good deal of this chapter reviewing the advantages of aftermarket blocks. The advantages by now should be obvious, but the downside is, of course, the price. The going rate for these new blocks range from around $1,800 to around $4,000 for an alloy version. While this sounds intimidating, it's worth investigating what you will spend to rejuvenate a used cylinder block. A bare minimum of machine work will include cleaning, Magnafluxing, boring and honing with a torque plate, an align hone, and resurfacing the decks. This will generally cost around $550 to $600. Add in the cost of converting to steel four-bolt main caps and the price jumps to somewhere around $1100. At this point, you have invested two-thirds of the cost of a brand new casting into a used block that offers no strength advantages.

Obviously, for roughly another $600 to $700, you will have a vastly stronger and higher-quality foundation that will offer years of durable service without worrying about whether it will be able to handle the power. The additional cost may be fiscally painful, but in the long run, investing in a quality casting is the first step in building a high-quality, big-inch small block that will deliver killer power and do it for a long time. Like most decisions in life, "you pays your money and you takes your chances."

Chapter 4

CRANKSHAFTS

In the grand scheme of things, the stroke is the other half of the displacement one-two punch. The easiest way to add displacement is to stuff a stroker crank in a stock block that will pump up a 4.030-inch bore 350 block to 383 cubic inches. This chapter will cover all the details that make up a crankshaft, what to look for, and what questions to ask when searching for the right crank. The incredible selection that is now available can make choosing a crank both easier and more difficult. Let's start with some crankshaft basics and then we can get into the romance of those cool 4340 stroker cranks.

Crank Basics

There are three basic ways to create a crankshaft — you can cast a crank, forge one, or machine one out of steel billet stock. Most production crankshafts are cast, but when Chevrolet first built the 265ci small block, it came with a forged crank. Later, manufacturers learned that they could build a very durable crankshaft out of nodular iron that was strong enough to survive well past 100,000 miles of daily use. Since the early 1970s, most production small-block Chevys have come down the assembly line with cast iron arms. Cast cranks offer great durability with the advantage of a low cost. Just like pistons however, a casting is not near-

The easiest way to tell a forged crank from a casting is by gently hitting a non-machined part of the crank with a small hammer. The forging will ring while a casting will have dull thump to it. You can also tell a forged crank by its wide forging mark at the crank centerline (right).

ly as strong as a forging. Chevy did install forged cranks in some small blocks, mostly high-performance engines and heavy-duty truck applications. While increased power levels do place more stress on the crankshaft, requiring a stronger unit, the most significant abuser of the crankshaft is engine speed. The horsepower equation makes it clear that the key to making more horsepower is spinning the engine faster. But that additional RPM also places dramatically greater stress on the crankshaft. If your plan calls for high RPM, then you'd better be looking for the best crank you can buy.

For an everyday street 383, several companies make excellent cast-iron 3.75-inch stroke cranks with your choice of either a one-piece or two-piece rear-main seal. These cranks are not only affordable, but also extremely durable.

In addition to the material, small-block Chevy crankshafts are also built in two different forms based on the rear-main seal design. The original 265 was built with a rope seal that surrounded the rear crank journal. Later, Chevy created a two-piece neoprene seal that served its purpose for almost 30 years. This seal design was not ideal, and with time it would eventually leak. Chevy converted to a one-piece rear-main seal in 1986, but this required a change to the rear flange on the crankshaft. The one-piece rear-main seal design also required a new block, as we've seen in Chapter 3.

Crankshafts

The biggest change to production crankshafts was in 1986 when Chevy changed to the one-piece rear-main seal. This change requires a new block, crank, seal, and oil pan.

With the increasing popularity of late-model, one-piece rear-main seal engines, there are now many variations on the 3.75-inch stroke cast or forged cranks for these engines.

The one-piece seal also dictated a smaller crankshaft flywheel/flexplate bolt pattern. So as you can see, this change affected quite a few other components and also clouds the issue of parts interchangeability. It is possible to use a two-piece rear-main seal crank in a one-piece rear-main seal block, but you cannot use a one-piece seal crank in a two-piece rear-main seal block.

Another point worth mentioning is crankshaft balance. The large counterweights on a crankshaft are there to offset the reciprocating weight of the piston, pin, rings, and the top half of the connecting rod. These counterweights generally increase in size with larger bore pistons and a longer stroke. These counterweights add mass to the crankshaft and contribute to internal stress and twist as RPM increases. There are essentially two ways to balance an engine's rotating forces. You can either do it internally or externally. Internally balanced engines employ all the balance weight using the crank counterweights. External balance engines, like the 400ci small block and the 454ci big-block Chevys use offset weight on the torsion damper and the flywheel/flexplate to create additional force at both ends of the crankshaft to balance the rotating assembly.

An interesting story revolves around the design of the original 400ci small block. Chevy engineers established a certain piston pin position with the 400ci small block with the 3.75-inch stroke. Packaged in the standard 9.025-inch deck height, this required a very short 5.565-inch connecting rod. This short rod design combined with long piston skirts limited the size of the crankshaft counterweights necessary to balance the engine. Since the counterweights couldn't get any larger, the engineers had no choice but to place the weight on both ends of the crank. One benefit is that the further you move the weight away from the centerline of the crank, the less weight you need to counteract the imbalance. Unfortunately, this additional weight on the ends of the crank also increases crank twist, especially at higher RPM. This points out that there are both advantages and disadvantages to external balancing. This isn't really a problem for low-speed passenger car engines, but certainly becomes a more critical issue with higher engine speeds.

With hundreds of custom rod and piston combinations possible, the subject of rod length is thereby dictated by deck height, stroke, and the minimum compression height of the piston. So for even a simple 406ci small block, increasing rod length to 6.0 inches allows the crankshaft maker to increase the size of his counterweights and produce an internally balanced 406. This internal balance not only hides an external clue to your 400-plus cubic inches of displacement, but this also reduces stress and twist on the crankshaft. This is especially important if you intend to make power above 6,500 rpm. Most crankshaft manufacturers prefer to minimize the weight of torsional dampers placed

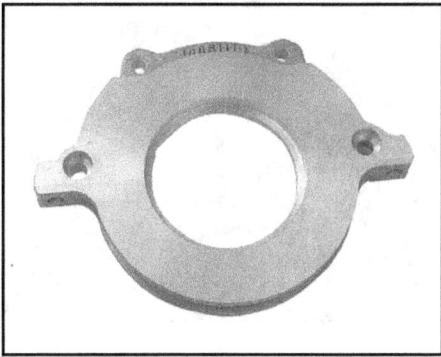

It is possible to use a two-piece rear-main seal crank in a one-piece seal block by using an adapter that's available through GM Performance Parts and several other companies like Moroso.

The 400 is the only production small block that requires external balancing with offset weights on the torsional damper and the flywheel/flexplate. These balancers are easily identified by the offset weight.

at the end of the crank. This imparts less twist back into the crankshaft. Therefore, building an internally balanced crank is preferable.

Cast Cranks

If we have to put an RPM limit on performance use for cast cranks, they are suitable for 6,000-rpm use, especially if this is not for extended periods of time. For example, there are several 3.75-inch stroke cast cranks for 383ci street engines that do an excellent job at an extremely low price. If this engine sees 6,000, or even 6,500 rpm, the engine will probably live a very long and healthy life. However, take that same crank and spin it to

Chapter 4

The 400 crank uses a 2.65-inch diameter main journal that is 0.200-inch larger than the standard 350 2.45-inch main journal. This additional diameter improves crank strength, although you can buy 3.75-inch and longer stroke cranks that employ a 2.45-inch main journal.

One way to lighten a crank is by eliminating weight in areas where it won't sacrifice strength. Many companies offer cranks with the rod and/or main journals drilled and finished.

Almost all the crank companies offer lightweight versions of almost every 4340 forged crank stroke option. While these lighter cranks improve acceleration, the stiff price of admission is usually not worth the performance advantage for a street engine. This is a Crower Ultra-Light crank.

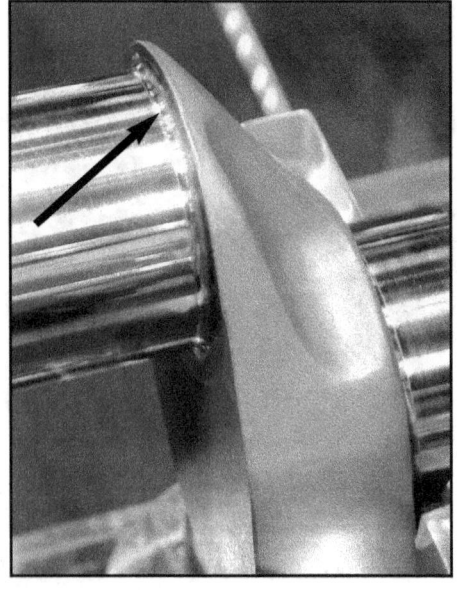

Crank strength lies in the radius between the journal and the cheek of the crank (arrow). Many aftermarket cranks create as much as a 0.125-inch radius in this area to improve crank strength and prevent stress cracks.

7,000 rpm or higher and you will radically shorten its lifespan. The forces placed on a crankshaft at these engine speeds are tremendous and a cast crank will eventually create stress cracks generated by the additional loads. Generally, these stress cracks will form near or on the radius between the rod journal and the cheek of the crank or the same location near a main journal. These are the areas where the stress on the crank is the greatest.

Some engine builders will have a crank hardened and/or stress relieved, both of which are excellent ideas to eliminate many surface stress crack possibilities. But this does not change the tensile strength of the basic crankshaft material. While nodular iron is more malleable than standard gray cast iron, the fact remains that cast iron does not have the strength to endure stresses imposed by high-RPM use. As the term implies, surface hardening only improves the surface strength of the bearing surface of the crank. It does little to improve overall toughness of the base material and its ability to withstand twist and deformation caused by high-RPM conditions.

If you wanted to build a street 383, the cast cranks mentioned above do offer significant advantages. First of all, original cast 400ci 3.75-inch crankshafts are almost impossible to find these days. Even if you find one that's in good shape, you will need to have the main journals ground down from the 2.65-inch 400 main journal diameter down to the 350 block's 2.45-inch main journal. The cost of the machine work alone will almost pay for a brand new crank from Eagle, Scat, or one of the other cast crank companies. These new cranks are already cut for the 2.45-inch 350 main journal size so no additional machining is required. As we mentioned, the fillet radius between the rod or main journal and the body of the crank is an area where stress can occur.

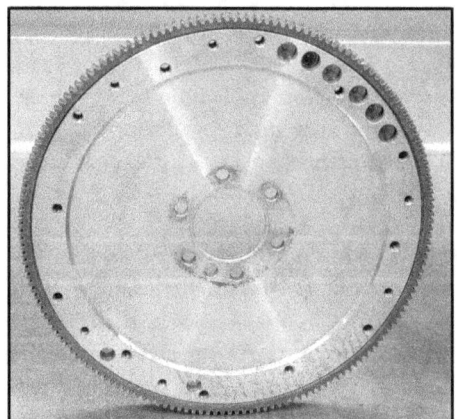

Externally balanced crankshafts require the use of offset weight in both the torsional damper and the flexplate/flywheel. This flywheel has been drilled to create offset weight for an externally balanced 406 small block.

Scat's 9000 series cranks, for example, offer a larger 0.125-inch fillet radius, which is significantly larger and therefore stronger than stock cranks. In addition, Scat offers 3.750-inch stroke cranks for either 5.7 or 6.0-inch rods as well as both two-piece and one-piece rear-main seal applications. You can

Crankshaft Alloys

This chart lists the popular steel alloys used in forged and billet crankshafts. We've listed them in ascending order of strength, with the weakest first and the strongest last. The Society of Automotive Engineers (SAE) identifies these numeric and alphanumeric designations. We'll save you the anguish of breaking each of these alloys down by element. All you really need to know is that 4340 is stronger than 5140 and so on. The rest you can leave up to the materials engineers. Most castings are nodular iron, while the forgings are comprised of the following alloy steels:

1010 — This is the basic alloy used in stock production crankshafts.

1053 — This is the next best alloy, used in some performance GM steel crankshafts sold through GM Performance Parts.

5140 — Even though the number implies a stronger alloy, 5140 is not as durable or as strong as 4340. This crankshaft material is a great compromise between ultimate strength and ductility. GM Performance Parts also sells some 5140 steel cranks.

4340 — This is the ultimate alloy to use in a high-performance crankshaft. There are higher-strength steels available, but they increase brittleness, which is not good in a component like a crankshaft that is subjected to significant bending and twisting forces.

Torsional dampers also play a significant role in crankshaft durability. A popular choice among most professional engines builders is the ATI Super Damper. It combines light weight with excellent damping characteristics.

If you are considering bolting a belt-driven supercharger on your big-inch small block, it's a simple procedure to order your forged crank with a larger big-block snout. Remember you will also need a special timing-chain cover, crank timing gear, and damper. Bo Laws makes 2-piece small-block covers with the larger snout diameter.

also get a 3.75-inch stroke crank for either a 350 or 400 block with 6.0-inch rod length capacity that is internally balanced. The best part is that none of these cranks cost more than about $275. The standard 383 crank sells for $200. That's tough to beat.

Forged Cranks

The next step up in strength is a forged crankshaft. As the name implies, rather than just pouring iron into a mold, high tensile strength steel is pressed together in a giant forge to create a much stronger crankshaft. There are a couple of ways to build a forged crankshaft — the twist and non-twist methods. The twist process involves building a less expensive flat mold in which the crank is forged. Then, while the crank is still hot, it is literally twisted to give it its four separate 90-degree throws for a V-8 engine. The non-twist process requires building a more complex die that accommodates all four throws necessary to forge the crankshaft into its final shape in one pressing. This also limits the length of the throw of the crank; requiring separate dies for different strokes. The companies building non-twist cranks contend that this process does not induce built-in internal stresses into the crankshaft by twisting it to achieve the final shape. As an example, all Crower cranks and the new Oliver crank are non-twist forgings. This is probably not a strength issue for street engines, but may have some impact on ultimate durability. We bring this up so that when you read about twist and non-twist crankshafts, you will know what these terms mean.

Not all forged cranks are made of the same material. This is where the subject gets a bit more complicated. We've included a small chart that lists the more popular steel alloys along with a short description of each. In essence, as you increase tensile strength with a stronger alloy you also increase brittleness. While there are a couple of alloys that offer a price advantage, if you are going to build a strong small block to make over 500 hp, the additional cost of using a 4340 forged steel crank is an excellent insurance policy. This leads us to billet cranks. A quality forging from companies like Callies, Crower, Manley, Oliver, Scat, and others offer more than enough strength for all but the most exotic performance application. The only reason for a billet crank would be for a one-off custom stroke application where no forging exists.

Most crank makers prefer to see a lighter, smaller-diameter torsional damper on the end of their crank. Twisting less weight on the end of the crank is a great way to improve crank life.

Many crank companies also undercut the counterweights (arrow) to decrease weight and improve engine acceleration.

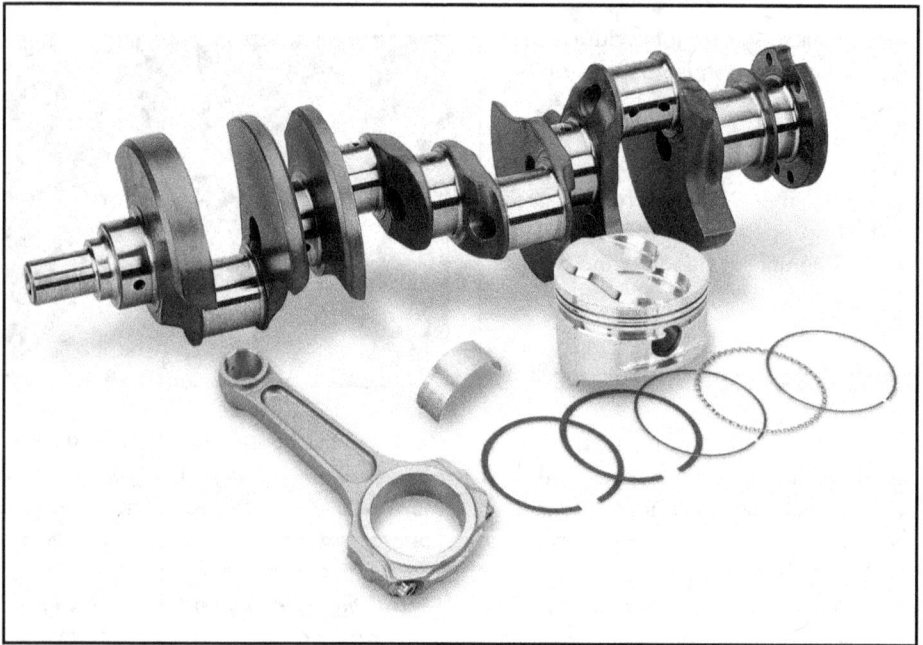

There are definite advantages to purchasing a complete rotating assembly (like this one from Lunati) when building a big-inch small block. Matched components prevent problems with bob weight and interference problems between the components.

companies offer lightweight versions of the same crank. Crower is probably the most prolific manufacturer in this area with four different versions of just about any stroke small-block crank that you can imagine. Crower offers Sportsman, Standard, Lightweight, and Ultra-Light configurations. The weight difference between the Sportsman and the Ultra-Light could be as much as 19 pounds, which is a huge gain in rotating mass. This is significant when you consider that it requires a certain amount of horsepower just to accelerate this rotating mass through its RPM range. The less weight the engine has to accelerate means that power can be applied to drive the rear tires.

There are several ways to reduce weight in a crankshaft and it makes a significant difference where the mass is removed. This is why an overall weight can be deceiving. For example, some companies remove weight from the center of the main journals. This reduces the overall heft of the crank but does very little in terms of reducing rotating weight. It is far more beneficial to remove weight from the point furthest from the crankshaft centerline. To illustrate this point, let's use a 1-pound weight tied to the end of a two-foot long string. It will require some amount of effort to swing this combination around in a circle over your head. Now let's make that a 3-pound weight. This will require a greater amount of effort (work) to accelerate that heavier weight up to the same speed. Add another foot to the length of the string and the effort increases again. This is an object lesson in the effect of what engineers call polar moment of inertia. Weight placed farther away from the pivot point or centerline of rotation requires more power to accelerate.

Given this, several crank companies undercut counterweights in order to reduce weight while still delivering sufficient bob weight. Of course, drilling the center of rod throws is another favorite trick to reduce weight. Lightweight cranks also eliminate the center counterweights. Keep in mind that while lightweight cranks are certainly an advantage, they are also more expensive that standard cranks.

Another area also worth investigating is heat treating. Each crankshaft manufacturer applies its own specific heat treating process to its crankshafts. The processes vary with the manufacturer that involves far too many details than we can get into in this chapter. It may be sufficient to say that each reputable crankshaft company has its own specific formula for heat treating and each process offers certain advantages that may be inherently beneficial. On the other hand, this information is so esoteric that you may find that trusting that the crankshaft company knows what they're doing is far easier and leave it at that. However, if you run into crankshaft durability issues with certain crankshafts, it may be a subject worth investigating.

Assuming you are going to go with a 4340 steel crank, weight and stroke are the next critical considerations. Obviously, a longer stroke crank will be heavier than a short stroke crank. But within a given stroke, most crankshaft

Crankshafts

Heat Treating

Hard Chroming — this process applies a relatively thick, hard chrome coating that creates an extremely durable finish on the crankshaft journal. Though it increases hardness, this process also reduces ductility, making the crankshaft more brittle. This is not recommended for either race or street crankshafts.

Nitriding — The process creates a relatively thin (0.005-0.010-inch) yet extremely hard surface by hardening the existing material. This is the most popular heat-treating process currently used by crankshaft manufacturers. Because the treatment works only on the surface of the crankshaft, the hardness can be removed by machining.

Deep Case Nitriding — This is the same process, but applied with more heat to extend the depth of the surface treatment. Unfortunately, this also creates a less ductile crankshaft that is difficult to repair.

Tufftriding — This is an older heat-treat process that used a salt bath that can cause chemical etching if not thoroughly removed. For environmental reasons, this process is no longer popular.

Stroke

This is the real meat of the reason we get into crankshafts. The longer the stroke, the more displacement we can build. But like most things in life, there is a limit to how far you can go. The variables include rod clearance for the camshaft, rod clearance around the oil-pan rail, rod length, piston compression height, counterweight-to-piston-skirt clearance, and the real issue of ensuring that a long-stroke, short-rod package doesn't pull the piston out of the bottom of the bore at bottom dead center (BDC). Some of these variables can be dealt with in more detail when we get into connecting rods and pistons, but they all should be addressed when deciding how big an arm you want to stuff into that small block.

But before we get into these details, there are some inherent strength considerations that are also important to cover. While the steel alloy is important when buying a crankshaft, there are other more subtle variables worth investigating. As you increase the stroke of a crankshaft, the amount of material that overlaps between the main journal and the rod journal decreases. This inherently weakens the crankshaft. When Chevrolet decided to build the 400 small block back in the late 1960s, one of the first decisions after they increased the stroke to 3.75-inches was to also increase the main bearing journal diameter from 2.45 to 2.65-inches. This 0.200-inch larger diameter increased the overlap between the rod and main journals, adding strength to the factory crankshaft.

You may have heard about how NASCAR engine builders, looking for that last bit of power from their engines, are reducing both rod journal and main journal diameters. While a smaller diameter journal does reduce bearing speed and therefore friction, we're talking very minimal numbers here. What is usually not discussed is how these smaller journal diameters also weaken the crankshaft. NASCAR engine builders are really only concerned with durability

It's difficult to see the difference between a twist and non-twist forged crank. This non-twist Oliver crankshaft is perhaps one of the strongest designs on the market, and it is also one of the most expensive.

When building a stroker motor, you have to watch out for things like interference between crank counterweight and the piston. Minimum clearance is 0.080-inch.

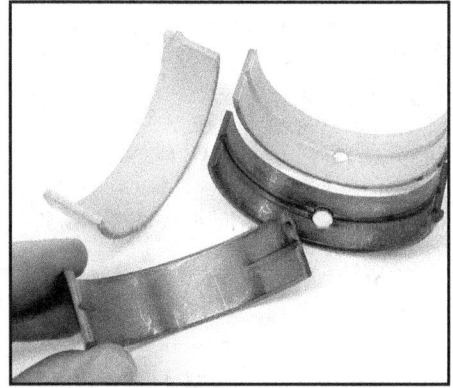

Today's main and rod bearings are drastically better engineered than materials even 10 years ago. These Federal-Mogul race bearings look questionable only because they have not been subjected to the flash coating that some engine builders prefer to eliminate.

Chapter 4

Knife edging is one way to profile the counterweight to reduce windage. Just as in car aerodynamics, it's important to carefully shape the trailing edge of the counterweight to reduce negative pressure turbulence at speed.

Just for fun, we thought you might like to see what you could call a seriously lightweight crank. This is a Kryptonite crank for a displacement-challenged small block that's under 240 cubic inches.

Balancing a crank often means increasing its weight to match the reciprocating weight of the pistons and rods. This means installing Mallory or heavy metal in the crank throws. This is an expensive process that should not be approached lightly.

for 500 to 700 miles. At the end of the race, the engine goes back to the shop and the entire rotating assembly is replaced with a new one for the next race! That's expensive and one reason why NASCAR racing is only for those with corporate-sized budgets. For a street or even a Sportsman-level competition engine, these tricks are unnecessary. While Honda rod bearing diameters of 1.780-inches may sound exotic, they aren't what you need for a long-stroke small block, no matter what the magazines may say.

For long-arm combinations, camshaft to connecting rod clearance can also become very tight. For example, if you want to build a 420ci small block with a 3.875-inch stroke, you will need to look at both rod clearance around a couple of lobes on the camshaft as well as block clearance for a standard pan-rail block. You'd be best served to build this engine with one of the high-strength aftermarket blocks since they offer additional material around the pan rail for clearance. This will also require some kind of stroker rod that offers more clearance around the big end for camshaft clearance. Even with these rods, a small base-circle camshaft is necessary.

It is possible to stuff a 4.00-inch stroke into a standard camshaft height block to build a 427ci, 434ci, or even s 454ci small block (depending upon bore size), but this is definitely pushing the boundaries of internal clearance. For example, the rod to cam lobe clearance is so tight that you should definitely install the camshaft first before bolting together the bottom end or you'll have to rotate the engine just to get the rods to clear the cam!

Another detail that comes up when building stroker engines is rod length. A rod that is too short can put more stress on both the piston and cylinder wall. Chevrolet spec'd a 5.565-inch rod when building the original 400 small block, and that, combined with the 3.75-inch stroke, could be considered as the minimum rod length-to-stroke ratio of 1.48:1. In addition, a rod that is too short can actually put the piston skirts dangerously close to the crankshaft counterweights! We'll get into that in more detail with the chapter on connecting rods, but this is a real consideration.

All of these details point out the hidden difficulties you will face when building a big-inch small block. If this is your first time buying or building a big-inch mouse motor, the usual approach is to buy the parts separately from different manufacturers. For example, you might buy a Scat crank, Manley rods, and JE pistons to build a your first 434ci small block. While this is certainly one way to do it, you run the risk of incompatibility unless you address every contingency.

Cranks By The Numbers

The following is a partial list of some of the more popular crankshaft designs listed by stroke and manufacturer. With the tremendous variations available from each of these companies, we don't have the room to list all the crankshaft options. Many companies like Crower will also grind a custom crank to your specifications. All specs are in inches.

Crower

Description	Stroke	Mains	Rod	Seal	Part Number
Standard 4340	3.750	*	*	2-pc.	95125
Standard 4340	3.875	*	*	2-pc.	95127
Lightweight 4340	3.750	*	*	2-pc.	LW95125
Lightweight 4340	4.000	*	*	2-pc.	LW95128

*Crower will build the crank to your main journal and rod length requirements

Eagle Specialty Products

Description	Stroke	Mains	Rod	Seal	Part Number
Cast 383, ext. bal.	3.750	2.45	5.7	2-pc.	103503750
Cast 383, ext. bal.	3.750	2.45	5.7	1-pc.	103523750
4340 383, int. bal.	3.750	2.45	6.0	2-pc.	43503750600
4340 383, int. bal.	3.750	2.45	5.7	1-pc.	435337505700
4340 383, int. bal.	3.750	2.45	6.0	2-pc.	4350375057LW

Elgin

Description	Stroke	Mains	Rod	Seal	PN
Cast 383, ext. bal.	3.750	2.45	6.0	2-pc.	CS383P6
Cast 383, int. bal.	3.750	2.45	6.0	2-pc.	CS383P6B
Cast 383, ext. bal.	3.750	2.45	5.7	1-pc.	CS383PL

Elgin cranks available through Competition Specialties

GM Performance Parts

Description	Stroke	Mains	Rod	Seal	PN
Raw forging, 4340	up to 4.00	2.65/2.45	any	2-pc	24502460
4340 383	3.75	2.45	5.7	2-pd	12489436

Manley

Description	Stroke	Mains	Rod	Seal	PN
Nodular iron	3.75	2.45	5.7	2 pc	18101
Nodular iron, light	3.75	2.45	6.0	2 pc	18102
Nodular iron,	3.75	2.65	5.7	2 pc	18103
Nodular iron, light	3.75	2.65	6.0	2 pc	18104

Scat

Description	Stroke	Mains	Rod	Seal	Part Number
Cast, 383 ext. bal.	3.75	2.45	5.7	2 pc	9-350-3750-5700
Cast, 383 int. bal.	3.75	2.45	6.0	2 pc	9-350-3750-6000
4340, int. bal., light	3.75	2.45	6.0	2-pc.	4-350-3750-6000-2
4340, int. bal., light	3.875	2.65	6.0	2-pc.	4-400-3875-6000-2
4340, int. bal., light	4.000	2.65	6.0	2-pc	4-400-4000-6000-2
4340, int. bal., std	3.75	2.45	6.0	2-pc	4-350-3750-6000

Strength in any crankshaft is affected by the overlap between the main and rod journals. This is why Chevy increased the main journal diameter to 2.65-inch on the 400 small block and why long-stroke cranks should have larger main journal diameters. Note the minimal overlap with this crank.

While reducing weight is important, Oliver cranks are designed with this ridge that ties the main and rod journal together. This increases strength without radically increasing weight.

The smarter plan is to purchase a complete rotating assembly from one company and use their experience to create the proper combination of parts to avoid most (if not all) of the hidden custom-stroke landmines. For example, Crower offers crank and rod packages combined with JE pistons and rings to complete your rotating assembly. Eagle, Manley, Scat, and several other companies also offer multiple options when it comes to locating the right parts. The prices for these kits are usually competitive and might just give you a leg up when it comes to a custom bottom end.

Torsional Dampers

The torsional damper (often called a harmonic balancer) is a necessary component that is pressed onto the front of the crankshaft to help prolong crankshaft life. Every time a cylinder fires in the engine, a certain amount of twist is imparted into the crankshaft. As each cylinder fires in turn, these pulses set up a frequency. Every engine will create a certain RPM where these frequencies become resonant, which means that all those minor twists add up to create a severe vibration that can literally crack a crankshaft. The torsional damper, as its name implies, dampens or quiets these vibrations.

Crankshaft stiffness (or its resistance to twist) is mostly a function of overall length, material, stroke, and rod/main overlap. Since all small blocks are the same length, the material, stroke, and overlap become the critical factors. By design, a 4.00-inch stroke crank will have far less overlap material between the rods and the mains than a 3-inch stroke crank. Drag race engines accelerate through the RPM band so quickly that they spend very little time at any one RPM. Therefore, these engines are far less susceptible to resonant frequency damage. Endurance engines or any engine that spends a long period of time at one particular RPM (like land speed racing) are engines that can benefit from a quality damper.

All GM production dampers are what are called elastomeric, which means they use a vulcanized rubber bond between the inner hub and an outer iron ring. The stiffness of this rubber band, if you will, is designed to dampen the crankshaft at a specific frequency. These dampers, however, are designed for specific engine packages such as a production 400 or 350 engine. When you build a custom-stroke small block, this new engine will create very specific frequencies that are probably not the same as a stock production 400.

The aftermarket has addressed this dilemma with several damper designs. Some emulate production elastomeric designs while others take a completely different approach. For example, the Fluidampr design employs a one-piece hub and outer case that is filled with a synthetic viscous fluid. This fluid supports an inner steel core that floats in the viscous fluid and moves to dampen the inherent frequencies. Unfortunately, this damper design is also heavy, making it less desirable. You should ask the crankshaft manufacturer whether he would recommend one or not.

The most popular damper with most professional engine builders and crankshaft manufacturers is the ATI Super Damper. This damper uses an inner hub and outer shell and an internal inertia weight that is fitted on both its inside and outside diameters with elastomeric O-rings. ATI refers to this design as two dampers in one since it utilizes two sets of O-rings. ATI also offers O-ring kits in 6 different durometers, allowing the end user to custom design his own torsional damper. Basically, the higher rated durometer rubber O-rings are designed for high-RPM, long-stroke applications. ATI also offers these dampers in two diameters using either steel or aluminum shells. Perhaps the best choice for a damper would be to talk to your specific crankshaft manufacturer and go with their recommendation. What you will find is that most will spec the lightest balancer they can that still offers sufficient frequency control.

Conclusion

As you can see, there's much more to crankshafts than just stroke and weight. We've gone into some detail so that you understand the complex relationship of a stroker crank to the rest of the engine and how one decision can affect the makeup of the rest of the engine. This is why it is important to understand the basics of each component before you set off in quest of that magical stroker engine.

Crankshafts

Bob Weight

When researching crankshafts, you will often see a spec called bob weight. This refers to the mass located on a single crankshaft rod journal. This takes into account the weight of two pistons, pins, locks, rings, both the reciprocating and rotating portions of the connecting rod, and the rod bearings. To calculate bob weight, you must measure the individual components.

Where this can get complex is with lightweight crankshafts. Most crank manufacturers will specify a bob weight that the crankshaft can support without an excessive amount of balancing. This is another good reason to purchase a complete rotating assembly since the manufacturer will have already done the homework to ensure that all the components will spin nicely together without the need for expensive Mallory metal.

Let's say we have an Eagle 4340 steel crank for a 350-main journal 383 that is spec'd for a 1900-gram bob weight. But if you want to go with the lightweight 383 crank package, you have a choice of bob weight at either 1750 or 1875 grams. The selection will depend upon the weight of your pistons and rods.

This is the place for a definition of bob weight so that you can properly choose the right components. Bob weight is divided into two parts — rotating weight and reciprocating weight. Reciprocating weight is the weight of the piston, pin, locks (if used), rings, and the small end of the connecting rod. Rotating weight is the large end of the rod and the bearings. Some balance shops also add a couple of grams for oil on the small end of the rod for wet sump engines.

Here's where it gets interesting. You don't just add rotating and reciprocating weight together. Bob weight for any common-pin V-type engine is 100 percent of the rotating weight and 50 percent of the reciprocating weight for each crank throw. For other engines, like a Chevy 90-degree V6 with offset rod journals, the formula is different. In order to come up with the bob weight, the balance shop must weigh a rod on both ends. Usually this is accomplished by using a gram scale with an adjacent pendulum or hook. First, weigh the big end of the rod on the scale with the small end suspended. Note this figure and then reverse it and weigh the small end with the big end suspended 90-degrees to the scale. The total of the two figures should equal the total weight of the rod.

Let's create an example: All weights are expressed in grams.

	Reciprocating Weight	Rotating Weight
Rod bearing		50
Rod big end		400
Piston	500	
Pin	70	
Locks	4	
Rings	40	
Rod small end	176	
Sub total	790	450

50% of reciprocating weight X 2 (2 pistons for each crank throw) = 790 grams

100% of rotating weight x 2 = 900 grams

790 + 900 = 1690 grams of bob weight for one crank throw
(1 ounce equals 28.35 grams)

Now this bob weight can be compared to the crankshaft bob weight figure. As an example, if the bob weight for the crankshaft is 1875 grams as in the above Eagle crank, this means that the total weight of your piston and rod assembly is less than that of the counterweight for each throw. That's good news because it is easy to lighten the crank by drilling. On the other hand, if the lightweight crankshaft you bought has a bob weight of 1650 grams, which is lighter than our 1690 gram example, then you are faced with a couple of choices. The easiest thing to do is change the bob weight on the piston side by using lightweight wrist pins. Wrist pins can vary in weight by as much as 20 to 30 grams depending upon the weight of the original pin.

The more difficult and perhaps more expensive alternative is adding Mallory metal to the crankshaft to increase its bob weight. Mallory metal is slightly more than twice the density of steel, which makes it valuable for balancing crankshafts. Begin by drilling a hole on the side of the counterweight. This removes metal, but then the Mallory is pressed into the hole, increasing the weight of the counterweight. For a 1/2-inch hole 3/4-inch deep, Mallory metal weighs 43 grams while the drilled hole removes 18.8 grams for a net gain of 24.2 grams. This process is then done for each counterweight. This is an expensive process because of the labor involved and the cost of the Mallory metal. It's very easy to wrap up hundreds of dollars in balancing mismatched pistons and rods to a crank. That's why it's critical to know the bob weights before you purchase individual components to create your own rotating assembly.

Even after you purchase a complete rotating assembly, you still need to have it balanced so that you can include the torsional damper and flywheel/flexplate. For big-inch small blocks, it's best to preassemble the rotating assembly in the engine before balancing. That way, if you have to massage a few rods to clear an obstruction, this will be accomplished before the system is balanced.

CHAPTER 5

CONNECTING RODS

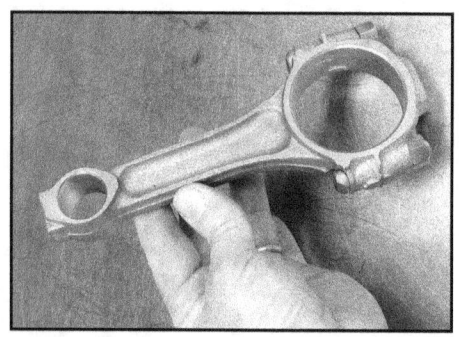

Stock small-block Chevy connecting rods for the 400 small block came in two lengths, 5.7 and 5.565-inches. Don't be lured in by the idea that the so-called "pink" rod is a stronger rod. The only thing the pink rods offered was that they were shot peened and Magnafluxed. Otherwise, they were forged of the same mild steel as other production rods.

The connecting rod is a simple enough part. While it accelerates and deccelerates at incredible speeds, it has no moving parts. As unassuming as it appears, the connecting rod is one of the most highly stressed and abused components in any internal combustion engine. Step into the world of high performance, high horsepower, and most importantly — high RPM, and it pays to spend some time to make the most of your connecting rods.

In stock street applications where engine speed rarely exceeds 6000 rpm, stock connecting rods do an excellent job of transferring the power from the piston to the crank. But add cylinder pressure, big cylinder heads, and long duration camshafts that require higher RPM to produce horsepower, and that's when we have to start paying closer attention to the lowly connecting rod.

STOCK RODS

When you talk about stock small-block Chevy connecting rods, the two most popular overall lengths are 5.7 and 5.565-inches. Go all the way back to the original 265ci mouse motor and you'll find that Chevy elected to use a 5.7-inch long connecting rod. As stroke increased from 3.00 to 3.25 to 3.48-inches, rod length remained the same. With the arrival of the 400 small block in 1970, there wasn't room to maintain the piston compression height that GM desired with a 5.7-inch rod, so the engineers shortened the rod by 0.135-inch to 5.565 inches. At the same time, the engineers also shortened the rod bolt slightly to create more clearance between the bolts and the cam. There is a third small-block rod used in the 350 H.O. and ZZ4 engines that is a 5.940-inch powdered metal (PM) rod that is every bit as strong as the original "pink" small-block rods. This rod was also used in the baby 265ci LT1-based engines from 1992 to 1994.

Production small-block rods are all constructed using a basic forged I-beam design with a stud-and-nut fastener. Gen

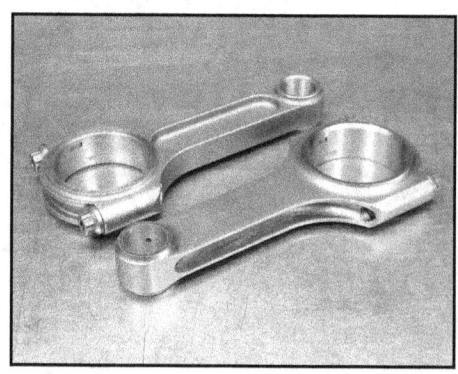

There are two basic connecting rod designs. The production-based I-beam rod (top) is the most popular, but the H-beam rod is now a popular performance alternative.

III small blocks also employ the powdered metal forging that is actually a little stronger. The other interesting technique employed in conjunction with these rods is the one-piece forging uses a cap that is broken off the main part of the beam. This jagged edge looks nasty but does a superior job of locating the cap to the rod, preventing what is generally referred to as cap walk. Unfortunately, it is not rebuildable since the jagged mating surface cannot be machined to make the big end smaller to resize it.

Stock rods work well on street engines that will not see more than 6,500 rpm and see that speed only for very short periods of time. But since high-performance engines are all pushing the

Connecting Rods

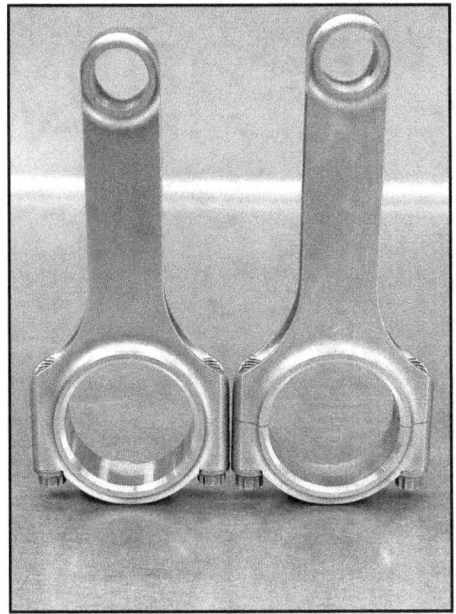

When you add stroke, it's best to increase the rod length at the same time in order to reduce the acute angle created by the longer arm on the crank. Popular long-rod lengths for the small block are 5.850, 6.000, and 6.125, but some companies make rods as long as 6.25 inches.

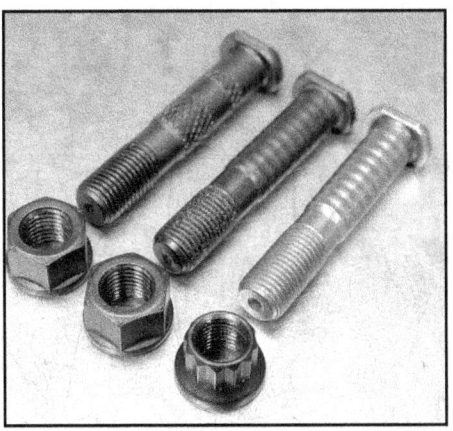

The most highly stressed fastener in any engine is the connecting-rod bolt. ARP offers rod bolts in three quality steps from the standard 190,000 psi 8740 bolt (left), to the Wave-Loc bolt (center), to the Pro Series Wave-Loc (right) made from a proprietary ARP 2000 material offering about 220,000 psi tensile strength.

Any time you replace rod bolts, you must also resize the rod in order to create the proper housing bore diameter. This housing bore diameter determines the proper inside diameter for the rod bearings in order to create the proper bearing clearance.

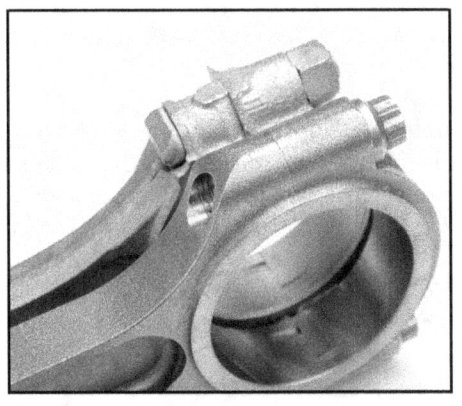

Longer strokes create problems with cam-to-rod clearance. This often requires the use of stroker rods that offer additional room in the area just above the rod bolt. As stroke grows, this clearance becomes increasingly tight.

envelope, there are better quality rods out there for such an attractive price that the aftermarket rods deserve significant attention. If you're on a tight budget and plan on using a 5.7 rod in an affordable 383 or 406ci small block, the smart move is to Magnaflux the rods for cracks, have your local machine shop install new ARP bolts, and then resize the big end of the rod. The big end must be resized anytime a new fastener is used since the new bolt will drastically alter the shape of the big end when it is torqued in place. You can also polish the side beams to prevent the formation of stress cracks.

Material

Stock Chevy rods are constructed of 1038 mild steel that offers decent strength combined with great ductility. Performance applications apply much more stress to the connecting rod than stock applications, so long ago companies like Carrillo, Oliver, and Crower started building extremely strong 4340 steel rods for racing applications. In the last few years, several new companies have jumped into the high-performance connecting rod market with inexpensive, yet high-quality 4340 and 4130 forged steel rods. For mild street engines, the next step up from stock would be the 4130 steel rods, and then on to the higher-quality 4340 forging.

There are several companies building 4340 steel rods. The difference in price can be substantial when you compare a Scat or Eagle 4340 steel rod to a rod like a Carrillo or Oliver. There's no disputing the quality of the Carrillo or Oliver rods, but the additional quality may or may not be worth the additional cost. Crower perhaps has the widest range of rods, all forged with 4340 steel, but varying widely in price and application. Selection then is more a question of application than price. For example, the Crower Sportsman is the entry-level 4340 chromoly steel rod that includes a 3/8-inch, 8740, 180,000 psi steel alloy bolt and nut. Increasing in price are the Sportsman Stroker, Billet, Billet Stroker, and Lightweight rods using through-style bolts and nuts. There are also Billet, Billet Stroker, and Midweight rods using cap screws. There's even an Ultra-Light cap screw rod. All told, Crower offers 14 different connecting rods for the small-block Chevy. All of these rods are built from 4340 steel, but vary dramatically in quality, application, and price. As you can see, there are plenty to choose from. But don't be misled into thinking that you need the trickest rod. The reality is probably the basic 5.7 or 6.0-inch Sportsman or Stroker rod would probably work best in most applications.

We mentioned billet rods as part of the Crower lineup. Oliver, Carrillo and others also offer billet rods, as do several other companies. A 4340-chromoly steel billet rod is generally considered to be the strongest, most durable rod made.

Chapter 5

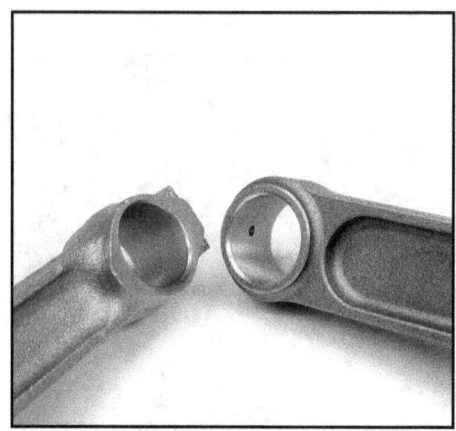

High performance rods are also available in either pressed pin (left) or full floating styles (right) identified by its bronze bushing. Full floating rods require using some type of piston locking rings to keep the pin inside the piston.

In order to determine bob weight, you must know the weight of both the big and small end of the rod. Each end is weighed using a fixture like this one. Those weights, when added together, must match the overall total weight of the rod.

ProForm makes a tool to remove the rod cap from a rod, but you can also use a rod vise. Loosen the nuts and then gently rock the rod until the cap loosens up.

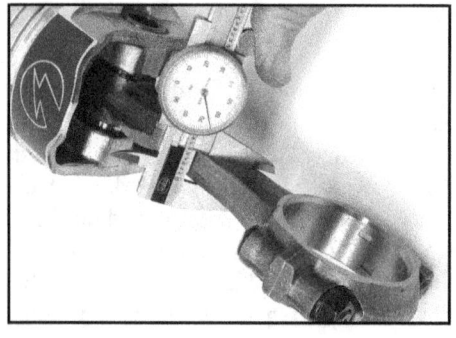

Another reason to not use stock rods is that in the mid 1980s, Chevy went to a thinner I-beam rod. The weights are the same, but the center portion of the rod is roughly 0.070-inch thinner. It's best to avoid these rods.

It comes in either through-bolt or cap-screw configurations. Billet rods are cut from pure parent material, as opposed to being pressed in a forge. This offers excellent flexibility in design, but dramatically increases the price. For street engines, billet rods would be considered a rather expensive luxury.

Pure drag race engines often employ aluminum rods in an effort to further reduce reciprocating weight. The only reason we mention them here is because some enthusiasts have the mistaken impression that there might be some advantage by employing aluminum connecting rods. Bill Miller Engineering (BME) contends that they have successfully used aluminum connecting rods in many street engines without failure, and we certainly are not in a position to refute those claims. However, any metallurgist will agree that even the best aluminum alloy is no match for 4340 chromoly steel in the strength department and that aluminum is far more prone to work hardening with use. These factors alone make an aluminum rod choice difficult to defend. The weight reduction may offer few, if any, advantages when it comes to creating a given bob weight. With all these considerations working against an aluminum rod, there are few credible reasons to support risking a rod failure.

STROKER RODS

The whole point of this book is to show you how to build a big-inch small block. One of the stumbling blocks to building a long-stroke mouse motor is camshaft-to-rod clearance. With the original 400, Chevy resorted to a shorter 5.565-inch rod with a shorter bolt. This produced plenty of cam clearance, but the short rod creates several problems when venturing beyond the factory 3.75-inch stroke. Because additional stroke makes the crankshaft counterweights larger, this also requires a longer rod in order to allow enough room for the piston to clear the counterweights at bottom dead center (BDC). Generally, a 5.7 or 6.0-inch rod is preferable, but you can find small-block rod lengths all the way up to 6.250-inches in length.

In addition to the length question, you will also need a rod with sufficient clearance around the upper portion of the big end. This is where the rod comes closest to the camshaft, just past top dead center (TDC). Stroker rods offer additional clearance around this area, making it easier to stuff a longer stroke crank into a standard deck-height block. It is possible to cram a 4.00-inch stroke crank into a standard cam-height block. The tightest clearance between the rods and the cam occur with rods 1,2, 5, and 6; but because of balance considerations, all the rods must be clearanced the same.

Many rod companies do not differentiate between their standard 4340 rods and stroker rods, so you need to contact the manufacturer to determine if the rods you want to use will clear the stroke you intend to employ. Crower's Stroker Sportsman rods are only available in 5.7 and 6.0-inch lengths but the stroker billet rod has more options ranging from 5.7 to 6.250-inches. Not only is the rod stronger, but also substantially heavier at 690 grams for a 6.0-inch rod compared to the Sportsman Stroker 6.0-inch rod that weighs only 615 grams. Clearly, the heavier billet rod is stronger,

Rod Length vs. Stroke

Mechanical engineers and hot rodders are always looking for a shorthand way to look at building a performance engine. There has been much debate in the high-performance world on the relative merits of connecting rod length. Long rod combinations have received a lot of support from famous engine builders like the late Smokey Yunick. Other race engine builders like Pro Stock drag racing engine builder David Reher contend that rod length plays almost no part in power. We have witnessed short rod lengths that tend to push the piston harder against the cylinder wall as evidenced by larger wear patterns in the cylinder's otherwise virgin cross-hatch.

It is easy to see that as stroke increases, the same length rod effectively becomes shorter in relationship to the stroke. The easiest way to look at this relationship is to use something called the rod-length-to-stroke ratio or L/R. The rod ratio is simply the length of the rod divided by the length of the stroke. For example, a stock 350ci small block with a rod length of 5.7-inches and a stroke of 3.48-inches has an L/R of 1.64:1. The equation dictates that as stroke increases, the rod length will also have to increase proportionately in order to maintain the same L/R or rod ratio.

Long stroke engines make increasing the rod length difficult since we are faced with the limitations of a given block deck height. For example, with a stock deck height of 9.025-inches, a

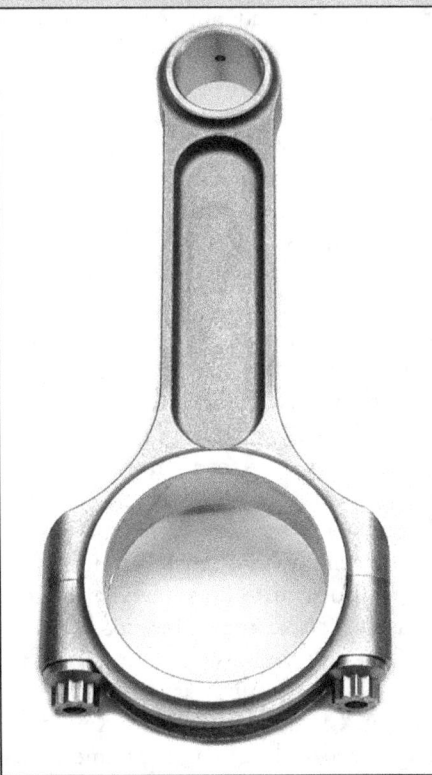

4.00-inch stroke, and a rod length of 6.0-inches, this leaves us with a compression height (the distance between the deck surface of the piston and the pin centerline — more on this in the next chapter on pistons) of 1.025 inch, which is the absolute bare minimum. Therefore, a longer rod is not possible unless we increase the deck height. A 6.0-inch rod in a 4.00-inch stroke engine only produces an L/R of 1.5:1, which is somewhat short. This means that the rod will tend push the piston harder into the thrust side of the block. This creates additional side load, friction, and wear. Despite this short L/R, there's little evidence to support that the engine loses horsepower due to this condition. We've included a chart that lists the L/R ratios for most popular stroke and rod length combinations. One of the disadvantages of a stock-deck small block is the physical limitation of a short deck height that prevents creating an acceptable L/R ratio with a long stroke engine. As stroke increases, the room left for a long rod is limited. Shoot for the longest rod you can squeeze into the engine without compromising the piston by moving the wrist pin too far up into the oil rings on the piston.

Stroke (inches)	Rod Length (inches)	L/R ratio
3.00	5.7	1.90:1
3.25	5.7	1.75:1
3.48	5.7	1.64:1
3.48	6.0	1.72:1
3.75	5.565	1.48:1
3.75	5.7	1.52:1
3.75	5.85	1.56:1
3.75	6.0	1.60:1
3.875	5.7	1.47:1
3.875	6.0	1.55:1
3.875	6.125	1.58:1
4.0	5.7	1.42:1
4.0	5.85	1.46:1
4.0	6.0	1.50:1
4.0	6.125	1.53:1
4.0	6.25	1.56:1

and much of its strength comes from its additional material. You must also consider rod clearance around the pan rail as well when shopping for a stroker connecting rod. Not all rods are shaped the same. Certainly, the stroker rods will offer some additional clearance is this area as well.

Fasteners

The most highly stressed fastener in the entire engine is the connecting-rod bolt. The sidebar on Strength vs. RPM will detail the loads imposed on a connecting rod and its fasteners, but the bottom line is that as the weight of the reciprocating system and RPM both increase, the forces that are trying to stretch the two bolts holding the cap on the connecting rod increase radically. Both weight and RPM are critical to this formula but certainly the most damaging is RPM. For example, a 4.0-inch bore, 3.875-inch stroke engine can

Chapter 5

Rod side clearance is one of those clearances that can be easily overlooked in the rush to assemble an engine. But if you are using all new parts, you absolutely must ensure that the clearances are within spec. Minimum rod side clearance for steel rods is between 0.010-0.012-inch. Greater clearance allows more oil to splash around the crankcase.

Always check that the chamfer on the rod bearing is adjacent to the fillet radius on the crank (arrow). More than one engine builder has inadvertently installed the rod backwards on the piston.

impose as much as 12,380 pounds of tensile load on the big end of the connecting rod as the rod accelerates away from TDC at 6,500 rpm. This happens every time the piston comes across TDC on the overlap stroke. When you consider the number of cycles an engine goes through (even though a majority are not at high RPM), this still requires tremendous rod-bolt strength.

Fasteners are a study unto themselves, but we'll try to condense the essentials down to a few simple paragraphs to give you the information you need to choose the right rod bolts. Most rod bolts are rated in terms of psi, which is the rating system used to define the stress or the load applied to the bolt divided by its cross-sectional area. This is why a larger diameter bolt made of the same material is stronger and offers more potential clamp load than a smaller fastener. Unfortunately, larger bolts weigh more so the ideal compromise is a strong material in a smaller bolt. The ultimate tensile strength is the maximum stress that a fastener can withstand without breaking. Each fastener also has a maximum amount of strength that it can withstand and return to its normal length. This is called the fastener's yield strength. If you exceed a fastener's yield strength, the fastener is ruined and should be replaced.

Extremely high tensile strength fasteners also tend to be somewhat brittle. That means that the difference between the fastener's yield strength and its ultimate tensile strength is a fairly small amount. Clamp load is force exerted by a tightened bolt and is the same as its preload. What makes life difficult for rod bolts is that they must have high yield and tensile strength but they must also be able to withstand well over a million cycles of tensile, or stretch, loads.

A high-quality connecting-rod fastener should therefore have a high enough tensile strength, but also have a fairly wide load range between its yield strength and its ultimate tensile strength. It is in this band where it may be asked to operate. This is why creating the proper preload or clamp load with a rod bolt is so important. This is most accurately measured in bolt stretch. Typically, ARP specifies a bolt stretch dimension that is 75 percent of the bolt's yield strength. So if a typical 3/8-inch ARP rod-bolt stretch figure is 0.006-inch, then its yield length is probably very close to 0.008-inch. The point here is to establish a clamping load that is far greater than the load imposed on the bolt during engine operation. During the point where the piston changes direction downward after top dead center (TDC) during the

Checking bearing clearance requires torquing the rod bolts outside the engine. Always use a rod vise when torquing the rods to prevent tweaking the rod. Make sure the vise supports both the cap and the beam of the rod.

overlap cycle, the crankshaft pulls down on the piston. This places the rod bolts in tension. At high RPM, this can actually deform the big end of the rod, making it oval and placing extreme loads on the rod bolts. This is why the clamping load is so important.

The only way to achieve this optimal stretch figure is to measure the bolt. This is accomplished with a rod-bolt stretch tool. Several companies, including ARP, sell this tool, which is really nothing more than a steel fixture mounted to a dial indicator. The dial indicator uses a heavier return spring than common dial indicators to help the tool remain in place on the rod bolt. This is helpful in the engine since this tool is most often used in the tight confines of a lower rotating assembly. The checking procedure is also simple. Place a box end wrench over the rod bolt with the fastener hand tight. Then position the stretch gauge so that you can read the dial indicator with the two points of the indicator located securely on the small divots on both ends of the fastener. These divots help hold the indicator points in position. Zero the indicator and then slowly tighten the rod-bolt nut until the desired stretch is achieved. This must be accomplished on all 16 rod bolts for a V8 engine.

If this sounds like way too much effort — it is. But if you are investing a couple thousand dollars in a quality rotating assembly, this is the only

Connecting Rods

Rod Strength

Most enthusiasts are under the mistaken impression that big horsepower numbers create greater stress on a connecting rod due to elevated cylinder pressures. It's true that cylinder pressure does place massive loads on a connecting rod. However, much like a column that is used to support a load of hundreds of thousands of pounds for a building, a connecting rod is designed to support a huge compressive load where the piston pushes straight down. A properly designed connecting rod can support these loads with very little stress on the main portion of the rod.

Where a rod is more highly stressed and has the greatest chance for failure exists has much more to do with reciprocating weight and engine speed than with horsepower. During engine operation, as the piston begins its downward path after top dead center (TDC), the crankshaft pulls down on the piston, accelerating the mass of the piston, rings, wrist pin, and small end of the rod. The heavier the reciprocating mass, the greater the force required to accelerate that mass away from TDC. The weight portion of this equation should be obvious, but RPM also plays a major role. Increasing engine speed also increases the force exerted on the rod, especially the big end where the fasteners must try to hold the rod together.

The next major factor is stroke. Let's say that you have a 350ci small block with a 3.48-inch stroke spinning at 6,000 rpm, which means the piston must travel 3.48 inches in a given amount of time. Now let's increase the stroke to 4.00 inches. At the same engine speed of 6,000 rpm, the 4.00-inch stroke piston must accelerate much quicker and travel at a higher speed in order to traverse that additional 0.520-inch longer distance in the same amount of time (6,000 rpm). So even though the engine is running at the same RPM, there are dramatically greater connecting rod loads inflicted upon a long-stroke motor compared to its short-stroke cousin.

RPM	Stroke (inches)	Average Speed (fps)
6500	3.48	125,070
6500	3.75	130,282
6500	4.00	135,107
6750	3.48	134,876
6750	3.75	140,496
6750	4.00	145,700
7000	3.48	145,052
7000	3.75	151,096
7000	4.00	156,692

Ironically, most rod manufacturers rate their connecting rods by horsepower first, and then by RPM. This is because most customers do not understand the extreme forces that the rod must endure. We thought we'd take a look at some simple numbers to give you an idea of what is occurring inside your engine. Let's take a look at several stroke and RPM combinations to evaluate average piston velocity.

The generally accepted maximum continuous use limit for an endurance engine is 150,000 fps.

As you can see, RPM has a huge affect on average piston speed. Add in the weight of a piston and rod assembly, and you start to see how a heavy piston and rod combined with high RPM can really put the hurt on a connecting rod. The place where this stress is the greatest is the mating surface of the cap and the rod. Maintaining this connection is the rod bolts' job. As an example, a 1360-gram piston and rod package would create almost 14,000 pounds of force in tension with an average piston speed of 150,000 fps. That means there is 14,000 pounds of force trying to rip the cap off the rod!

Clearly, weight of the reciprocating package and RPM are the two most important factors in connecting rod stress. A high-quality rod with an acceptable rotating weight that is spun below 7,000 rpm will probably live for a long time. Keep in mind that this 150,000 fps piston speed is rated for maximum continuous RPM. Revving the engine at a higher RPM for very short periods of time is still stressful to the engine, but may not result in engine damage. Knowing all this might at least get you to think twice before buzzing that stroker motor to the moon.

Chapter 5

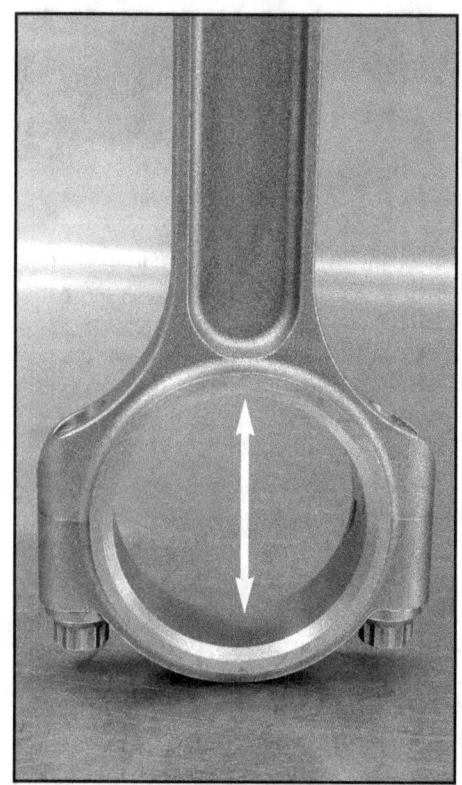

Always measure bearing clearance in the vertical. All engine bearings employ a certain amount of taper towards the horizontal component. Measuring the inner diameter of the rod at the parting line will produce an erroneous wide clearance.

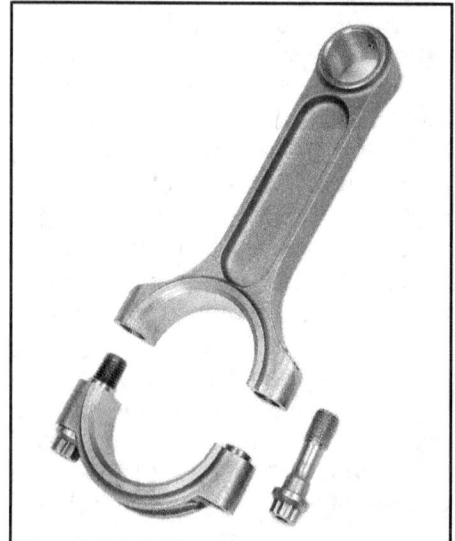

Many higher-quality rods employ cap screws rather than bolts and nuts. The cap screws offer certain height advantages for stroker applications and can be measured for bolt stretch just like any other rod bolt.

Another advantage to using a higher-quality aftermarket rod is these locating dowels that prevent rod cap walk under high-RPM applications.

Cycling the rod bolt several times also helps seat the rod bolt in the rod. Sometimes the machine shop does not fully seat the bolt in the rod due to a tight fit between the bolt and rod. Torquing will usually fully seat the bolt in place.

acceptable way to ensure that the rod bolts are adequately loaded. Some may contend that using a torque wrench is sufficient, but the reality is that there are entirely too many variables that affect bolt torque that have little to do with stretching the bolt. For example, ARP specifies a torque setting intended to be used only in conjunction with ARP's moly lubricant. This lubricant offers a reduced coefficient of friction than motor oil, which is why the lubricant torque is always less than the torque specified when using oil. We have tested these torque figures against actual bolt stretch and because ARP cannot account for all the variables, we've found the ARP torque figure usually creates a bolt stretch that is less than the optimal spec. We have tested this on several occasions and we consistently come up at least 0.0008 to 0.0010-inch shy of ARP's specified bolt-stretch figure. This is why measuring the actual bolt stretch is the only way to go.

There are actually no excuses for not using a rod-bolt stretch tool. These tools are not that expensive (usually around $100) and are easy to use. However, in an emergency, you certainly can merely torque the rod bolts in place. If you are using brand new fasteners, ARP recommends torquing each fastener at least five times before the final torque is applied during assembly. This is because new fasteners need to establish a wear pattern between the nut and bolt and within the threads. This may also take into consideration the rare time when a rod bolt is not fully seated in the rod. Torquing the fastener at least five times should seat the bolt in the rod and establish a reasonable wear pattern that will allow more of the actual torque to create bolt stretch as opposed to merely overcoming friction.

Torque wrench accuracy is another variable that affects the fastener torque and stretch. It is not uncommon to find a torque wrench that is off by as much as 10 ft-lbs when checked for accuracy. If you have not had your wrench calibrated, have it checked at the specified torque setting for the rod bolts. That way you can at least account for this variable.

If you really want to know if a rod bolt has been stretched beyond its yield point, then you need to also keep track of the relaxed length of each fastener when it was new. During subsequent teardown, the bolts can be re-checked for length. If a used bolt is even as little as 0.001-inch longer than its original relaxed length, it has been stretched beyond its yield point and must be replaced. We've expended a significant amount of this chapter on rod bolts and their use because of the catastrophic damage that can occur if these specifications are not followed. Spend time making sure this area is assembled properly and you can avoid most of the expensive problems.

Connecting Rods

This cutaway shows just how close all the rotating parts are when you stuff a long-stroke crank and long rods in a small block. The minimum clearance for the rod to the camshaft is 0.050-inch.

If you must torque rod bolts in place rather than using a stretch gauge, ARP recommends you torque the rod bolts at least three to five times. This burnishes and smooths the threads and the rod-nut to rod interface, which creates less friction. Also be sure to use only the rod-bolt moly lube that comes with the ARP bolts.

How to Measure Stretch

With all the hype about rod-bolt stretch, you'd think that there would be some kind of elaborate procedure to go along with all the technical hoopla. The good news is that measuring stretch is almost as easy as tightening the bolt. To start off, slip all the piston/rod assemblies in the engine, install the rod caps, and hand tighten all the rod nuts in place. Next, slip a box-end wrench over the rod-bolt nut. Now place the rod-bolt stretch gauge over the rod bolt and position the points on both ends of the gauge into the small divots in the bolt. This is probably the most important step, since you want to ensure the gauge is accurately located on the bolt. Zero the dial indicator and now you're ready to start tightening.

We've found that we often need a pipe over the end of a short end wrench in order to create the torque necessary to achieve the bolt stretch figure. Work slowly and make sure the wrench doesn't contact the gauge fixture, which could create an erroneous reading. We like to start at the front of the engine and slowly work to the rear. After the last rod nut, check each rod bolt nut with a torque wrench to ensure you didn't miss one but reduce your rated torque spec by 10 ft-lb so you don't over torque. That's it.

A torque wrench only approximates bolt clamp load by measuring friction. The far more accurate method is to use a rod bolt stretch gauge like this one from ARP. Any given bolt will offer maximum clamp load when stretched slightly less than its yield point.

I-Beam, H-Beam

In addition to all the other variables involved with connecting rods, the aftermarket has also begun offering a different style of rod called the H-beam rod. H-beam rods were developed for racing engine use and were designed to be stronger in high-RPM use where the rod's ability to withstand increased load in tension are an advantage.

The traditional connecting rod design is the I-beam style, which, according to the manufacturers that we've interviewed, is stronger in compression compared to the H-beam rod, mainly due to reduced stress concentrations. Since most large displacement small blocks will be built more as torque engines rather than stratospheric-RPM powerplants, the I-beam rod appears to be the more sensible choice. However, there is certainly nothing wrong with using H-beam rods in almost any application and the differences in strength are probably not going to make a difference in terms of a potential failure.

After wading through all this material on connecting rods, hopefully you've gained a greater appreciation for both selection and application of this often-overlooked component. Connecting rods are not generally associated with massive power improvements, but they do play an essential role in making sure that all the power you do make is created durably and reliably.

CHAPTER 6

PISTONS AND RINGS

In the simplest of terms, a piston is just a slug of aluminum that moves up and down in the cylinder and takes the brunt of the cylinder pressure. But in reality, there's more than a little engineering that goes into that alloy slug. We'll spend a few pages on these cam-shaped pieces that attract more than their share of attention from engine builders and enthusiasts alike.

MATERIALS AND PROCESSES

For your basic street engine, cast pistons work just fine. But we're interested in more than just pedestrian street power plants. For any performance application, forgings are the only pistons worth discussing. Cast pistons offer minimal strength; and hypereutectic pistons, while stronger, are very brittle and react to detonation by shattering, which is not what you want in any power plant, let alone a high-output performance engine. Given these limitations, forging is the only realistic choice. But there's much more to ordering pistons than just picking a compression ratio.

Cast and Hypereutectic

We will spend a limited amount of time with these pistons since they represent such a small portion of the big-inch small-block market. First of all, there's no reason to even consider a cast piston for any kind of performance engine buildup. Cast pistons have their place in low-performance, stock production engines because they are inexpensive to build and are durable within the realm of low-RPM engines. The problem with cast pistons is that they are both heavy and brittle. The weak link with cast pistons is the ring lands. Combine a heavy dose of cylinder pressure with even mild detonation and the ring land will break every time. When cast pistons fail, they virtually explode due to their brittle construction. As a result, those pieces help destroy the rest of the engine. At least with forged pistons, if there is a problem, the piston tends to deform rather than break, which limits the damage to that cylinder, as opposed to trashing the rest of the engine.

Hypereutectic pistons came on the market several years ago as a bridge between cast and forged pistons. The Keith Black hypereutectic pistons were the first, followed shortly by Federal-Mogul. Hypereutectic pistons are essen-

There are several common piston definitions worth knowing: (A) compression height, (B) ring land, (C) skirt, (D) top ring groove, (E) second ring groove, (F) oil ring groove.

Cast pistons (left) are best left for stock applications because they are very brittle. Hypereutectic pistons like this KB (center) are slightly stronger and are offered in a few stroker applications. The best pistons for performance use are forgings such as this one from Federal-Mogul (right).

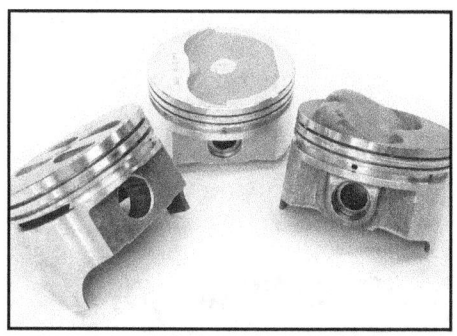

Flat-top pistons (left) often employ four valve reliefs so that the same piston can be used in all eight cylinders. Dished pistons (center) offer additional chamber volume to reduce static compression on long-stroke engines. The only time you would use domed pistons (right) on a big-inch small block is for a pure race motor where more than 12:1 compression is desired.

tially cast aluminum pistons made with a high silicon content alloy that is significantly stronger than a typical casting. So much so, that machining hypereutectic pistons must be accomplished using diamond tooling. However, these are still cast pistons, and as a result are susceptible to breakage under detonation. The concept was that hypereutectic pistons were less expensive than forgings and were offered in several different rod length applications for stroker combos like the popular 383.

Where the hypereutectic piston fills a need is with a budget-oriented 383 small block where the engine is built with a cast crank, stock rods, and a mild cam and cylinder heads. Since this engine will not see a lot of RPM or high cylinder pressures, the hypereutectic piston is a good choice. Cost should always be a consideration as well. Hypereutectic pistons cost around $250 to $300 depending upon the application, which is less than a good forged SRP piston, for example, but about the same price as a budget forging. If you can find a forging for a budget application like this for the same price as a hypereutectic piston, then the forging will always be the better deal. This holds true even if the forging is slightly heavier than the hypereutectic. A stronger piston is always a better choice.

Forgings

The first forged pistons were merely stronger clones of OEM castings. Forged pistons are created using a stronger-alloy aluminum squeezed in a press with thousands of pounds of force. Pressing the material eliminates voids in the material and creates a stronger base that is able to handle the stresses imposed by high cylinder pressures and engine speeds. Ironically, the old original TRW pistons weren't actually forgings, but rather an extrusion, that wasn't quite as strong as a true forging. Many race engines employed these pistons mainly because they were the only alternative to expensive custom-made pistons. Later, high-production pistons were created as forgings in the basic shape that required only minimal machine work to complete the rings, skirt shape, and pin boss size. While strong, these pistons tend to be heavy and are only offered in a limited selection when it comes to rod length, ring thickness, and other options.

Federal-Mogul carries on the tradition of excellent forgings at an affordable price with a tremendous general performance selection of pistons in its PowerForged lineup. Most of these pistons are constructed of what they call a VMS-75 alloy. This is an aluminum alloy that includes 11 percent silicon to add toughness and give the piston excellent skirt-area scuff resistance as well as reduced ring-groove wear. One additional advantage to these pistons is a high production rate that allows them to be attractively priced. Unfortunately, Federal-Mogul offers a limited selection when it comes to big-inch small block applications other than 377, 383, and 406 displacements with either 5.7- or 6.0-inch rod lengths.

Custom pistons aren't part of the Federal-Mogul lineup, but recently the company has added a few CNC-machined 2618 alloy race pistons. For example, the LW2604 383 piston, is designed for a 5.850-inch rod-length. It offers close to 10:1 compression ratio with a 64cc chamber, minimal deck height, and weighs a mere 441 grams. With the 2618 material, Federal-Mogul

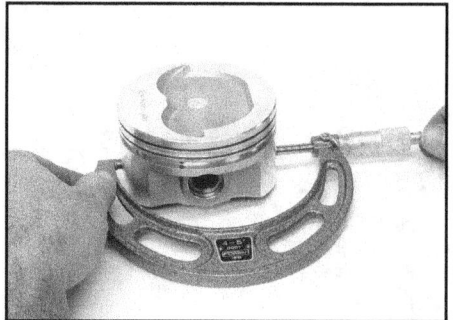

Pistons are cam ground, which means the widest point of the piston is the area roughly at or just below and 90 degrees to the wrist-pin centerline. This is the best place to measure for piston-to-wall clearance.

considers this a race-style piston and doesn't recommend it for the street.

This brings us to the 2618 aluminum-alloy material that begins life as a forged chunk and is fully CNC-machined into its final shape. While this has been the playground of the custom piston companies like Diamond, JE, Ross, Venolia, Wiseco, and others, even Federal-Mogul is now playing in this arena. There is evidence to support the fact that 2618 is not as scuff resistant as the 11-percent silicon-style pistons, and therefore perhaps not as durable for daily street operation. For a 100,000-mile engine, this is probably true. However, few of the engines that will be covered in this book are intended as high mileage powerplants. Most hot street and track engines will probably see far less than 20,000 miles in their lifetime before a teardown and inspection. The advantage offered by the 2618 alloy is its excellent ductility, which allows it to withstand the pounding of high cylinder pressures without cracking.

Another, perhaps less well known piston alloy is 4032, which is similar in most respects to Federal-Mogul's VMS-75. The 4032 alloy is enhanced with 12-percent silicon that adds scuff resistance and excellent durability. While not well publicized, many of the custom piston manufacturers like JE, SRP, and Wiseco offer both the 2618 and 4032 alloy pistons. Using 4032 instead of 2618 really comes down to application. If the piston

Chapter 6

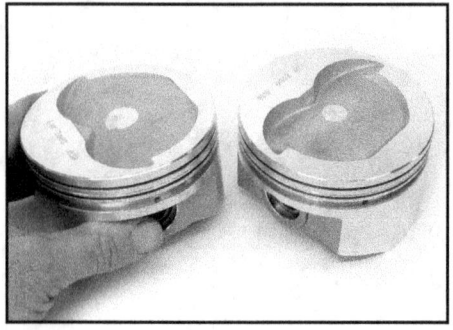

The best dished pistons utilize what JE calls a reverse dome. The flat portion of the piston creates an excellent quench area that can actually allow dialing in more static compression and yet reduce the engine's total ignition timing requirements.

It's almost impossible to look at a CNC-machined piston and be able to tell if it is a 2618 or a 4032 alloy piston. This happens to be a 2618 dished 400 piston from Federal-Mogul.

Compression height is the distance from the centerline of the wrist pin to the flat portion (not the dome) of the piston. Compression height, rod length, block deck height, and stroke must be properly matched when building a big-inch small block.

will see a majority of street use with some track time, the high silicon content 4032 piston is probably the better choice. If the engine will see limited street use and more track time, then the selection of a 2618 alloy piston may be the better way to go. Not all piston companies offer the 4032 alloy, but if you intend to build a big-inch street engine, you may want to ask your piston manufacturer if your piston choice is offered in this material.

Dished or Domed?

The first thing everyone wants to know about any particular piston is the compression that it generates. While the piston helps generate the ultimate compression ratio, piston configuration is only one part of a greater equation determined by bore, stroke, deck height, combustion chamber, and head gasket volumes. We'll deal with how to determine compression ratio in the accompanying sidebar, but a rule of thumb for any engine is that even a small change in bore or stroke with a big-inch engine tends to really bump the compression. As an example, let's say we have a 418ci small block with a 4.155 bore, a 3.850-inch stroke, 20cc-dished pistons, a deck height of 0.005-inch, a 64cc chamber, and a 0.041-inch thick head gasket. This creates a compression ratio of 10.08:1. Increase the bore to 4.185-inch and the compression jumps to 10.20 for an increase of 0.12 of a ratio. Tickle the stroke from 3.85 to 4.00 and the compression spikes to 10.43:1. In both cases we have increased the volume that the piston squeezes.

Since big-inch small blocks larger than 383 or 406 inches are only now becoming popular, the demand has not been sufficient to warrant off-the-shelf pistons. This means that a big-inch small block may need a piston with a 20cc or larger dish in order to place the compression around 10.5:1 with the increasingly popular 64cc chamber. An inspection of the major piston manufacturer catalogs reveals very few dished pistons with bore sizes larger than 4.155-inch as on-the-shelf items. This means these pistons would have to be custom ordered. With the widespread use of CNC machines, this does not mean the pistons will be extremely expensive, but you can expect to pay at least $600 for a set, depending upon your specific requirements.

For the sake of discussion, domed pistons aren't really even a consideration with large displacement engines unless you are looking for a compression ratio above 14:1. As an example, just adding flat top pistons to our original 418ci example engine creates 12.5:1 compression. Obviously, as the displacement increases, there is less need for domed pistons, unless you are aiming at pure, drag-race compression ratios. This is another advantage of the large-displacement small block over a rat motor where a 100cc chamber is considered small. With 119cc chambers, rat motors require a domed piston just to bump the compression to around 10:1. Piston domes tend to get in the way of the flame front, which is why using flattop or dished pistons with small chambers is a much cleaner way to make compression.

It's worth it at this point to discuss what JE calls inverted dome or D-cup style dished pistons. In the early days of piston design, the piston dish extended

Pistons and Rings

Ring placement is best left to the manufacturer, and is often dictated by the compression height of the piston. Most piston manufacturers prefer to set the top ring at least 0.200-inch down from the top or more, if the piston will see nitrous action.

Lightweight pistons are certainly beneficial, but don't go overboard, especially for a street engine. There is strength in weight. Matching piston weight to the crankshaft bob weight is also a major variable that must be considered.

Almost all performance pistons now come with 1/16th, 1/16th, and 3/16th-in ring grooves, since this style of ring is far superior to 5/64th-in ring widths.

across the entire top of the piston. But since the small-block Chevy employs a wedge-style combustion chamber with a quench or flat portion facing the piston, designers quickly adopted the D shaped dish that leaves a flat portion mirroring the quench portion of the head. The dish ends up shaped like a D, which is where the "D-cup" moniker originated. The reason for the piston's flat portion is to create turbulence within the combustion space as the piston approaches TDC. These matching flat portions squish or push the air-fuel mixture into the chamber, creating dramatic mixture movement that helps create a more homogenous air-fuel mixture in the combustion space above the piston. An ideal combustion situation would be where the fuel droplets are all very small in diameter and they are evenly distributed throughout the entire combustion space. This homogenous mixture would be easier to light and would burn much faster than a mixture comprised of large and small fuel droplets that are unevenly distributed in the combustion space. Since smaller fuel droplets burn more quickly than large droplets, there is a significant power advantage to enhancing a more homogeneous mixture. A better mix of fuel and air in the combustion area creates an engine that is smoother and less susceptible to the onset of detonation.

This efficiency of this squish or quench movement is determined mainly by the piston-to-head clearance. Here's a case where tighter is better. Obviously, we are limited by a safe piston-to-head clearance to prevent the piston from smacking the cylinder head. But after polling several professional race engine builders, it appears that the safest piston-to-head clearance for optimal quench movement is in the neighborhood of 0.037 to 0.039-inch. Anything tighter than this runs the risk of damage to the piston, while greater clearance reduces the quench effect. You can run as tight at 0.037-inch, but this assumes a rather tight piston-to-wall clearance to

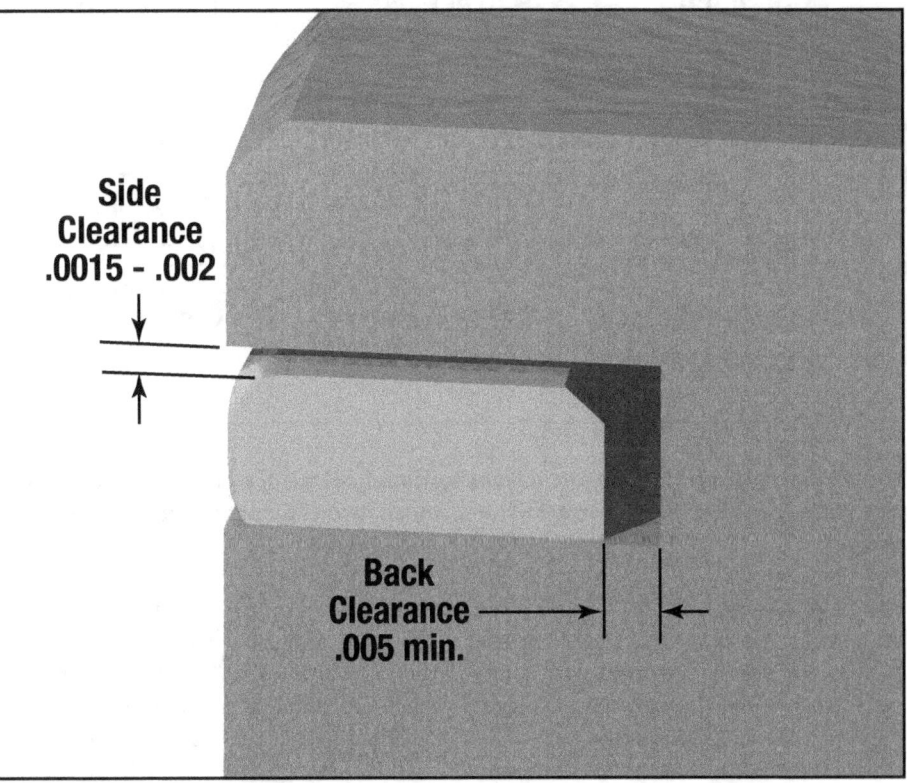

One clearance many non-professional engine builders overlook is ring side and back side clearance. If you can attain the tight side of 0.0015 to 0.002-inch side clearance, you're doing well. Back clearance is important to prevent the ring from extending past the ring groove, the spec is less important than the fact that there is clearance.

Chapter 6

Most performance piston manufacturers are now creating this pressure accumulator groove between the top and second ring. Some also create an anti-detonation groove between the top ring land and the top of the piston.

Low-tension oil rings receive a lot of attention, but for street engines, most professional engine builders recommend sticking with standard oil-tension rings. Make sure the ends of the expander do not overlap. Install the stainless expander first, and then slip the top rail in before the bottom rail.

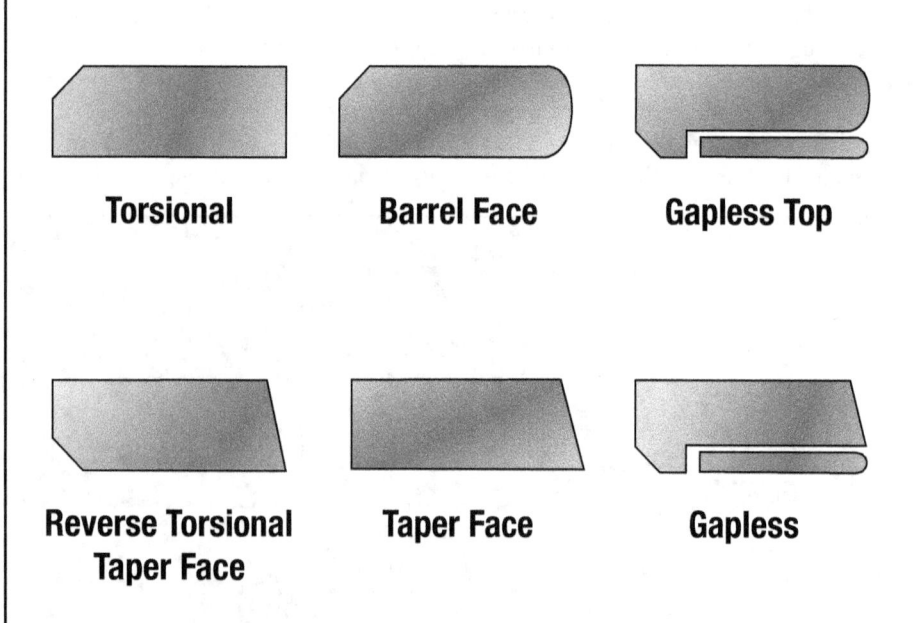

Top or compression ring styles include the torsional, barrel face, or gapless. For the second ring, there are the reverse torsional taper face ring, taper face, and gapless designs.

reduce piston rock at TDC. The benefit of a tight quench area and enhanced mixture motion in the chamber is a dramatic decrease in the engine's sensitivity to detonation. This means you could run a slightly higher static compression ratio with pump gas and still run the maximum amount of ignition timing the engine demands. An interesting benefit of running tight quench clearances is a reduction in total ignition timing required to attain maximum power. For example, a tight quench engine could demand only 32 to 34 degrees of total timing as opposed to 36 to 38 degrees of lead to make the same power in an engine with a greater quench area. These tighter quench clearances also reduce the engine's sensitivity to detonation. Combustion chamber shape also plays a big part in this equation, with the kidney or heart-shaped chambers the most popular right now. Keep in mind that less ignition advance can itself improve power by reducing pumping losses.

Compression Height

One of the many limitations placed on a big-inch small block engine builder is the distance between the top of the piston and the centerline of the wrist pin. This is called the piston's compression height. This is important stuff because we are trying to stuff 10 pounds of displacement into a stock deck height block's five-pound bag. Let's say, for example, that you want to build a 434ci small block with a 4.155-inch bore and a 4.00-inch stroke in a standard 9.025-inch deck height small block. The formula for determining compression height is easy. Add the rod length and half the stroke together and then subtract this sum from the deck height:

$$[\text{Deck Height} - (\text{Rod length} + 1/2 \text{ Stroke})] = \text{Piston Compression Height}$$

Based on this equation, if we wanted to run a 5.850-inch long connecting rod in this 4.00-inch stroke engine with a stock deck height block, the compression height would be:

$$[9.025 - (5.850 + 2.00)] = 1.175\text{-inches}$$

Compression height must include all three piston rings while also leaving sufficient room between the top ring and the top of the piston. The absolute minimum compression height is 1.00 inch, but most engine builders prefer heights of between 1.125 to 1.250 inch. This creates more room between the rings as well as moving the top ring down from the top of the piston. This is important since the closer the top ring is to the top of the piston, the more combustion heat is transferred to the ring itself. Elevated ring temperatures are a main cause of ring distortion and loss of seal. This is also hell on the wrist pin and bushing.

All of this is important since several factors affect piston design. As we learned in the chapter on connecting rods, rod length is important to reduce

Pistons and Rings

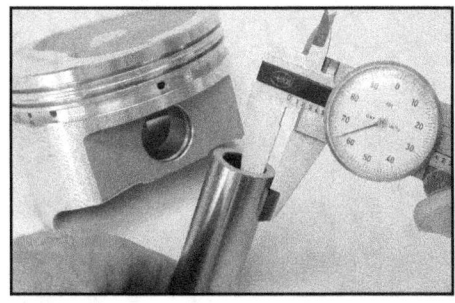

Piston pins come in various weights, which can be handy when trying to reduce piston weight to match a crankshaft bob weight. There are several variations of tapered wall pins available.

an acute angle of the rod to the piston after TDC. Given this, as stroke increases (as in our 4.00-inch stroke example) we'd love to have a 6.00-inch long rod in this package to create a decent 1.5:1 rod ratio. If we plug this into our compression height equation, we discover that this requires a 1.025-inch compression height. Not only does this squeeze the ring package together on the piston, but is also moves the wrist pin into the oil ring groove. This requires an oil rail support to ensure the oil ring remains stable across the gap created by the wrist pin hole entering the oil ring groove. For street engines, this will work, but it's not ideal.

The solution for this particular problem is to use a tall-deck block that measures 9.325 inches. This adds 0.300-inch to the height of the block, which now means we can have our 6.000-inch rod with a 4.00-inch stroke and generate a more stable compression height of 1.325 inch. But keep in mind that adding this deck height also means a raised cam bore and other changes to the standard small block that you must take into consideration before making that decision. This taller block also creates other problems. For example, this will also raise the cylinder heads, which means that even if you wanted to use production exhaust headers, they probably won't fit the chassis because the taller deck moves the exhaust ports farther out and up relative to the chassis. Things can get very complicated very quickly when you get into non-stock applications. None of this is impossible to overcome, it just means more work and added cost.

While we could get into a discussion of determining the exact spacing of the ring package between the wrist pin and the top of the piston, this is best left to the piston manufacturer. The most important consideration, and the only one that we will address here, is the distance between the top ring land and the top of the piston. Naturally aspirated drag race engine builders prefer to place the top ring land very close to the top of the piston, often less than 0.100-inch. For street engines, this distance should be increased to at least 0.200-inch mere-

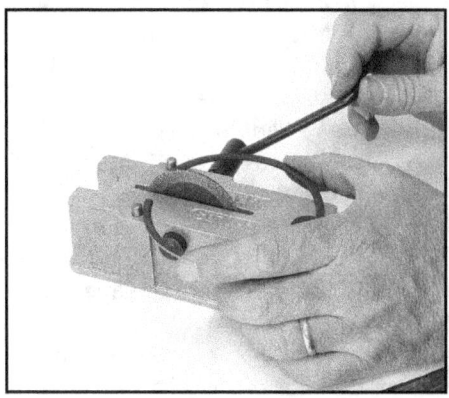

For most engine builders, this manual ring grinder does a great job at cutting ring end gaps. Work slowly and remember to keep the ring parallel to the grinder.

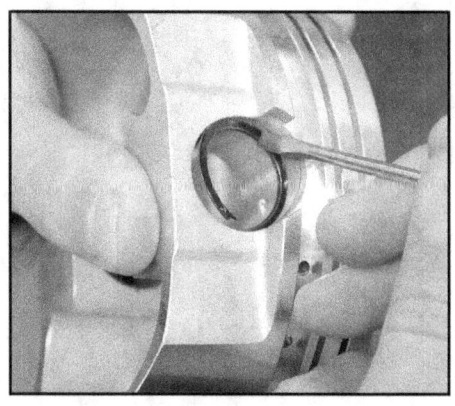

For engine builders using free-floating wrist pins, Spirolocks are the best way to secure them. However, Spirolocks require some skill to install and a special tool to help remove them.

All performance ring sets come in 0.005-inch oversize dimensions that allow the engine builder to set his own ring end gap.

Computing Compression

To determine static compression, you need to know several dimensions: bore, stroke, combustion chamber volume, head gasket volume, ring-land crevice volume, the volume displaced by the piston, and the piston deck height. Simply put, the compression ratio is the ratio of the volume of the cylinder with the piston at bottom dead center (BDC) compared to the volume of the cylinder with the piston at top dead center (TDC).

We will show you how to figure compression mathematically because it's always good to know how to compute compression in long hand just in case you're stranded on a desert island in an episode of Survivor and one of your tasks is to determine the compression ratio of a big-inch mouse motor mysteriously left by drag racing gypsies. But before we do that, we thought you'd like to know the easy way to do all this work quickly and efficiently. Rather than search for your calculator, fire up your computer instead and log onto www.performancetrends.com. This website offers a free, downloadable compression-ratio program that will calculate compression as fast as you can enter the data. You can purchase a slightly expanded version of the program if you so desire, but the free version works great. The speed of the calculator also allows you to play all kinds of what-if games that would otherwise take hours the old fashioned way. Of course, the idea is that you like Kevin Gertgen's free program so much that you'll be predisposed to buy one of Performance Trends' other interesting programs. To satisfy the naturally curious, let's dive into how to compute compression the way your grandfather did it with pencil and paper.

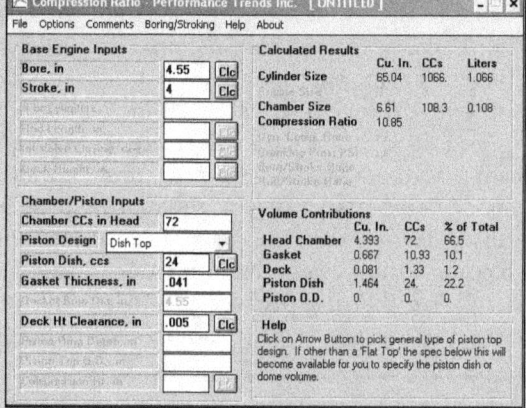

Most importantly, we need to remember to keep all computed values the same. If you mix cubic centimeters (cc) with cubic inches (ci), you'll never come up with the right answer. This means converting any value in cc's to cubic inches. To start, we'll need to know the bore and stroke to obtain the swept volume of the cylinder:

Bore x Bore x Stroke x .7854 = Swept Volume in cubic inches.
Example: 4.25 x 4.25 x 4 x .7854 = 56.74ci

Next we need to convert the combustion chamber volume from cc's to ci's. To do this, multiply cc's x 0.061. Just for the record, to convert ci to cc just multiply by 16.41. For our combination, let's say we have a 64cc chamber. To make this cubic inches:

64 x 0.061 = 3.9ci

Our next step is to compute head gasket thickness. This is easy because all head gasket manufacturers give you the gasket volume on the package. But don't fret if you threw the package away and only know the compressed thickness. Use the same volume equation for computing cylinder volume. In our example, the specs are for a 4.250-inch bore Fel-Pro gasket with a compressed thickness of 0.051-inch.

Bore x Bore x Gasket Thickness x 0.7854 = Gasket Volume in cubic inches
4.25 x 4.25 x 0.051 x 0.7854 = 0.72ci

Use the manufacturer's actual compressed volume when possible because the gasket opening is often larger than the bore. In our case, the calculated volume is within 0.005 of a cubic inch (0.08 of a cc), so we're okay.

Deck height is calculated the same way as gasket thickness. For our example, let's assume a negative deck height where the piston is below the deck surface by a value of 0.005-inch. If the piston is above the deck, we calculate the volume the same way but subtract it from the rest of the volumes rather than add it. You do this because the piston would actually be subtracting from the chamber volume. For a small-block Chevy, this is very rare since we have to be concerned with piston-to-head clearance.

$$\text{Bore} \times \text{Bore} \times \text{Deck Height} \times 0.7854 = \text{Deck Height Volume in Cubic Inches.}$$
$$4.25 \times 4.25 \times 0.005 \times 0.7854 = 0.07 \text{ci}$$

The final piece of the compression ratio puzzle is piston top volume. Most piston manufacturers list the volume of their domes, dishes, and even the valve relief volume for flat top pistons. If you don't know how much your pistons displace, the easiest way to find out is to measure it just like you would a combustion chamber. Place the piston in the bore exactly 1/2-inch down, use a flat piece of plastic with a hole drilled in it that will cover the entire bore, and then pour in a colored liquid from a graduated burette. Comp Cams sells an inexpensive (less than $25) cc kit that you can use. Compare the measured volume of this cylinder against a calculated volume of a pure cylinder of the bore and the 1/2-inch depth. If the measured volume is more by 20 cc's, for example, then that is the volume of the dish in the piston. Obviously, if the measured volume is less than the calculated amount, you have a domed piston. Our 20cc dish volume must also be converted to cubic inches:

$$20 \text{cc} \times 0.061 = 1.22 \text{ci}$$

Now we can do the actual calculation. First let's compute the overall swept volume of the cylinder at TDC:

$$\text{Chamber} + \text{Gasket} + \text{Deck Height} + \text{Piston Dish} = \text{Volume at TDC}$$
$$3.9\text{ci} + 0.72\text{ci} + 0.07\text{ci} + 1.22\text{ci} = 5.91\text{ci}$$

Next, let's determine the volume of the cylinder with the piston at BDC:

$$\text{Cyl.} + \text{Chamber} + \text{Gasket} + \text{Deck} + \text{Piston Deck} = \text{Volume at BDC}$$
$$56.74\text{ci} + 3.9\text{ci} + 0.72\text{ci} + 0.07\text{ci} + 1.22\text{ci} = 62.65\text{ci}$$

Now we divide the volume at BDC by the volume at TDC:

$$62.65\text{ci} / 5.91\text{ci} = 10.60:1$$

The compression ratio for this engine is 10.60:1.

---

ly to protect the top ring from the elevated temperature of combustion. Supercharged, turbocharged, or nitrous-injected engines should place the top ring land farther down from the top of the piston. Consult your piston manufacturer for their recommendation for these applications.

Weight

The question of weight is especially important when it comes to pistons. The compromise comes on several different levels. While reducing weight reduces the g-force load imparted to the connecting rod, excessively lightened pistons also sacrifice strength and durability. Ultra-lightweight pistons may survive in a drag racing environment with minimal run time, but they would not last long in an endurance, road race, or street application. The other area to consider is crankshaft bob weight. The reciprocating weight of the piston, rings, pin, and the top half of the rod must come close to the crank bob weight or you will have to spend money on balancing. Piston weights vary dramatically based on variables such as piston configuration (dished vs. flat top), rod length, and several other details.

As an example, we compared a flat-top, Federal-Mogul, 406 style-piston, to a JE flat top with a slightly shorter compression height and discovered a 54-gram difference between the two pistons (526 vs. 472, respectively). Another interesting point is that dished pistons tend to be slightly heavier than pure flat-top pistons because the dished pistons require a thicker top. A flat-top JE piston with a 1.125-inch compression height comes in at a mere 431 grams, but a dished JE piston with the same compression height is 526 grams — a 95-gram difference. As you can see, it pays to have all the information before you decide which piston is best for your application.

Rings

While it may appear that rings have a simple task to perform, the physics of what piston rings have to withstand makes their job difficult at best. Con-

Long strokes and long rods combine to create very tight compression heights that push the wrist pin up into the oil ring. This requires oil ring supports to ensure the oil ring works properly when spanning the gap.

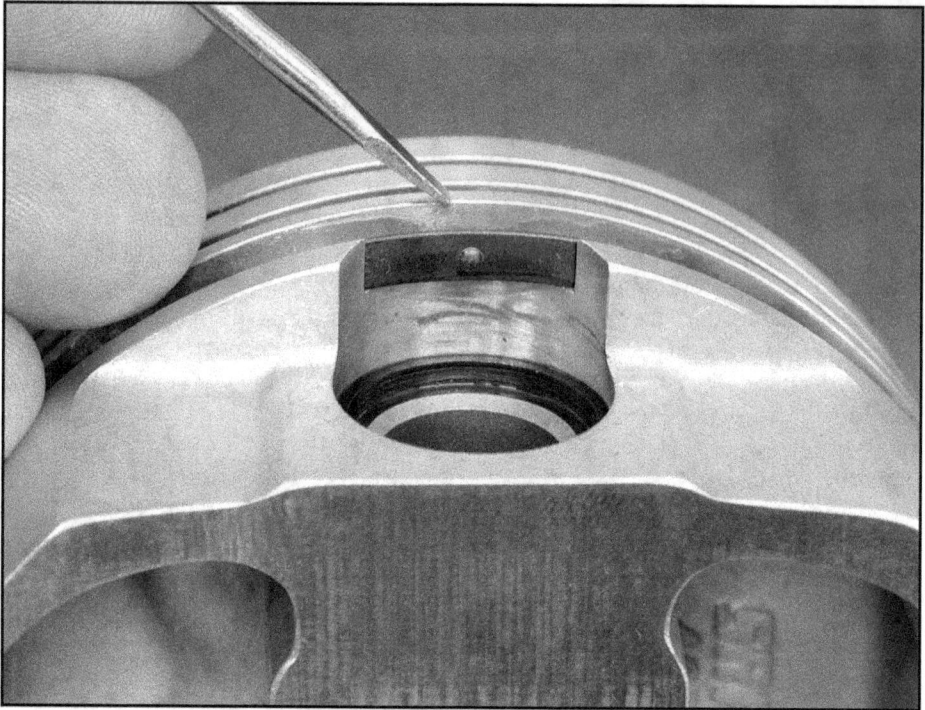

ventional pistons utilize a three-ring configuration that seems to perform best. Some drag race engines can get by with a two-ring set, but these are the exception. For the more typical three-ring set, there is plenty of engineering that goes into the material, design, shape, and performance of these rings. There are volumes of Society of Automotive Engineers (SAE) papers on the subject, but we'll spare you the tedium and cut right to the chase.

The top ring is called the compression ring and its job is simply to seal as much cylinder pressure above the ring as possible so that the pressure can be converted into torque and horsepower. The ring shape, material, weight, and ring gap all contribute to how well the ring can do this job. The second ring is easily the most misunderstood ring. While most consider it a secondary compression ring, the second ring's primary mandate is to act as an oil scraper to prevent oil from reaching the top ring and polluting the combustion chamber. This ring's secondary job is to also function as a secondary compression ring and to prevent blow-by, which is combustion pressure and carbon that enter the crankcase, neither of which is positive.

The third ring is the oil ring, whose job is to actually lubricate the piston, rings, and wrist pin assembly and to not allow oil to enter the combustion area. Oil rings also help in controlling piston temperature by using oil to pull heat away from the piston top. Many performance pistons actually employ wrist pin oilers that drill a lubrication path between the backside of the oil ring groove and the wrist pin hole. Piston movement then forces the oil through the path, which keeps the wrist pins lubricated.

The first area to cover in more depth should probably be ring material. Production engines use cast iron rings that do an admirable job at a low cost. For performance applications, the more malleable ductile iron is the next step up and is often used in mild performance applications. The most popular street ring system uses a ductile-iron ring with a moly face. The moly is usually sprayed into a small slot milled into the ring. The moly creates a better ring seal that seats to the cylinder wall very quickly. Beyond coated ductile iron rings, we get into the specialized world of race engine rings. For example, Total Seal offers a steel top ring designed for nitrous and other heavily loaded engines with extremely high specific outputs. These rings are designed for specific applications, but it is worth noting that these very hard rings also contribute to increased bore wear, which is a good reason not to use them in a street application, especially when there are plenty of ductile-iron, moly-filled rings from which to choose.

Ring width is a popular subject and also a source of some confusion. Until recently, production small-block Chevy engines have always used a 5/64-inch ring width. These large rings did an admirable job, but were heavy and required a significant amount of radial tension to seal properly. This increased tension is the primary source of internal engine friction. We've seen estimates of up to 60 percent of total engine friction attributed to the interface between the

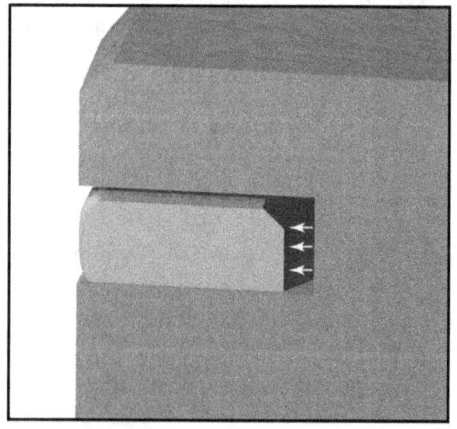

Piston rings use cylinder pressure to push the ring into the cylinder wall for an optimal seal. Pressure works on both the top and the back of the ring.

piston, rings, and the cylinder wall. Because of this, performance engine builders, and now even the OEM, are moving to increasingly thinner rings. As an example, many GM production engines now employ 1.5-millimeter (0.0590-inch) thick top and second rings, which equate to a ring thickness that is slightly thinner than a 1/16-inch (0.0625-inch).

The most popular performance ring thickness is the 1/16-inch thick top and second ring combined with a 3/16-inch oil ring. The difference in ring drag between a 5/64-inch ring package and a 1/16-inch ring package is nothing less than amazing. You can actually measure this with nothing more complicated than a simple fish scale hooked to the bottom of a piston with the rings installed and fitted in a cylinder. The reason that the thinner rings create less drag has to do with radial ring tension. With a given radial tension, a thicker ring presents more area to the cylinder bore, creating a given unit loading pressure on the bore. A thinner ring width offers less contact area to the bore, which means the ring designer can reduce the radial tension until the unit loading pressure is similar to the previous load. The gain is less ring drag due to the reduced ring thickness.

Another way to reduce ring drag is with low-tension oil rings. Another popular trick for drag race engines where the engine builder has more latitude, is to reduce the amount of oil ring tension. The down side to this is a thicker film of oil left on the cylinder wall that tends to create oil control problems for the second ring. Ultimately, a small amount of oil could be left on the cylinder wall that could contaminate the combustion process. The problem is that residual oil in the chamber increases the chances of detonation, which is never a good thing. You may want to investigate reduced-tension oil rings since many manufacturers offer several different grades. For street and endurance engines, standard-tension oil rings may be a better choice to ensure adequate oil control.

Ring Style

There are probably as many different ring designs as there are rabid University of Georgia Bulldog football fans. In order to save our sanity, we'll limit our discussion to a few of the more popular designs that have a place in performance street engines. The accompanying illustrations will help you to better understand how each of these rings is shaped. The most popular performance top or compression ring is the tapered face ring. This ring employs a slight chamfer on the upper inside edge of the ring that creates a twist when installed in the bore. This twist then pushes the lower edge of the face of the ring into the cylinder wall. This, along with cylinder pressure applied to the top and inside of the top ring is what seals the ring to the cylinder wall as the piston travels down the cylinder during the power stroke. Cylinder pressure does the main job of sealing the ring during the power stroke. Twist is still important however because excellent ring seal is also critical during the intake stroke when the piston is again traveling down the cylinder, but this time cylinder pressure is not present to help ring seal.

Another variation of this design is

Clearance Check

Each manufacturer has its own requirements for how and where to check the piston outside diameter to establish piston-to-wall clearance. It should come as no surprise that all of the major piston companies specify a different place to check the piston. Because pistons are eccentric by design, measuring in the proper place is essential to establishing the proper piston clearance. We have concentrated on the major piston companies, ignoring stock replacement and hypereutectic pistons. The widest point of any piston is at the piston skirt 90-degrees to the wrist pin. However, because of the taper built into every piston, each has its own specific place to be measured. Keep in mind that all these pistons should be measured at room temperature (around 72 degrees F). Significant temperature fluctuations can have a big effect on aluminum. Higher temperatures will cause the piston to expand while lower temperatures will shrink the piston.

Manufacturer	Measurement Position
Federal-Mogul 2618	0.750-inch below the bottom of oil ring groove
Federal-Mogul PowerForged	Wrist-pin centerline
JE	0.500-inch above bottom of skirt
Ross (A design)	Bottom sill of side relief
Ross (B design)	0.200-inch from bottom of skirt
Wiseco	1.30-inch below oil-ring groove

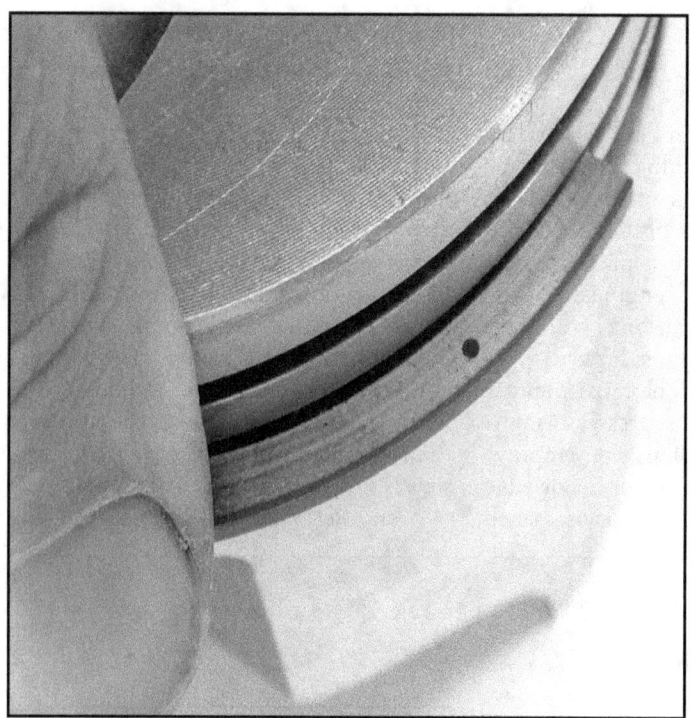 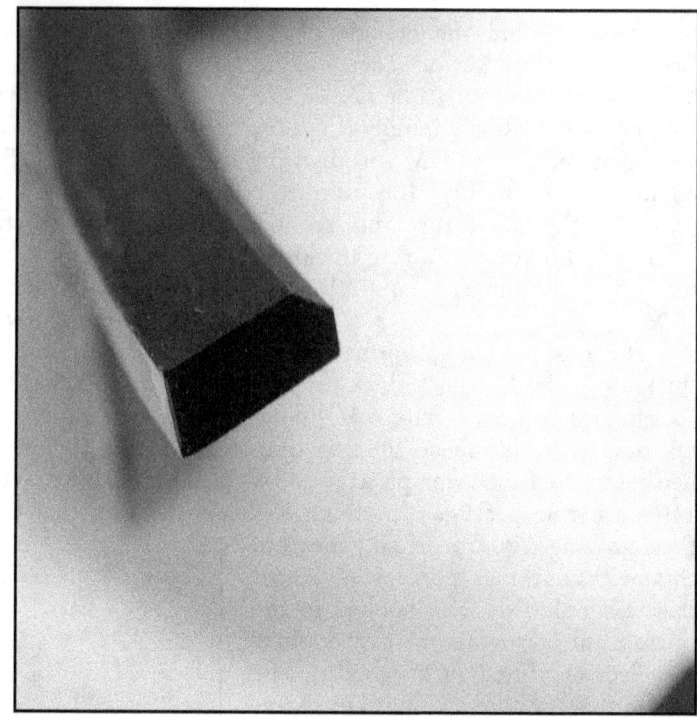

Most top compression rings use a chamfer on the top inside edge of the ring to create a torsional twist to help seal the ring during the combustion process. These rings indicate which side is up with a pip or divot in the ring. The pip always goes up.

the barrel face top ring that eliminates both sharp edges that come in contact with the cylinder wall. This ring also employs the twist by virtue of the upper inside chamber. A favorite of the drag race crowd is the Dykes top ring that uses a wide face thickness that is reduced where the ring fits into the piston ring land to further reduce ring weight.

For the second ring, there is a taper-faced ring that creates a scraper-like face to increase the amount of oil that can be removed from the cylinder wall. A variation on this idea is the combination of a taper face with a torsion twist. The placement of the torsion twist chamfer on the second ring is the opposite from top ring, however. Note that the chamfer is on the bottom inside diameter of the second ring. This is because we want the second ring to apply the sharp edge of the taper face toward the cylinder wall during the piston down stroke. This is why the chamfer is always placed up on the top ring and down on the second ring. Most ring manufacturers will indicate the top side of either a top or second ring with a pip mark. In all cases when you see a pip mark on a ring, that means it should be installed with the pip mark facing up. If there is no pip (which is often the case on the second ring) then it can be installed in either direction. This usually means it is not a taper face or a torsion twist ring.

Ring Seal

There has been quite a bit of noise about the advantages of gapless rings within the engine building community. The net goal with any gapless ring is to increase cylinder pressure by minimizing pressure loss past the rings during the power stroke. Gapless rings are supposed to minimize this pressure loss. It is worth mentioning that the ring end gap established on typical gapped rings when the ring is slid into the bore is much wider than the gap that occurs during combustion. As heat builds in the cylinder during combustion, ring temperature increases which makes the ring expand. The ring end gap is created to ensure that the ring ends do not meet, or butt. If this happens, radial load increases radically which can create excessive ring wear, ring-land erosion, and cylinder wall scuffing, not to mention a drastic loss in cylinder sealing.

Clearly, ring butting is to be avoided. However, it is possible to have as little as a few thousandths of an inch of dynamic ring end gap during engine operation, which will allow very little cylinder pressure to escape past the gap.

There is also some information to suggest that while a tight top ring end gap is beneficial to good ring seal, increasing the gap on the second ring may actually increase top ring seal, and therefore performance. The idea is that no top ring is 100 percent efficient in sealing cylinder pressure. As a result, a certain amount of cylinder pressure exists between the top and second ring. Any ring manufacturer will tell you that the greater the pressure differential between the top and second ring is what helps seal the top ring. If sufficient pressure exits in this captured area, top ring seal can be compromised. The theory suggests that increasing the gap in the second compression ring increases this pressure differential (reducing the pressure between the first and second rings) improving top ring seal. This is a rather simple thing to accomplish and the best part is that it's free. All you have to do is open the gap up on the rings as you are file-fitting them to the cylinder. This

Pistons and Rings

Ring End Gap Recommendations

Application	Top Ring (inches)	Second Ring (inches)	Oil Ring Rail (inches)
Street/Strip	Bore x 0.0045	Bore x 0.0050	Min 0.015
Nitrous to 150 hp	Bore x 0.006	Bore x 0.0055	Min. 0.015
Nitrous over 150 hp	Bore x 0.008	Bore x 0.0065	Min. 0.015
Blown gasoline	Bore x 0.0055	Bore x 0.0050	Min. 0.015

Example: 4.200-inch bore normally aspirated street engine
Top Ring   = 4.2 x 0.0045 = 0.019-inch
Second Ring = 4.2 x 0.0050 = 0.021-inch

This is a merely a guideline, please refer to piston and ring manufacturer's specific recommendations to prevent ring end butting. This is especially important with high-silicon content pistons.

is also the reason you will see a machined indentation in the ring land between the top and second ring of many performance pistons. If nothing else, it makes for a great bench racing topic that could last for hours.

There is also evidence to suggest that the Gapless top and/or second rings sold by Total Seal and the Zero Gap Second rings sold by Childs & Albert do in fact perform at the level that their proponents suggest. The author has witnessed tests where the C&A rings have both reduced crankcase pressure and actually generated a slight torque and horsepower increase. In theory, a big-inch street engine could benefit from a gapless ring package if for no other reason than to reduce crankcase pressure and crankshaft windage. The jury is still very much undecided when it comes to these ring packages from a power standpoint. However, what is clear is these rings are generally about twice the price of a standard moly ring package.

There's plenty more to the subject of pistons and rings. If you do your homework and apply the information presented here, you should be able to avoid most of the common problems associated with big-inch small blocks. If you do this, you'll end up with an outstandingly durable and powerful street engine that will make you the talk (or is that the torque) of the town.

Pin oilers use the scraping action of the ring to force oil into the piston pin boss to lubricate the pin. Production engines relied on splash oiling but performance engines need a little more help.

Oil must be allowed to escape from the oil ring once it's removed from the cylinder wall. The best performance pistons use multiple holes instead of slots since the holes create a stronger piston. However, slotted pistons can usually be run with tighter piston-to-wall clearance.

How To Build Big-Inch Chevy Small-Blocks

Chapter 7

Camshafts

Camshafts are the brain center for any engine. Without a signal dictating when and for how long to open the valves, an engine won't make power. The operation seems simple enough — just design an eccentric that converts rotary motion into linear motion and time it so the valves open and close at the proper moment. But as simple as that seems, the camshaft learning curve seems to be getting steeper rather than easier.

The big question is not really lift, duration, or even lobe design. The current challenge is to create a camshaft system that will make the most overall power over an increasingly wider RPM band. Engines intended for street operation comprise the most difficult cam challenge because street engines operate over an extremely wide RPM band. A typical street engine is required to function from an idle of 900 rpm all the way through to a peak horsepower point of 6,500 to perhaps 6,800 rpm. That's a bandwidth of 5,600 to 5,900 rpm. In contrast, a drag race engine may only operate within a 2,000-rpm band, while a road race engine may be wider at between 3,000 and 4,000 rpm.

Clearly, this effort requires a significant compromise to satisfy the demands of a performance street engine. It is difficult to make great torque at 2,500 rpm and still make outstanding horsepower at 6,500 rpm. But one thing that we have going for us is size. A big-inch small block enjoys the luxury of a large displacement that makes excellent torque at

The two most common types of camshafts are flat tappet (bottom) and roller (top). Either can use solid or hydraulic lifters. Solid-lifter cams require a valve lash while hydraulic cams run with a slight preload to the lifter.

lower engine speeds. This allows the cam designer and engine builder to sacrifice a bit of low-speed torque in order to make more top-end power. The question is, how much do you give up, and where?

This chapter will deal with the basics of camshaft design and function. You'll learn all the basic camshaft information as well as some nuances that you may not know exist. We'll also cover the advantages and disadvantages of flat tappet versus roller cams and some of the details you must know in order to take advantage of these different cams. We'll also throw in some very practical and useful information on roller and flat tappet cams that may just make a little power, keep you out of trouble, and prevent camshaft confusion all at the same

Cam styles are dictated by lifter design. Roller cams require a much harder steel core camshaft, which is one reason they are more expensive. Most flat-tappet cams like the one shown here are merely hardened cast or ductile iron.

time. But first, as always, we need to cover the basics.

Flat and Roller

There are two styles of camshafts used in V8 engines like the small-block Chevy. The oldest and most popular is the flat tappet. As the name implies, the tappet, or cam follower, is flat on the end that slides along the lobe face. Actually, this is a bit of a misnomer, since all flat tappets are actually built with a slightly convex face. This forces the tappet to spin, which helps longevity. The cam lobe itself induces this spin. Alternate lobes on the cam are ground with a slight taper, forcing the cam to the rear of the engine. This taper makes the tap-

Camshafts

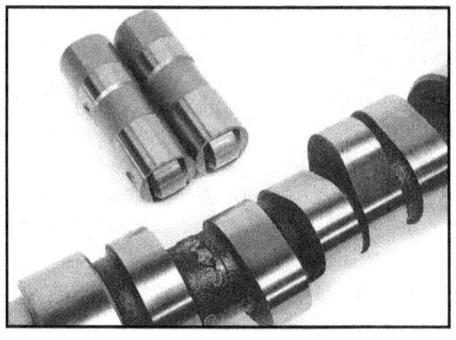

While hydraulic roller cams offer significant duration and lift advantages over flat-tappet cams, the lifters are also measurably heavier, requiring more spring pressure to control. This makes hydraulic roller cammed engines RPM limited. These are stock-type hydraulic roller tappets.

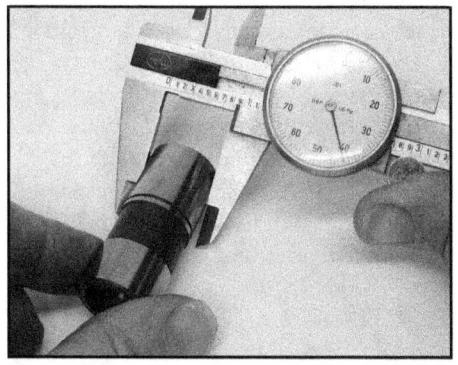

Flat-tappet cams are velocity limited by the diameter of the lifter. Small-block Chevy lifters are the smallest of the big-three companies with a 0.842-inch diameter. Small-block Ford lifters enjoy a bit of an advantage since their lifters are 0.875-inch in diameter.

pet spin and also forces the camshaft to the rear. This is why a cam button, which limits camshaft movement, is not necessary with flat tappet cams.

Within the flat tappet cam family, there are two versions — the hydraulic and the mechanical, or solid lifter. Mechanical lifters are merely solid chunks of steel that impart all movement from the lobe to the pushrod. In the small block, these lifters also direct oil from the lifter galley to the pushrod and then up to the rocker arm. The latest versions of the solid lifter utilize a small oiling hole in the middle of the face that touches the lobe to help lube the lifter and cam interface. This is not necessary for street engines unless you use a long duration, high-RPM cam that requires heavy spring loads. Solid lifters require a clearance, or lash, within the entire valvetrain that is used to account for component growth during warm up as well as to produce a little clearance to prevent holding the valve open when it should be closed. This lash is set between the rocker arm and the valve tip using a feeler gauge with the lobe on its base circle.

Hydraulic flat-tappet lifters are similar in shape and appearance to solid lifters but utilize a small piston and spring that sit in a bore inside the lifter body. This piston assembly is retained with a clip on the top of the pushrod cup. Oil fills the area underneath the piston and acts as a hydraulic cushion between the pushrod and the lifter body. No lash is used with a hydraulic tappet. Instead, hydraulic tappets operate with a certain amount of preload that compresses the piston against the spring and oil in the bore. This preload then accommodates changes in dimension in the engine during warm up and also accounts for dynamic changes during engine operation. Most cam manufacturers specify a small amount of preload of around 0.020-inch, which is set with the lifter on the base circle of the lobe. This is set by eliminating all the clearance in the valvetrain and then tightening the rocker stud adjustment nut an additional 1/2 to 3/4 turn.

Roller lifters are the high-tech style cam follower. As the name implies, roller tappets employ a roller follower that eliminates much of the friction of a flat tappet follower. This is also a much more expensive style of cam follower because of the design and complexity of the roller, but also because the roller, by design, has a much smaller contact patch on the cam. Because of this, the unit loading pressure skyrockets, requiring a much stronger steel core cam instead of the flat tappet's cast iron core. The lifter must also be much stronger, requiring tiny roller bearings to support the load of the lifter wheel and prevent it from seizing. These stronger steel roller cams and roller tappets are also much more expensive than flat-tappet designs.

Almost all four-stroke engines spin the camshaft at exactly half crankshaft speed. Each tooth on this particular Comp Cams gear is a spread of a little more than 8 degrees, which is why properly locating the cam gear is so important.

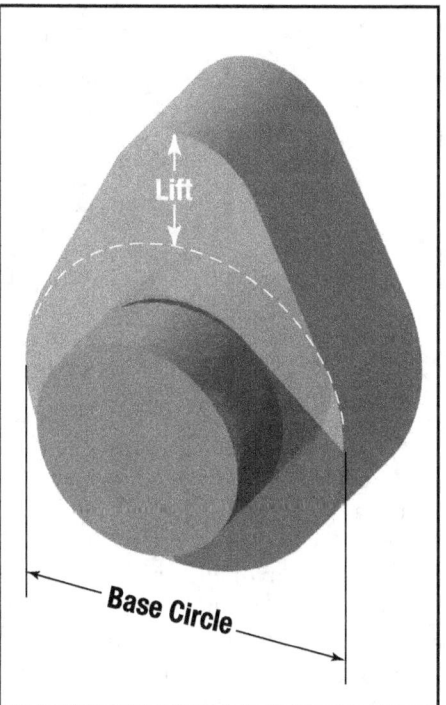

Lift is generated by adding a bump, or eccentric, that creates lift greater than the length of the radius of the circle. This lobe generates linear movement from rotating motion.

How To Build Big-Inch Chevy Small-Blocks

Chapter 7

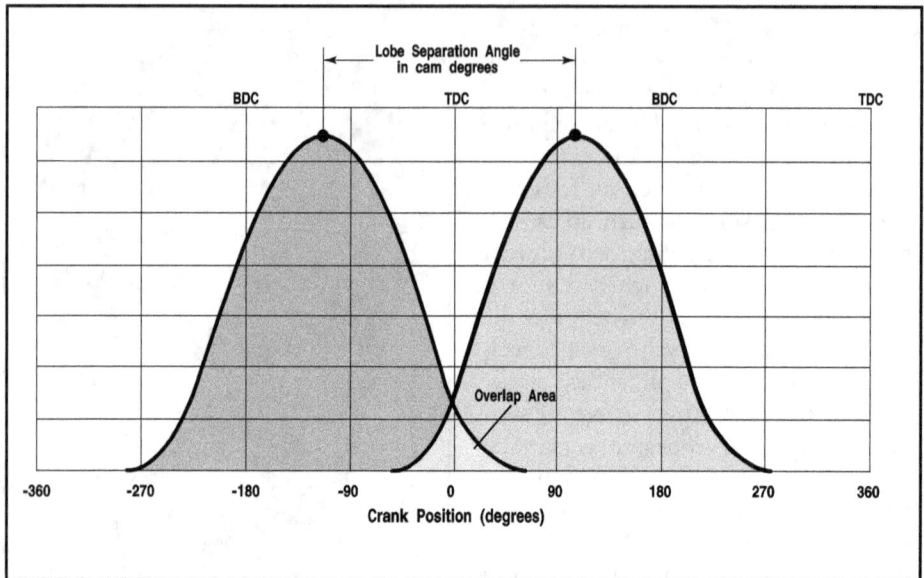

Studying this illustration will probably do more to help you understand camshaft operation than any other photo in this entire book. Duration can be advertised by a manufacturer at 0.006-inch tappet lift from opening to closing. Duration can also be expressed in duration at 0.050-inch tappet lift, which his shorter, but can be used to compare cams from different companies.

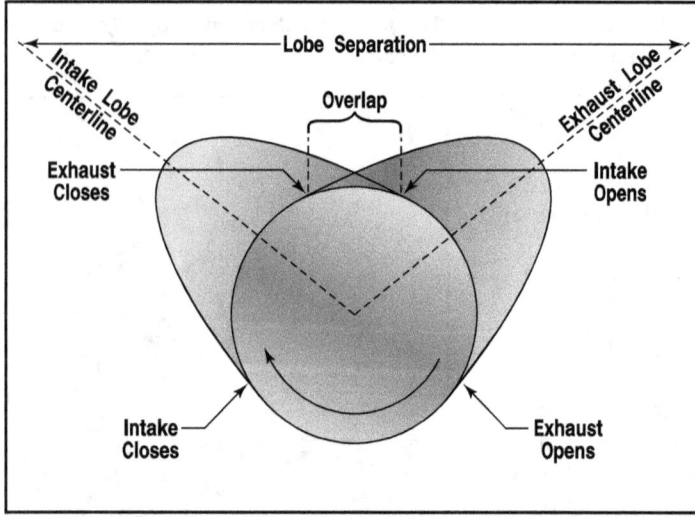

The lobe separation angle establishes overlap and is expressed as the number of camshaft degrees between intake and exhaust lobe centerlines. The only way to change a cam's lobe separation angle is by grinding a new cam.

As with flat-tappet cams, roller cams are offered in both solid and hydraulic versions. Around 1987, GM began using hydraulic roller cams in many of its production small-block engines in an attempt to improve fuel mileage by reducing internal friction. While there is only a negligible improvement in fuel mileage with hydraulic roller followers, this did push the aftermarket into employing the hydraulic roller-tappet system. Aftermarket companies before this had already been offering mechanical roller systems for years, with the majority of them being targeted at race engines.

We will get into the relative advantages and disadvantages of rollers versus flat-tappet cams later in this chapter, but one interesting side note is that it is impossible to create a taper with a roller-cam lobe, which means that all roller cams are ground with flat lobes. Since small and big-block Chevys use the cam to drive the oil pump and the distributor with a gear located on the back of the cam, this drive mechanism imparts a rearward thrust to the camshaft. Post 1986 factory hydraulic roller-cam blocks employ a thrust limiter plate just behind the camshaft drive gear that prevents cam movement. Earlier small blocks do not offer this feature, so the engine builder must employ a cam button that uses the back side of the timing chain cover to limit forward cam movement. We'll discuss this in more detail in a sidebar on cam thrust buttons.

Eccentric Info

The details of cam timing must start using a simple circle. If you imagine a camshaft lobe first as a circle, then you can add an eccentric to that circle to create lift. Lift is defined at the amount of rise in the eccentric over the radius of the circle called the base circle. If we have a camshaft with a cam lobe lift of 0.300-inch, then this is the amount of rise created by the eccentric rising up from the base circle. This lift is not created with a single sharp step up from the base circle. Instead, cam lift is made up of a gentle incline or slope that rises from the base circle, achieves its peak, and then gently slides back to the base circle. Since a circle is made up of 360 degrees, we can measure the amount of time, or duration, in degrees required to create that lobe. This would be the duration of the lobe expressed in degrees. All camshaft grinders express camshaft duration in crankshaft degrees, which is twice the actual figure of camshaft degrees, because the camshaft spins at half crankshaft speed. Crankshaft degrees are used because the easiest way to check a camshaft is in the engine. We'll show you how to do that later.

In order to have duration, you must begin and end at some specific point. Since the slope is very gentle at the beginning and end of its travel, one trick used in expressing duration is to start at a reasonable point of say 3 to 5 degrees into the lift curve. This makes the checking process easier to accomplish. But not all cam companies start measuring at the same point to determine what is called advertised duration. For example, Crane specifies its advertised duration for flat-tappet hydraulic cams at 0.004-inch of tappet rise, while Comp Cams uses

Camshafts

You can change when a cam opens and closes the valves by advancing or retarding the cam. This moves the entire cam, which moves all four opening and closing points (IO, IC, EO, and EC). This can be accomplished with cam bushing eccentrics, a multiple position crank gear, or an adjustable cam gear.

Factory small blocks built after 1986 incorporate dedicated cam limiter plates that prevent cam walk. The cam on the left is for a late-model block, using the step in the cam to locate it on the plate.

0.006-inch. The SAE spec is actually 0.009-inch of valve lift, which can mean different dimensions at the cam based on rocker ratio. Since there is significant crankshaft movement between 0.004 and 0.006-inch of tappet rise, it's difficult to compare these camshafts since the cam with duration specs at 0.004-inch will appear longer in duration than

It is virtually impossible to tell by looking which cam is the race roller and which is the street roller. Race cams offer much more aggressive lobe profiles that tend to be very abusive to the valvetrain for street operation.

a cam spec'd at 0.006-inch.

The solution was to choose a specific tappet lift point where all cams would be measured so that eager camshaft fans could compare apples to apples. Harvey Crane, the originator of Crane Cams, is the man who is given credit for deciding this point should be 0.050-inch of tappet lift. This is the only spec where camshaft of different origins can be compared. For example, a Comp Cams Extreme Energy XE274 hydraulic flat tappet cam offers 274 degrees of advertised duration measured at 0.006-inch tappet lift. At 0.050-inch of tappet lift, this same camshaft generates 230 degrees of duration. See how that works?

One caveat to working with duration at 0.050-inch tappet numbers is that the only thing the engine cares about is what happens at the valve. So if you are thinking in terms of duration or overlap at 0.050-inch tappet lift, the engine sees overlap, valve opening, and valve closing points at checking heights, if not before. This is not a critical problem, but one worth making a point to remember.

Each cylinder uses an intake and an exhaust valve, so each cylinder also requires two cam lobes. Each lobe will have a centerline, expressed as the exact midpoint of the duration of the lobe. This centerline is expressed in crankshaft degrees in relation to top dead center (TDC). For the intake lobe, this figure is generally between 104 and 114 degrees after top dead center (ATDC). For the exhaust lobe, this will generally be between 118 and 110 degrees before top dead center (BTDC). These centerlines establish the relative positions of each lobe to the crankshaft. You can think of this as their positioning of when to open and close.

Intake Centerline

Intake centerline is generally used to position the camshaft in the engine. For example, an intake centerline of 106 degrees indicates where the cam is located relative to the number 1 cylinder. This can be changed by moving the camshaft in relationship to the number 1 cylinder. This is known as cam phasing or degreeing. By moving the cam's position, we can either advance it, which means the intake and exhaust valves all open earlier than the base position, or we can retard it by opening and closing the valves later than our initial position. Using the 106-degree intake centerline example, let's say we wanted to advance the cam by 2 degrees. This means we will open the valves sooner, which means the intake centerline moves to 104 degrees ATDC. This might seem confusing, but remember we are talking about degrees ATDC. If we advance the cam, we are moving the centerline of the cam back toward TDC, which would reduce the number of degrees.

If we wanted to retard the cam four degrees from the original 106-degree point, the new intake centerline would be 110 degrees ATDC. Remember that we are moving entire camshaft here. This means all eight intake and all eight exhaust valve opening and closing points will move when we change the intake centerline of the cam.

Lobe Separation Angle

Another important specification is the lobe separation angle. This is the spread in camshaft degrees between the lobe centerlines of the intake and exhaust for one cylinder. Let's say we have a camshaft with an intake lobe centerline of 106 degrees ATDC and an exhaust lobe centerline of 114 degrees BTDC. Add these two together and divide by 2

Long-stroke cranks in standard deck height blocks will require a camshaft with a small base circle in order to clear a couple of rods in the engine that come dangerously close to the base circle of the cam.

For the more sophisticated cam buyer, you may consider building your own personal grind based on cam lobe designs usually found in the back of most cam company catalogs. Crane offers a separate book, while Comp Cams lists all its lobe designs in its main catalog.

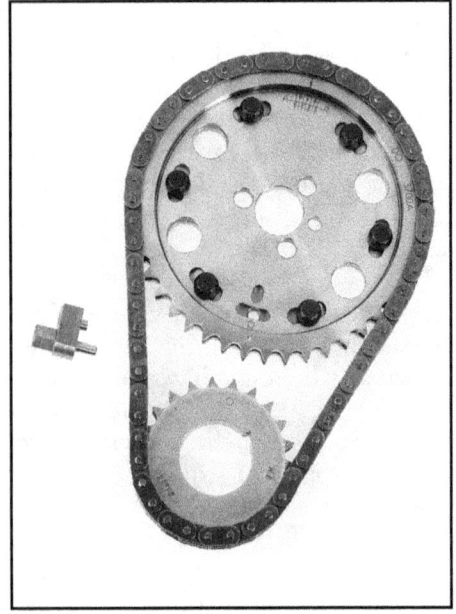

Most cam companies, along with specialty companies like Cloyes, offer steel chain and gear sets that are stronger and more durable. This Comp Cams unit is also adjustable. Just loosen the six bolts, move the cam the desired amount, and tighten everything back down.

(to get camshaft degrees, because the cam spins at half crankshaft speed) and we have: 106 + 114 = 220/2 = 110 degree lobe separation angle.

This is an important value because it establishes the amount of overlap between the intake and exhaust valves in the engine. If you remember your basic 4-stroke cycle, the exhaust valve is just closing as the piston approaches TDC. Most engines run best when the intake valve begins to open before the exhaust valve fully closes. This time overlap (expressed in crankshaft degrees) affects engine operation throughout the entire RPM band, which makes it a critical component to understanding camshafts and how they work.

Lobe separation angle is a confusing but necessary element in engine tuning. First of all, this angle is machined into the camshaft when it is ground. Using our 110-degree example, moving the intake centerline relative to the engine does not alter the lobe separation angle. The only way the lobe separation angle can be altered is by grinding a new camshaft. As an example, move the intake centerline closer to the exhaust lobe and the angle will become tighter, expressed as a smaller angle, like 108 degrees. Moving the exhaust lobe away from the intake lobe by advancing the exhaust centerline increases the lobe separation angle to something like a 112-degree angle.

Tightening the lobe separation angle increases the amount of overlap. This seemingly simple step offers massive changes to engine operation. For any engine, changes to the lobe separation angle affect the entire curve. For street engines, increasing overlap decreases idle quality, making the engine idle much rougher. This also tends to hurt mid-range torque in favor of increased power at the top of the RPM curve. This occurs because at high RPM there is much less time to accomplish filling the cylinder. So by increasing the amount of time (in camshaft degrees) at this RPM point, the engine has a better chance to breathe.

What makes the lobe separation angle more confusing has to do with the amount of the cam's duration. Keep in mind that lobe separation angle and overlap is expressed in crankshaft degrees. As an example, a single pattern cam with 220 degrees at 0.050-inch tappet lift with a 110-degree lobe separation angle offers a given amount of overlap. If you increase duration to 240 degrees at 0.050-inch tappet lift and retain the same lobe separation angle, the number of degrees of overlap increases by 10 degrees — a significant amount as measured in crankshaft degrees. This is why you will see longer duration camshafts often with wider 112-degree lobe separation angles. From this, you should be able to see that it's not really the lobe separation angle but the amount of overlap that is really important.

It requires no great shakes to see that there are four critical components to the four stroke cycle — in order they are: exhaust opening (EO), intake opening (IO), exhaust closing (EC), and intake closing (IC). Exhaust opening occurs near the middle of the power stroke and affects the power curve in a couple of ways. Once the exhaust is open, it uses cylinder pressure to force the exhaust out of the cylinder. Opening the exhaust valve sooner may bleed off cylinder pressure that could still add to the power stroke at low RPM but it may also give more time to remove the exhaust at higher RPM. A later EO can create low-RPM torque.

Intake opening is our second valve event. This begins the overlap event and an early IO increases overlap, and can also maximize lift at peak piston velocity depending upon the engine's stroke. An early IO also decreases low-speed torque and can create reversion in the intake manifold by allowing residual exhaust gas pressure to travel up the intake tract. If you've ever seen what

Camshafts

Lately, belt-drive systems have become more popular from companies like Jesel, Comp Cams, and others. Some engine builders feel these drives are more accurate and reduce torsional vibration through the cam from the crankshaft firing pulses.

Many companies offer roller bearings to use behind the cam drive gear. Some professional engine builders prefer solid bronze washers because if the Torrington bearing cage fails, those tiny roller bearings end up jammed in the oil pump and throughout the engine.

Setting Roller Cam End Play

As mentioned, roller camshafts must use some type of end-play limiter to prevent the camshaft from moving forward at high RPM. If the end play is too great, the camshaft has a nasty habit of surging rearward during high-RPM operation. When this occurs, the load from the oil pump drive imparts a forward motion into the cam from the helical cut gears. As the cam moves forward, this retards ignition timing again as a result of the helical cut gears on the cam and distributor. Ignition timing can retard as much as 10 to 15 degrees depending upon the distance the camshaft moves.

A simple cam thrust button or limiter is used to keep the cam in one place. There are several different styles of cam buttons, but the best is a roller button sold by several cam companies like Comp, Crane, and others. These roller buttons employ a roller bearing to reduce wear and friction and are also height-adjustable using tiny shims.

The best approach is to use a reinforced timing chain cover, such as an aluminum casting that is able to withstand the slight amount of pressure applied by the cam. Another idea involves reinforcing a stock tin timing cover with a welded plate and then using a short aluminum water pump with an adjustable tab bolted on the bottom of the pump that limits the cam movement. Edelbrock is one source for this style of aluminum water pump. Note that this is only available on the short-style pump. Long water pumps do not offer this feature.

Checking camshaft end play is relatively easy when assembling an engine. Install the crank and cam in the block along with the timing set you will be using. Be sure to include the timing cover gasket with the cover. Certain aftermarket aluminum covers like the Bow Laws (BLP) cover are equipped with a small tapped hole that allows you to place a dial indicator on the cam gear to read the cam thrust clearance. If you are not using one of these covers, you can place the dial indicator on the back of the camshaft with the rear cam plug removed.

Once the dial indicator is in place to measure fore-aft movement, carefully force the cam fore and aft with a large screwdriver pushed up against a lobe. The thrust button will limit forward movement while the back of the timing gear will limit rear movement. Cam thrust clearance is between 0.005 and 0.010-inch with the ideal around 0.008-inch.

The best cam button to use is the roller style; it can be adjusted using small shims supplied with the button.

looks like exhaust soot or smudge in the intake port, that's reversion usually caused by the IO coming too early. A later opening intake decreases overlap, which creates a more stable idle and usually improves low-speed torque.

Exhaust closing is our next point on the duration curve and ends the overlap event. A late EC increases overlap and tends to hurt low-speed torque and idle quality. An early EC has the opposite effect and improves low-speed torque but also runs the risk of not allowing sufficient time for most of the exhaust gas to exit the chamber. If this happens, you'll have built-in exhaust gas recirculation (EGR), which is often not a good thing, especially if this occurs in the RPM range where you want to make power.

Intake closing (IC) is by far the most important of the valve events. It

Chapter 7

Cam Tuning Techniques

Most street roller cams, either flat or hydraulic, now offer an iron distributor cam drive gear on the back of otherwise steel cams. This allows the engine builder to use a stock iron distributor drive gear. Otherwise you must use a silicon-bronze gear on steel camshafts to prevent quick wear of the iron gear on the steel cam.

If you plan to run a mechanical fuel pump on your steel roller cam, be sure to use a special-tipped fuel-pump pushrod. Comp Cams offers several different types, including this bronze-tipped pushrod that prevents cam wear.

If you are interested in optimizing your combination beyond your first effort at matching a cam to the heads, intake, and exhaust system, there are several approaches. The typical modifications include advancing or retarding the cam, changing the lash (assuming this is a solid lifter engine), changing lift, creating a new lobe separation angle, or modifying the duration. Of these, you can advance or retard the cam, or change lift, without removing the cam from the engine. We'll explain these first.

While advancing or retarding the cam moves all four of the valve events, the predominant effect is achieved with moving the intake valve. Most changes are accomplished by moving the cam at least two degrees and even then the effect will be limited. If we decide to advance the cam, this tends to increase low-speed torque usually at the cost of some high-speed power by closing the intake valve sooner. It should be obvious that retarding the cam then closes the intake valve later, which improves top-end power. Regardless of which way you move the cam, since the intake closing point is the most important, it's probably a good idea to check the intake closing point as a reference to advancing or retarding the timing. Intake centerline is okay, but it's still a good idea to double-check intake closing as well.

The next technique only relates to mechanical camshafts, either flat tappet or roller, since hydraulic cams do not require lash in the system. Lash is the amount of clearance established between the valve tip and the rocker arm with the cam on its base circle. Changing lash can be a great way to learn more about your camshaft and how it relates to the rest of the engine combination. Changing the lash effectively modifies the amount of duration by changing the point at which the valve is actuated by the cam.

Let's say the lash established by the cam manufacturer is 0.020-inch. If we tighten the lash 0.004-inch, this actuates the valve sooner, since there is less clearance between the rocker and the valve. This effectively lengthens the duration and adds 0.004-inch of valve lift. Loosening the lash creates a slightly shorter lobe. This is a significant move to learn how close the cam is to creating the power curve you desire. If you tighten the lash on the intake lobe, this opens the intake valve sooner and closes it later. If the power increases across the power band, this means you could use a longer duration camshaft. If the power only increases at the very top with an equal or greater loss of torque in the middle, then you must evaluate the overall power change to see if that is what you desire.

takes precedence over all the other events. Earlier closing intake events create better low-speed power by trapping the air in the cylinder. This is why short duration cams make more low-speed torque. The down side to this is that at high RPM, the intake valve closes too early before the air and fuel column has a chance to completely fill the cylinder. This is because there is much less time to do so. Conversely, later closing intake valves allow more time to fill the cylinder at higher engine speeds to make more power. However, this doesn't come without a price. The later IC also means that at lower engine speeds, the air and fuel will tend to be pushed back out the intake valve back into the intake manifold as the piston ascends. This hurts cylinder filling, reducing low and mid-range torque. It's all a compromise.

So now when we talk about duration and lift, you need to think in terms of individual timing events. For example, think of a long duration cam not as having more duration, but rather as an intake lobe with a late closing intake valve. Are there other ways to do this? Sure, you could use a shorter duration lobe and retard the intake centerline so that you had a later closing intake point. With no other changes, this would also decrease the overlap. However, for a street engine, you have to be careful with this since a later closing intake really hurts low-speed power.

But before we give up on that, what would happen if you also advanced the exhaust lobe at the same time? This would decrease the overlap and improve low-speed torque while opening the exhaust valve sooner which

Camshafts

You can also change the lash on the exhaust lobe as well. A looser lash on the exhaust produces a later EO and an earlier EC. Changing the exhaust lobe may not create great changes unless the camshaft has substantially missed the mark. Don't be surprised if changes to the exhaust lash produce minimal power curve differences. To make this interesting, we've also included rule of thumb changes to camshaft duration based on the amount of lash changes. Keep in mind that you should limit your lash changes to a tighter lash to about 0.004 to 0.005 inch. You can increase the lash beyond that point, but only for a quick test. You should not run the cam beyond the lash recommendation for any length of time since the additional lash can quickly harm the valvetrain.

Effect of Lash Change on Valve Duration

Lobe Lift (inches)	Loosen Lash 0.004-inch Change (degrees)	Tighten Lash 0.004-inch Change (degrees)
Seat	-6	+6
0.010	-5	+5
0.020	-4	+4
0.050	-2	+2
0.200	-1	+1

Changing the lift is easily accomplished by changing the rocker ratio. Increasing the rocker ratio by 0.10-ratio such as going from 1.5 to 1.6:1 rockers will generally add 0.030 inch of gross valve lift. Changing rocker ratio also has the effect of increasing duration slightly, since the lobe achieves the lift sooner in the curve. If your cylinder heads offer increased airflow above the current lift, this may be an advantage. But often this additional lift produces negligible results. The effort can be attempted on the intake, exhaust, or both, in an effort to learn how the camshaft matches the engine package.

Modifying the lobe separation angle is one way to change an engine's power characteristics without changing the duration. The opportunities here are somewhat confusing since you can move one lobe or both in either direction. We won't run through all the possibilities since that would be complex and beyond the scope of this chapter. But let's look at one possibility and that should give you an idea of what's possible. Keep in mind that any change to lobe separation angle requires a new camshaft.

Let's say you have a hydraulic flat-tappet cam with 245 degrees of duration at 0.050-inch tappet lift with a lobe separation angle of 110 degrees and an intake centerline of 106 degrees. Let's say that you'd like to close just the intake valve four degrees later while leaving the exhaust lobe where it is. This will retard the intake lobe, moving the intake opening point four degrees later in the cycle. This creates an intake centerline of 110 degrees ATDC, which also changes the lobe separation angle from 110 to 112 degrees while the exhaust lobe centerline remains the same at 114 degrees. Remember, lobe separation angle is expressed in camshaft degrees, so a change of four degrees at the crank is only two degrees at the cam (110 + 114 = 224 / 2 = 112 degrees lobe separation angle).

Closing the intake valve later also spreads the lobe separation angle apart, which reduces overlap. This alters several operations at the cylinder since not only does the intake valve open and close four degrees later, but the exhaust and intake valves spend less time open simultaneously. This may hurt mid-range torque because of the later IO, but improve top-end power with the delayed IC. Ultimately, your individual engine requirements will dictate whether this is a good change or not.

Changing the duration is where most engine builders head first, even before they go through the above experiments. If the centerline, lash, or lift changes indicate that the cam is either too short or too long, this is when you should consider changing duration. As we've mentioned previously, a longer-duration cam tends to hurt low and mid-range power, while improving top-end horsepower. With big-inch small blocks that employ relatively small intake port dimensions, it's possible to add a slightly longer duration cam to help improve top-end power since the ports will tend to increase mid-range torque. However, it's very easy to go too far. A cam with excessive duration will kill power everywhere. Conversely, a cam with too little duration will make massive low and mid-range torque but run out of steam early, peaking before your anticipated peak horsepower RPM.

Chapter 7

Roller vs. Flat Tappet

It may appear at first blush that roller tappets have the advantage in terms of performance. But this isn't the whole truth. The best approach is to look at all the pro's and con's and then make your decision.

Flat tappet cams have the advantage in terms of cost, with a complete cam and lifter package price out around $150, depending upon where you get it and who makes it. Add in pushrods, good springs, retainers, and a set of roller rockers, and you have around $900 for a roller cam system with both roller lifters and roller rockers. That's probably slightly on the high side, depending upon the spring you need.

Cost aside, flat-tappet cams are limited to a certain amount of lift per degree that is determined by the diameter of the lifter. With a 0.842-inch diameter stock flat-tappet follower, a small block (or big block) is limited to 0.007-inch of lift per degree of lobe movement. Move up to a larger diameter lifter like a Ford 0.875-inch diameter lifter and the lift-per-degree spec inches up to 0.0755. This may not sound like much, but it's worth some significantly quicker acceleration rates and more lift for the same duration. This is so important that NASCAR specifies that all Winston Cup engines use the larger Ford lifter diameter — even the Chevys and the Mopars. The Chrysler guys are less than thrilled about this because their production lifter diameter happens to be larger at 0.904-inch — hence the level playing field.

Are there advantages to the larger Ford style lifter? There are, but only if you employ a lobe that can take advantage of the enhanced lift-per-degree. You'd have to tell the cam folks to put a Ford lobe on a Chevy cam blank, which is certainly possible. There's enough room to squeeze the larger Ford lifter in between the lobes after machining the lifter bores. The advantages would also be limited, and few street engine builders have gone this far.

Another advantage of flat-tappet cams, besides lower initial cost, is that they have a stronger acceleration rate off the base circle than a roller cam. This means that shorter duration cams (smaller than 225 degrees of duration at 0.050) enjoy a slight advantage over their roller cam cousins. But once you get above this duration figure, the valve lift cards are certainly stacked in favor of the roller cam.

On the roller side, we've already addressed the cost factor, which is significant. Roller cams enjoy a dramatically better lift-per-degree figure of 0.009 to 0.010-inch-per-degree depending upon the base circle diameter. Cam designers will tell you that, initially, the roller gets a slow start off the base circle. But at around 0.200-inch of tappet lift, the roller is clearly in the lead in terms of valve lift. This means that the roller achieves valve lift sooner, and holds it open longer than a flat-tappet cam. This means the engine builder can spec a slightly shorter duration and still achieve the lift numbers to help build power.

Let's look at an example to illustrate our point. We'll use intake lobes at the same 0.050-inch checking height for our comparison. Note that we've listed two hydraulic roller lobes; the second is more aggressive over the nose, requiring more spring pressure or less RPM. This lobe would work best with a 1.5:1 rocker.

Lobe	Advertised Duration	Duration @ 0.050	Duration @ 0.200	Lift @1.5	Lift @1.6
Hyd. Roller	282	230	151	0.510	0.544
Hyd. Roller	282	230	157	0.584	0.622
Flat Tappet	274	230	140	0.455	0.485
Mech. Roller	268	230	153	0.552	0.589

The first point worth noting is that the flat-tappet cam offers a shorter hydraulic intensity or the number of degrees between the advertised duration point and the 0.050-inch checking point. The flat-tappet cam required only 44 degrees between these two points while the hydraulic roller requires 52 degrees, or 8 degrees more time. This is because the hydraulic roller is acceleration-limited off the seat. This is why it needs more seat duration to achieve the same 0.050 numbers.

Comparing duration at 0.200-inch tappet lift shows us that the more aggressive lobe offers 17 more degrees of duration between the two 0.200-inch tappet lift numbers. Looking at the comparison of the two lobes on the overlapping lobe profiles makes this additional duration obvious.

The most obvious advantage of the hydraulic roller is the additional lift. The more aggressive of the two lobes offers a staggering 0.129-inch of additional lift compared to the flat-tappet cam! This is an astounding amount of lift and again points to the potential power increase. Even the milder of the two hydraulic roller profiles still offers 0.055-inch additional lift over the flat-tappet profile.

Camshafts

Comparing the mechanical roller to the flat-tappet hydraulic really isn't fair, especially since the mechanical appears to have a shorter advertised duration. This is the result of the mechanical cam being checked at 0.015-inch tappet lift instead of 0.006-inch. However, the mechanical offers 13 degrees more duration at 0.200-inch tappet lift and a stout 0.097-inch of additional lift at 1.5 rocker ratio. This is a street roller intake lobe. If we were to dial in a more aggressive race roller, the disparity would be even larger. It's not a good idea to use a drag race profile on the street however, since these lobes tend to beat up on valvesprings, roller tappets, and rocker arms.

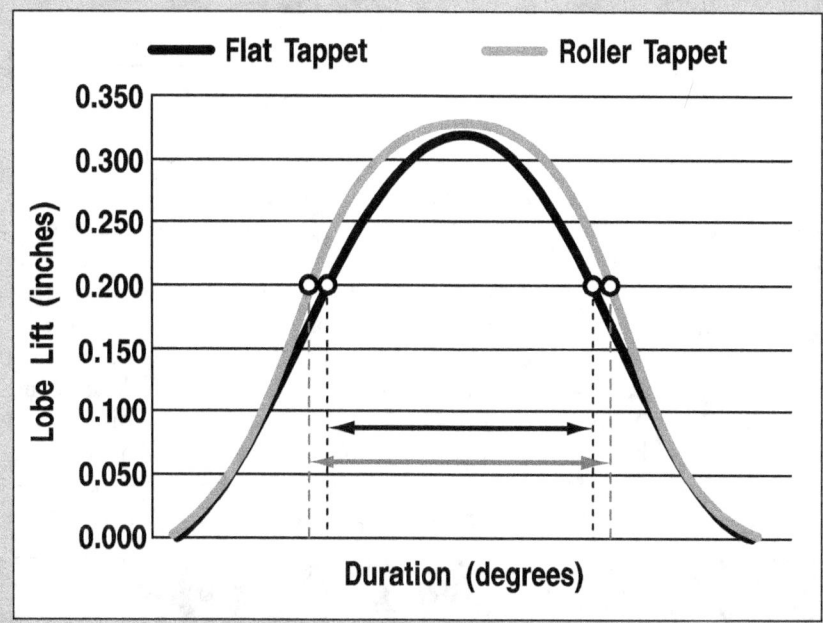

Flat tappet cams offer a slight advantage over hydraulic roller cams, especially with cams shorter than 220 degrees at 0.050. However, with larger cams, the roller enjoys superior lift as well as longer duration between the 0.200-inch tappet lift areas.

would hurt torque at the bottom slightly but would create less pumping losses in the mid-range and help power up high. What you would need is more static compression ratio to help the bottom and mid-range because of the later closing intake.

What this idea represents is exactly what Chevrolet has been doing with the later model LS1 and LS6 engines. If you've ever wondered why these engines can perform so well with high static compression ratios and not have knock problems, this is one reason. The factory LS1 and LS6 cams feature much later closing intake valves, combined with wide lobe separation angles in order to create that dead-smooth idle that is so important to a production vehicle. The late closing intake tends to bleed off some cylinder pressure down low, so the engineers make up for that low-speed loss by squeezing what is left at low speeds with a higher compression ratio. Combine this with an excellent combustion chamber and really good flowing heads and it is no wonder these engines make such great power and get excellent fuel mileage. If there is one detriment, it may be that these engines idle way too smooth, so they don't sound like a performance engine. However, if you don't consider that a problem, there may be some advantage to running a wide lobe separation angle cam with a later closing intake valve and a higher compression ratio. It's just a thought.

Theory contends that you should always close the intake valve at the exact point that the pressure inside the cylinder equals that of the pressure in the intake tract. If you close the valve at exactly that point, the cylinder will be filled and you will make maximum power. Unfortunately, there are dynamic considerations that make that very difficult. For example, air tends to have an inertia. Not unlike a train, once that column of air and fuel begins to move, it is not that easy to stop. This inertia will continue to fill the cylinder even after that theoretical 100 percent volumetric efficiency has been achieved. This is the advantage to later closing intake valves at higher engine speeds. You need that longer intake duration to initiate the intake flow and to give it time to move the air into the cylinder. This begins to lead into cylinder head and intake tract development, like the size of the intake runners. This is all discussed in another chapter, but we mention it here to emphasize the importance of matched components and creating the best cam for the parts you've chosen — the system approach.

CHAPTER 8

VALVETRAINS

There's quite a bit of discussion in the performance arena about how Chevrolet continues to use "antiquated" pushrod engines when the future seems clearly in favor of overhead cam engines that eliminate the "monkey motion" of pushrods and rocker arms. Clearly, these agitators have evidently never watched a NASCAR race where 358ci small-block Chevys run up to and over 9,000 rpm for 500 miles making well in excess of 700 hp. And the rules even require them to run flat-tappet camshafts!

The reason the small block continues to be popular is because of sheer volume. The volume is there because the engines make great power and are incredibly reliable. Given this volume of parts and the small block's incredible reputation for reliability, companies continue to build more parts in an attempt to extract more and more power. This sets up an interesting battle of sorts between the cam designers who continually push the boundaries of valvetrain dynamics and those long-suffering valvetrain engineers who are assigned the task of making the rest of the motion chain survive.

This chapter will address every component in the valvetrain including lifters, pushrods, guideplates, studs, rocker arms, retainers, locks, springs, spring seats, seals, and valves. There's much to cover in this section so we'd best get started.

LIFTERS

The cam follower is a crucial component where it's best to invest in the highest quality tappet possible. We've

The factory small-block hydraulic roller-tappet system uses 8 cast bars that slip over matching flats on the lifter body to prevent the lifter from spinning in the bore. Then a lightweight spring spider is bolted to the middle of the lifter valley to maintain pressure on the bars and prevent them from slipping off.

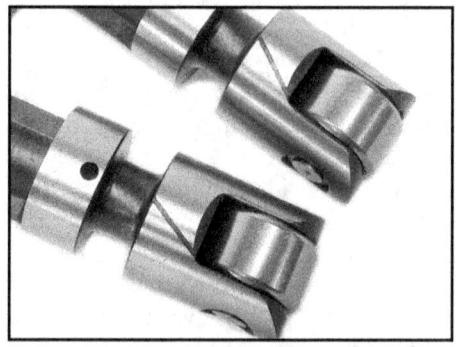

Mechanical roller lifters are designed to be used with high spring pressures that affect durability. One way to ensure durability is Comp Cams' Endurex roller lifters that have a machined passage that directs pressurized oil path aimed at the roller bearings to ensure proper lubrication. Crane's roller lifters use an internal oil path for this same reason.

Valvetrains

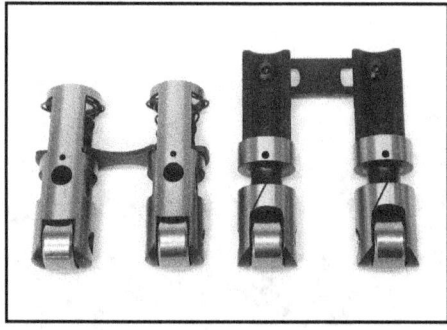

For aftermarket roller lifters, there are both horizontal and vertical tie bars. Crane's horizontal tie bars push up on the lifter when the pushrod is removed. This pulls the lifter away from the cam far enough to allow cam changes without removing the intake manifold.

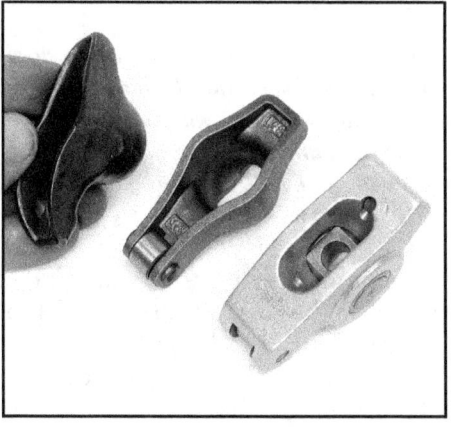

From left to right are a stamped steel 1.5 rocker, a roller-tipped rocker, and a full roller rocker. The only rocker worth investing in is the full roller rocker for a serious big-inch small block, especially with a roller cam.

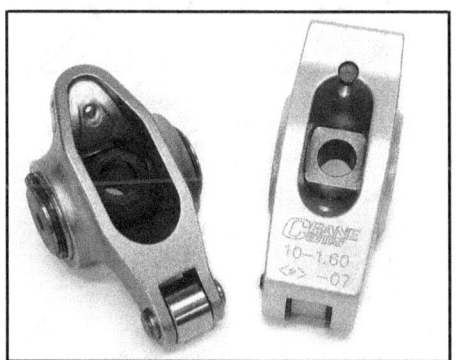

Comp's high-end roller rockers are constructed of stainless steel and are rebuildable (left). Crane's Gold Race rockers are aluminum and somewhat lighter (right).

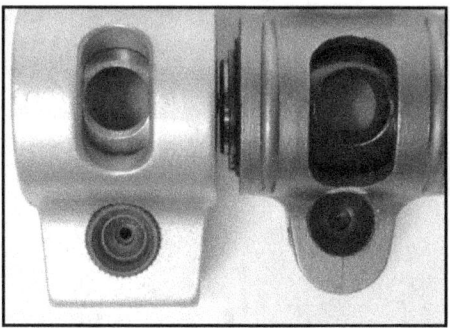

The distance between the fulcrum centerline and the valve tip is a fixed length, so increasing the rocker ratio means shortening the distance between the pushrod cup and the fulcrum. The 1.6 rocker distance (right) is shorter than the 1.5 rocker (left).

already covered the differences between flat, roller, hydraulic, and mechanical tappets in the cam section, but with flat-tappet hydraulics there are some subtle differences worth noting. Hydraulic lifters were originally developed to quiet engine operation. The hydraulic flat tappet incorporates a hydraulic piston inside the lifter that balances oil pressure and valvespring pressure to maintain a cushion of sorts that also compensates for expansion as the engine achieves operating temperature. The clearance inside the lifter between the piston and the tappet body are critical to the bleed-down rate of the lifter. These clearances determine the amount of oil that eventually bleeds off and returns to the pan. The best lifters have critical internal dimensions that limit this bleed-down rate and contribute to more precise valve control at high RPM.

So-called "bleed-down" lifters, like the original Rhodes lifter, offer an interesting alternative to the standard tight clearance lifter. These lifters, like the Crane Hi Intensity or the Comp Cams Hi Tech Hydraulic offer a greater bleed down rate. At idle and low engine speeds, the lifter becomes a lost motion device. Lift begins on the opening side of the lobe, but the greater clearance between the piston and the lifter pumps a small amount of oil out of the reservoir, which means the lifter body moves upward but the pushrod does not. Eventually, the piston does actuate the pushrod and the valve, but in the meantime the bleed-down lifter has shortened the cam's effective duration and lift. These lifters are used as a crutch or band-aid to improve idle quality on street engines with long-duration camshafts. Tests have shown improvements of around 1 to 1.5 inches and sometimes as much as 3 inches of manifold vacuum.

A more robust pushrod cup retainer clip on the top of the lifter can often identify high-quality hydraulic lifters. Stock lifters use a small square retainer ring that can, on occasion, pop out and allow the lifter to come apart. The better quality lifters often use an internal snap ring that does a better job of ensuring the lifter stays together. These lifters are often called "anti pump-up" lifters because of their tighter tolerances. Comp Cams, for example, specifies a minimal 0.002 to 0.004-inch preload on their Pro Magnum lifter to create optimal performance. This limits the travel the internal piston can move when it pumps up during high-RPM valvetrain instability.

The main advantage to hydraulic flat-tappet lifters is their weight. These tappets are considerably lighter than their hydraulic roller cousins. This weight advantage carries over into the flat-tappet mechanical lifters as well. Comp offers a Hi-Tech Lite (HTL) lifter that is approximately 20 grams lighter than a typical solid lifter. These lifters are also machined without the edge chamfer at the bottom of the lifter to maximize effective diameter. These are also very expensive lifters. For street operation, these lifters are not necessary unless you are intrigued with that last 100 rpm of engine speed.

Comp also offers an interesting solid flat-tappet lifter with a precision-drilled hole in the lifter face for improved lubrication between the lifter and the cam. These lifters are probably not necessary for most street-destined engines, but you could use them if you desire the added durability. Remember, most V8 engines rely on splash oiling the lifter-to-cam interface, and high spring pressures certainly make that job difficult. While we're on that subject, Comp also makes a lifter bore grooving tool that cuts a small slot in the lifter

Chapter 8

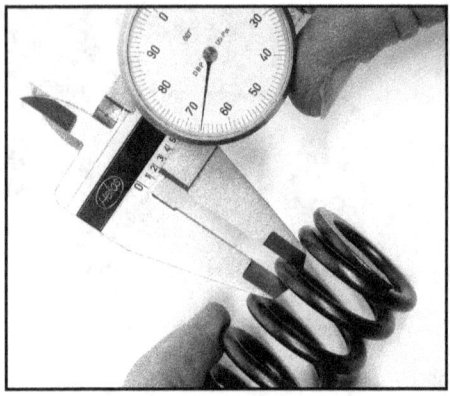

One of the latest innovations in spring design is ovate wire, which is oval. This allows more lift before coil bind. This is a more expensive spring to build, but you will probably see more of this spring in the future.

The easiest way to bump up valvespring pressure is to increase the spring's diameter. With the same wire diameter, a larger o.d. spring will increase the rate.

The spring on the far left is a single wire valvespring. The middle spring is a larger diameter single spring with a damper. The spring on the far right is a true dual spring also with a damper. Dual springs can also use a damper. The spring rate for a dual spring is found by adding the rates of the two springs together.

bore that directs oil to the cam and lifter to increase lubrication to the lifter. This is a great idea for flat-tappet cams.

There's probably enough information on roller lifters to overwhelm even a lifter engineer, so we'll limit our discussion to the more streetable lifters. Perhaps the most important thing to remember is that the roller must always remain parallel to the lobe. This is why all roller tappets use some type of tie bar arrangement that usually ties two lifters together to remain aligned. This has created several different alignment arrangements.

The factory hydraulic roller system uses flat spots on the lifter body to accommodate two-hole retainers that fit down over the lifter body to keep the lifter parallel to the lobe. Used alone, these retainers could easily pop off the lifter body. So the factory uses a spring steel spider that bolts to the center of the lifter valley. It uses eight separate legs to place a load in the center of each of the eight tie bars. This system works well in stock applications and for engine speeds below 6,500 rpm, as long as you maintain valvetrain stability. We have also seen the spider bend in 6,800 to 7,000 rpm use. This allowed the tie bars to jump off the lifters due to valve float, which destroyed the lifters and the cam. This system does work well for mild street use, but requires three bosses in the center of the lifter valley to mount the spider. So without major work, this design cannot be used in pre-1987 blocks.

Retrofit roller lifters use specifically designed tie bars to precisely locate the lifters. These tie bars are offered in either vertical or horizontal configurations. Most roller lifters come with vertical tie bars, but Crane offers both standard and pro-series horizontal spring-loaded tie

Before you buy that set of killer dual springs, make sure that the inner spring's inside diameter (i.d.) will clear the valve guide boss and the valve guide seal. The seal will not live if the spring constantly rubs against it.

bars that lift the tappet body up off the cam when the pushrod is removed. The horizontal tie bar design allows cam changes without having to remove the intake manifold. However, Bow Tie blocks often come with a tall lifter bore area that can interfere with the horizontal tie bar. These blocks must be machined in order to clear the tie bar.

Another important point to consider with mechanical roller lifters is proper lubrication. Comp has created its Endurex mechanical roller lifter with a machined oiling groove that directs pressurized oil at the roller bearings to improve lubrication, especially at low street engine speeds. For street engines, this is especially important since solid roller engines generally employ higher spring pressures, which place additional load on the entire valvetrain, not just the lifter.

The disadvantage to hydraulic roller tappets is their inherent weight. Hydraulic roller-tappets weigh significantly more than a typical mechanical roller tappet and or a flat tappet. This means that the valvespring is forced to control additional weight. Valvespring pressures become especially important on street engines if you intend to run a rather aggressive cam profile, or if you intend on running higher-ratio rocker arms.

This does cause grief when it comes to building engines that will spin past 6500 rpm. The heavier roller lifters require more spring pressure, which can often cause the hydraulic lifter to pump down at high RPM. This becomes evident after a high-RPM run, when the engine runs rough and clatters terribly because the spring pressure and inertial loads have caused the lifter plunger to purge all the oil out of the lifter.

One fix for this is a system is the Hydra-Rev, offered by AirFlow Research. The Hydra-Rev system uses additional springs in the lifter valley to control only the hydraulic roller lifter. This allows the builder to run slightly less spring pressure on the valvespring, preventing lifter pump down. This system has proven powerful in certain applications with significant power gains above 6,000 rpm. However, other tests were inconclusive.

Perhaps what should be discussed at this point is the relative disadvantage of a hydraulic roller tappet over a mechanical roller. The only real advantage for the hydraulic seems to be the reduced maintenance. Solid cams, either roller or flat tappet, require maintenance, such as periodic lash adjustments. However, our experience with several mechanical roller street engines (albeit relatively low mileage engines), is that lash maintenance is a relatively minor thing. One engine with over 5,000 street miles required very little adjustment. The use of poly locks on all rocker arms maintains the lash adjustment, and unless there is a problem, constant valve lash adjustments appear to be more of a wives tale than anything else.

In addition to the mechanical tappet's weight advantage, it also offers the engine builder/tuner the advantage to do perform lash changes to evaluate slight changes to the camshaft that cannot be accomplished with a hydraulic roller lifters. This is an advantage that is also useful with flat-tappet lifters as well. This is something that should be considered when deciding upon which cam to use in your street small block.

Spring Rate

The original calculation of spring rate is a rather complex formula, which really isn't necessary. What is easy to determine is spring rate given two set measurements. Spring rate is expressed in pounds per inch (lbs/in). A common error is to express spring rate as psi, (pounds per square inch) which is a pressure, but different from spring pressure, which is merely a load. Most coil springs are linear, which means that for every inch the spring is compressed, the load will increase by the same amount. Let's say that you have a spring sitting on the bench but you're not sure of its rate. Let's say that you've measured the seat load at 120 pounds at an installed height of 1.700-inch. Using the spring pressure tool, compress the spring to 1.200-inch for a spring travel of 0.500-inch and read a load of 270 pounds. Subtract the seat load from the open load (270 - 120 = 150 pounds). Since we have a spring travel of 0.500-inch, if we double the spring load (150 pounds x 2 = 300) we will get the spring's rate based on the change of load between the two points. For dual spring assemblies, merely add the two rates together to get the combined rate. If the outer spring has a rate of 320 and the inner spring a rate of 120, then the total spring rate would be 320 + 120 = 440 lbs/in.

It's also possible to figure out open load pressure if you know the rate and the installed height load. As an example, let's say the seat pressure is 120 lbs and the rate is 450 lbs/in. We'll make valve lift 0.500-inch to keep the math simple. To determine open load pressure, we merely add half the spring rate (1/2-inch of valve lift, or 225 lbs + 120 lbs seat pressure = 345 lbs of open pressure).

If you want to know what adding a shim is worth, merely multiply the spring rate times the thickness of the shim. For example, adding a .030-inch shim under a 400 lb/in spring increases the seat pressure by 12 pounds (400 x .03 = 12 lbs). Or if you increase the installed height on this same spring by 0.050-inch, this would reduce the seat pressure by 20 lbs (400 x -0.05 = -20 lbs).

To determine the rate for a typical coil spring, you need to know its outside diameter, wire diameter, and the number of active coils.

PUSHRODS AND GUIDEPLATES

The pushrod tends to play a big part in valvetrain geometry, since its length establishes the amount of rocker-arm travel across the valve tip. It should be obvious that any engine builder desires to minimize rocker-tip travel across the top of the valve. We'll get into setting pushrod length in the accompanying sidebar.

The pushrod should be as stiff as possible, but like most components, adding stiffness also adds weight. Most professional engine builders will tell you that despite the additional weight, a stiffer pushrod is always a good idea. The alternative is a flexible pushrod that actually becomes more like a track meet vaulting pole that bends in the center. When this happens, the valve is no longer following the cam profile. With a

Chapter 8

flexible pushrod, the valve lags behind the acceleration side of the cam. Cam profiling is a careful science, since the cam must slow the valve down and actually stop it at max lobe lift before it starts its descent. After the pushrod bends, the stored energy in the pushrod is released at the point where the lobe is attempting to slow the valve down. This has the affect of launching the valve off the end of the lobe, drastically increasing valve lift. Unfortunately, this also often results in smashing the valve into the piston since valve lift is drastically increased over the cam specs. This is most apparent with drag-race style lobes, but it can happen with aggressive street cams using higher spring pressures.

Stiffer pushrods work great at deterring this problem. Stock small-block pushrods are 5/16-inch in diameter. Several companies offer 3/8-inch diameter small-block pushrods, but before you step up to these much larger pieces, let's take a look at ways to strengthen a typical 5/16-inch diameter pushrod. Pushrods made from 4130 chromoly steel are a great way to improve strength using a much stiffer material. Both Crane and Comp Cams build an 0.080-inch wall thickness, one-piece pushrod in 4130 for small blocks. These pushrods are available in 0.050-inch increments, which allow the engine builder to establish valvetrain geometry perfectly. Even better, the Comp pushrods are laser etched with the exact pushrod length, which helps prevent mix-ups. One-piece pushrods are a better idea than three-piece pushrods, which feature welded balls on the ends. These three-piece pushrods are not as strong as a one-piece design.

Of course, all of these pushrods are also hardened to ensure that they are durable enough for use with a guideplate. Guideplates are intended to help center the rocker over the valve tip by limiting lateral movement of the pushrod. This is accomplished in stock small-block Chevys by drilling small holes in the cylinder head, which help limit lateral pushrod movement. The pushrods did not have to be hardened because cast iron is soft. One trick worth mentioning is that you should

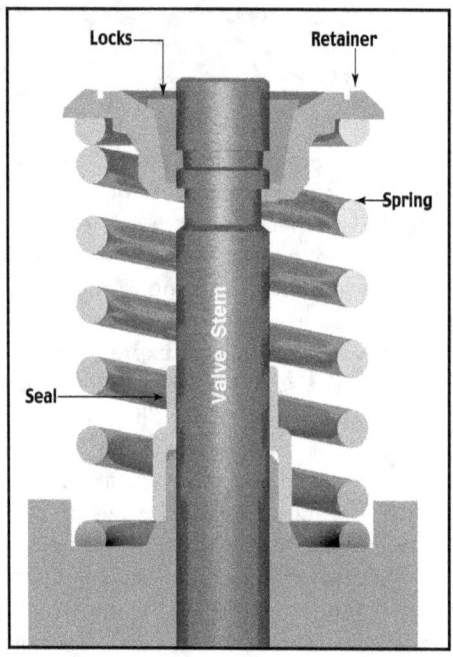

This cutaway reveals the relationship between the spring, retainer, locks, seal, and valve. Retainer-to-seal clearance is an important spec you should check, especially with high-lift cams.

An easily overlooked spec is the retainer-to-seal clearance. This should be at least 0.050-inch more than the net valve lift. As an example, if the net lift is 0.500-inch, there must be 0.550-inch between the retainer and the seal at installed height. If not, you may have to machine the guide boss down to create the clearance.

Coil bind is easy to visualize. Most cam companies require 0.060-inch clearance to coil bind. If net valve lift is 0.500-inch, then maximum spring travel must be able to accommodate at least 0.560-inch. With the cam manufacturer's coil spring information, this is easy to determine.

Valvetrains

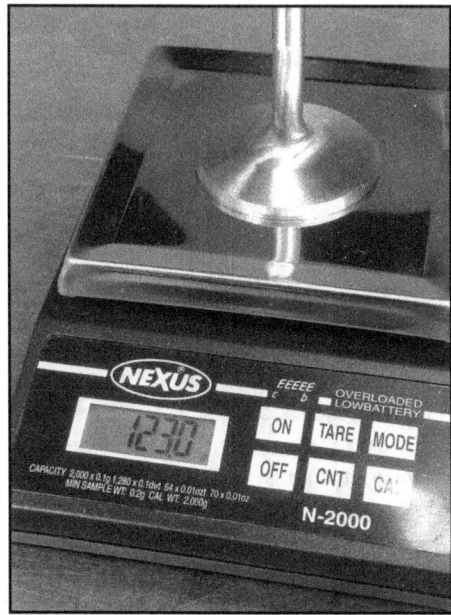

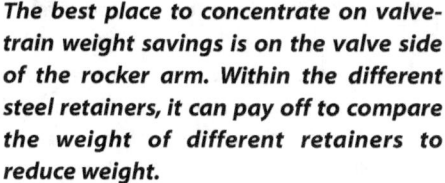

The best place to concentrate on valvetrain weight savings is on the valve side of the rocker arm. Within the different steel retainers, it can pay off to compare the weight of different retainers to reduce weight.

Spring pressure is best checked with a simple gauge if you are in doubt about the springs in your engine. Use only enough spring pressure to keep the lifter on the nose of the cam and to prevent the valve from bouncing off the seat on closing. Intake valves require more pressure because they are larger and heavier.

Jesel, Comp, and Crane offer budget-based rocker shaft systems for the small block. Rocker shaft systems are designed for specific heads based on the geometry of that particular head. These systems reduce valvetrain deflection, optimize rocker-to-valve geometry, and can be worth both power and improved valvetrain durability. This is an example of the Comp Cams shaft rockers.

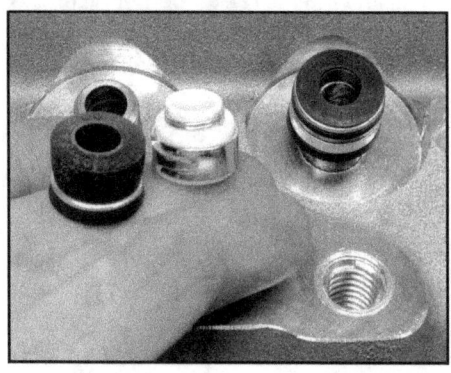

Trash those old white plastic valve guide seals and invest in a set of high-quality Viton rubber positive seals. These new generation seals come in both 0.560 and 0.530-inch guide diameters for small-block 11/32-inch valve stem diameters. Keep in mind they may not clear a dual-spring application.

carefully inspect the pushrod alignment with the valve. Often you can merely slide the pushrod guideplate laterally to help align the rockers with its valve. Often this isn't possible, which means you may have to cut the guideplate and then weld it back together. Isky makes this easy with an adjustable guideplate. This allows the engine builder to set the desired distance between the pushrod slots in the plate. It also requires the plates to be welded.

Retainers

Here's an area that is receiving an increased amount of attention. We will be continually discussing weight in this chapter since it has such a dramatic effect on valvetrain performance. Larger diameter springs require a bigger retainer that weighs more. Weight in the retainer makes life more difficult for the valvespring, which is why you hear so much about titanium retainers. The weight difference may seem insignificant, but titanium retainers are 40 percent lighter than steel, and this is usually worth 100 to as much as 200 rpm of valve stability. This can be enough to prevent the negative effects of valve float.

Regardless of material, it is essential that the retainer be matched perfectly with the valvespring. This isn't nearly as critical with single wire springs as it is with dual springs. Dual springs increase pressure yet act and must be treated like separate springs. That means that the retainer must accurately locate the inner as well as the outer spring. The steps built into the retainer accomplish this. The innermost step must fit snugly into the inside diameter (i.d.) of the inner spring, while the next step locates the i.d. of the outer spring. The top of the retainer should cover the outside diameter (o.d.) of the spring. These connections need to be secure and tight since the spring cannot be allowed to move around the retainer.

There are also options for the type of keeper that can be used with the retainer. Before we get into that, it should be noted that the tang in the keeper that rides in the slot in the valve is not what locks the retainer to the valve. This notch merely locates the keeper on the valve, while the outside taper angle is what actually locks the retainer to the valve. The more pressure that is exerted on the taper only increases the clamping load on the retainer. You should always look for a slight gap between the two keepers when installed in the retainer. If the two keepers butt against each other on both ends, this means the keepers are too large for the retainer. Keepers that are too small will leave a gap between the middle of the lock and o.d. of the valve stem. All locks

Pushrod Length

This may be the most overlooked and misunderstood system of the small-block Chevy valvetrain. If you study any rocker arm, it becomes clear very quickly that the rocker-arm tip moves in an arc as it creates lift. This arc creates movement across the valvestem tip. The small block's stud-mounted rocker arms rely on pushrod length to establish the proper pushrod geometry. This minimizes rocker-arm tip movement across the valve tip. While there are some that demand that the rocker tip be positioned in the middle of the valve tip at half lift with the rocker perpendicular to the valve, there are others who only look to minimize the rocker tip travel across the valve tip.

It is beyond the scope of this chapter to get into all the details necessary to investigate these relationships. What we have found is a simple trick that works about 90 percent of the time, requires few specialty tools, and is a reliable indicator of pushrod length but this only works with rocker arms that use a roller tip. Pull a valve cover and roll the engine over until you have a rocker arm on the base circle of the cam. Remove the rocker and clean the oil off the valve-stem tip. Using a black, felt-tip marker, color the entire tip. Now replace the rocker arm and wiggle the rocker over the valve tip, making a witness mark. Now remove the rocker arm and look for the mark on the valve-stem tip. If the pushrod length is correct, the mark will be about one-third of the way in from the intake side of the valve tip.

If the mark is farther outboard toward the exhaust side of the engine, then the pushrod is too long. If the mark is too far inboard, then the pushrod is too short. If the pushrod length is incorrect, the best way to determine the proper length is to use an adjustable pushrod. Comp Cams makes a great adjustable pushrod that indicates its actual length right on the side of the pushrod with graduated lengths set up like a micrometer. Measuring pushrods is difficult because the length is measured from the radius of the tip. Comp Cams eliminates that variable by taking that into account with its adjustable pushrod. The pushrod is graduated in 0.050-inch increments, as are Comp's custom pushrod lengths. Generally, it takes a change of at least 0.100-inch to make a difference in the pushrod geometry.

It's also important to note that just checking one valve/rocker assembly does not ensure that the rest of the valvetrain will want the same pushrod length. Especially with roller camshafts, if you are checking the intake rocker/valve combination, the exhaust lobe on the cam is often ground on a different base circle. This can change the pushrod length by 0.050-inch or more, so you need to check both the intake and the exhaust. Variables like overall valve length, depth of the valve job, clearance between the rocker stud hole and the stud, rocker stud concentricity, block deck height, amount of head milling, and head gasket thickness all play a part in establishing proper pushrod geometry. The idea is to limit the total rocker tip travel across the valve tip. High-quality rocker shaft systems will limit rocker travel to as little as 0.020-inch across the valve tip.

If we were building an all-out, competition engine, we would make sure all those variables were checked. However, for a street engine, minimizing rocker tip travel across the valvestem tip may not be worth the effort, since this may not represent significant power at street engine speeds. If you're really serious about valvetrain geometry, it's worth noting that many of these problems are eliminated with a shaft rocker system, although a proper length pushrod is still required.

The witness mark will tell you if the pushrod is the proper length. The witness mark seen here indicates a too-long pushrod that has pushed the roller tip outboard toward the exhaust side of the head. Shortening the pushrod so that the mark falls on the inboard third of the valve tip is preferable. The ideal rocker tip movement across the face of the valve tip is zero travel, but 0.060-inch or less is a good spec.

Comp Cams sells this handy little adjustable pushrod that allows you to set the overall length of the pushrod and then read the length based on the gauge imprinted on the side of the pushrod.

Valvetrains

Spring seats do more than just protect an aluminum head from damage from the spring. Both o.d. and i.d. springs seats locate the spring to prevent it from moving around at engine speed.

should be test fitted before final assembly to ensure that they fit properly.

One interesting twist on the lock theme is the placement of the tang in the lock. Most companies place the tang directly in the middle of the lock. However, not every company does so, which will change the vertical position of the retainer on the valve. This affects the installed height of the valvespring. For example, Crane builds machined steel, 7-degree locks in three different installed heights that will add or subtract 0.050-inch of height from the standard position. This allows the engine builder to customize the installed height of the valvespring, which we will discuss later in this chapter. Machined locks are far stronger than stamped-steel locks. It's also important to ensure the retainers you've ordered are for the right size valve stem. Retainers are sized to fit a valve stem, with the stock small-block stem size being 11/32-inch.

VALVESPRINGS

Here's where things really get interesting. You can invest in nothing but the best parts for your big-inch small block, but if you choose the wrong valvesprings, all that money will never overcome the shortcomings of a weak or misapplied spring. In its simplest definition, the spring only has to control the action of the valve by maintaining the valvetrain in contact with the cam lobe. But that's easier said than done.

Titanium retainers can save roughly 40 percent of the weight of a steel retainer. A few grams may not seem like much, but titanium retainers are often worth as much as 100 to 200 additional RPM.

In its simplest form, a single wire valvespring creates a load based on how much it is squeezed. Spring rate is a function of the number of active (non-touching) coils, the wire diameter, and the spring's outside diameter. Larger spring diameter, larger wire, and fewer numbers of active coils all contribute to increasing the spring rate. However, there are plenty of limitations. The first is the outside diameter (o.d.) of the spring, which is limited by space between the valves and other components like head bolts. Stock small-block Chevy springs measure 1.250-inch in diameter, but most performance heads, especially for use with roller cams, will specify a 1.450 or 1.550-inch spring o.d. These larger diameter springs allow for larger wire diameters, which create space for an inner spring.

Dual-spring assemblies should not be confused with single springs that include a flat wire damper. These dampers are flat wire inserts used to dampen the spring's natural frequency. This natural frequency can lead to loss of valve control at a certain RPM. The insert or damper tends to help minimize this spring oscillation. You will see these dampers used in all types of springs. They do not contribute to the spring rate, but are important to spring durability nonetheless.

Spring rate is the most important aspect when it comes to choosing valvesprings. The higher the rate, the more load the spring places on the valve. In order to create load, you must compress the spring. The installed height is the distance between the spring pad on the cylinder head and the bottom of the spring retainer with the valve closed. The standard installed height for a small-block Chevy is 1.750-inch, but that can change with aftermarket heads, especially if longer valves are used. The

Spec Chart

Application	Spec (inches)
Coil bind clearance	0.060
Retainer to seal	0.050
Stamped rocker slot to stud	0.060
Rocker arm to retainer	0.040
Spring to spring cup interference	no more than 0.005
Hydraulic lifter preload	.040 to 0.050
Mechanical lifter lash	manufacturer's recommendation
Valve-to-piston clearance	Int. 0.080, Exh. 0.100
Lifter to bore clearance	0.0015-0.0020

How To Build Big-Inch Chevy Small-Blocks

Chapter 8

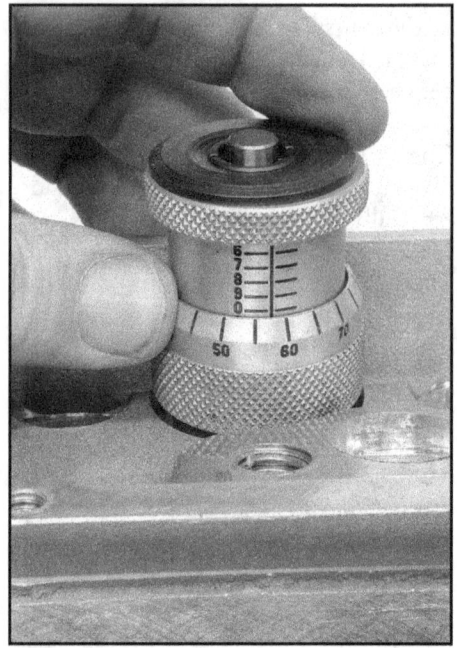

It's also important to use the specific retainer and keepers for each valve to establish the actual installed height of each spring. The height mic makes this job easy.

When assembling the valvetrain, you must check for retainer-to-rocker clearance. This must be checked on all 16 rocker/spring combos since production tolerances may create problems on only one or two.

installed height will load a spring to anywhere from a stock application of 90 to 210 pounds per inch (lbs/in) or more for a dual-roller spring assembly.

The next spring spec worth noting is the open load pressure when the valve is at maximum lift. This load will be a percentage of the spring rate added to the seat pressure. For most valvesprings, load will increase linearly as the spring is compressed. In other words, the rate will increase at a set rate until the spring is fully compressed. One way to increase the overall load on the valvetrain without changing springs is to increase the starting pressure. This can be done by reducing the installed height, assuming there is sufficient clearance to prevent coil bind.

This brings us to several clearances that must be checked when assembling the valvetrain to ensure the engine does not break parts. The first clearance to check is coil bind height. Coil bind height is the height of the spring once it has been fully compressed and all the coils are touching. In any cam catalog, the company will list a spring's coil bind height. Subtracting the coil bind height from the installed height will give you the total amount of valve spring travel. Let's say the installed height is 1.800-inch and coil bind height is 1.250-inch. This produces a total spring travel of 0.550-inch. This appears we have enough spring travel to accommodate 0.550-inch valve lift. But this would be running dangerously close to coil bind, which will break rocker studs, bend pushrods, mangle rocker arms, and generally cause chaos. To be safe, the minimum clearance is 0.0060-inch, or about 0.015-inch of clearance between each active coil. It's worth it to actually check the spring height at coil bind by placing it in a vise. We've discovered that manufacturer's specs can often be on the safe side. In other words, the coil bind spec might be 1.200-inch, when in fact the actual spring will compress to as short as 1.150-inch. This gives the engine builder another 0.050-inch of clearance.

The next dimension to check is the retainer-to-seal clearance. Checking this involves assembling a valveguide seal, valve, retainer, and keepers on a head. The distance between the lowest portion of the retainer and the top of the seal installed on the guide must be at least 0.050-inch more than the maximum valve lift. This prevents smashing the retainer into the seal at maximum valve lift. This minimum clearance of 0.050-inch does not prevent the retainer from smashing the seal if the engine goes into valve float. This is why it's best to check all these clearances before you assemble the heads for the final time. Increasing the installed height will increase this clearance, but the tradeoff is a loss of spring pressure.

ROCKER ARMS

There's plenty to talk about rocker arms, but we will focus our attention on roller rocker arms since with a big-inch small block, there's little call for stamped steel rockers. The only thing to say about

Valvetrains

Upgrading to 7/16-inch rocker studs instead of the stock 3/8-inch would be wise if you intend to run a solid roller cam with big spring pressures. The increase in stiffness will prevent rocker-arm deflection.

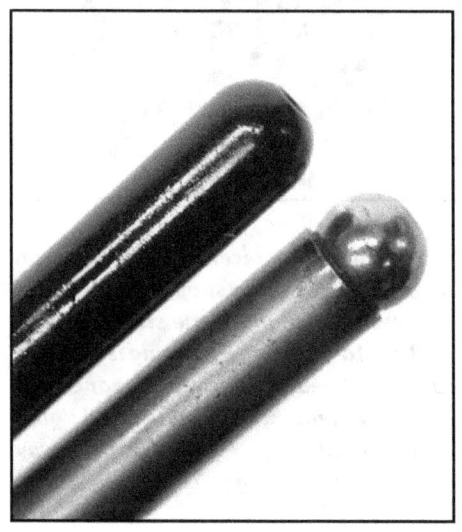

It may seem counterproductive to move to a thicker-walled (heavier) pushrod. But consider that the pushrod is itself a spring, with the possibility to allow deflection. Stiffer pushrods will create an overall better valvetrain that may be worth both power and reliability

Valvespring Load Recommendations

This information was taken from Crane's suggestions for spring load based on camshaft configuration and usage. These pressures are for serious small-block street/strip engines based on using stock or lightweight components. Lighter components require less pressure. Open pressures of around 380 to over 400 pounds require quality components and billet steel roller-tappet bodies. Valvetrain component durability for street engines is inversely proportional to spring pressure when you get over 360 to 380 pounds open pressure. Circle track and drag racing applications will require higher pressures on both the seat and the open pressures.

Camshaft	Seat Pressure (lbs)	Open Pressure (lbs)
Flat tappet	105 to 125	260 to 280
Roller hydraulic	120 to 145	300 to 400
Roller mechanical	165 to 180	350 to 400

the roller-tipped ball stud rockers is that the roller tip does not really roll over the end of the valve stem as you might think. The unit loading pressure exerted on the end of the valve by the roller tip is exceptionally high. Remember, we're talking about a small roller where only a fraction of its diameter actually touches the valve tip. Therefore, the pressure (in pounds per square inch — psi) is enormous. This is also true of full-roller rockers. The tip does not roll, but rather slides across the stem tip. The disadvantage to the roller-tipped rocker is that is still generates high oil temperature because of the friction at the ball fulcrum.

Full-roller, stud-mounted rockers come in a variety of materials, designs, and ratios. The full-roller bearing fulcrum reduces friction compared to the ball fulcrum and also improves ratio control. Roller rockers come in both extruded aluminum and in steel configurations. Aluminum was originally used because of its light weight. While weight is important, aluminum will also deflect more under load than steel. By using less steel over the valve tip, a rocker like the Comp Cams Hi-Tech Stainless rocker can be used with excellent durability. These rockers are also rebuildable, while most aluminum rockers are not. Because the steel roller rockers use less material out over the valve, this also increases the clearance between the rocker arm and the retainer when using large diameter springs on a small block.

Ratio selection is another excellent reason to choose roller rockers. The stock small-block rocker ratio is 1.5:1, but most companies offer roller rockers in ratios including 1.52, 1.55, 1.6, 1.65, 1.7, and even some 1.8:1 ratios. Each 0.10-ratio change is worth about 0.030-inch of increased valve lift. So that means that increasing the ratio from 1.5 to 1.6 would take a 0.450-inch valve lift cam to around 0.480-inch. A less well-publicized advantage of a ratio increase is its affect on duration. While the opening and closing points remain the same, an increased rocker ratio lifts the valve sooner in its curve, effectively making the cam look bigger to the engine. This has been estimated to be the equivalent of increasing the duration by 2 or 3 degrees.

Just as there is no free lunch, there are drawbacks to higher-ratio rocker arms. It may seem that the trick of the week would be to use a relatively short duration cam and then stuff a 1.7 or 1.8:1 rocker ratio to max out the lift. That's not a good idea for several reasons. First, the valvetrain must be able to accommodate the additional lift. Coil bind, retainer-to-seal interference, and valve-to-piston clearance must all be accounted for with increased valve lift. Another potential drawback to increasing rocker ratio is the radical increase in valve acceleration that occurs with a ratio increase. Cam designers create a camshaft with the expectation that the end user may put one additional ratio in the rocker arm over stock. For a small block, that would be a jump from 1.5 to 1.6:1. Beyond that, the valve acceleration may exceed the spring's ability to control the valve at higher engine speeds.

How To Build Big-Inch Chevy Small-Blocks

Chapter 8

To set lash, turn the engine over until the exhaust valve just begins to open and adjust the intake. Then rotate the engine until the intake is half closed and set the exhaust valve. The shorthand way to remember this is EO - IC. This procedure puts each lobe on its base circle so that the lash can be set.

Comp Cams has recently introduced an ovate wire, beehive shaped spring that reduces the weight of the spring as well as the retainer. Plus, the spring is variable rate, which reduces spring resonance and surge problems and perhaps could signal a new trend in spring design and away from massive spring pressures.

It's a given that increasing rocker ratio will lower the RPM at which valve float occurs. The net result of this would be, at best, a loss of power. The worst-case scenario would be a bent valve or two from contact with the piston because the valve smacked the piston during float.

If you really wanted to run a 1.7 or higher rocker ratio, the best move would be to talk to your cam grinder to get input on a lobe design that would allow you to run these kinds of ratios. It has been done, but generally this is with engines that will spin no more than 5,500 to 6,000 rpm. The simpler plan might be to increase the spring pressure to keep things glued together, but more spring pressure generally abuses the valvetrain by placing additional stress on all the components. Of course, this will cause deflection, which only reduces the valve lift you're trying to create.

You also need to decide which size rocker stud you wish to run. If you are contemplating higher spring pressures with a mechanical roller cam, you might want to step up from the stock small block 3/8-inch diameter stud to a larger 7/16-inch stud. This offers additional strength against deflection, which makes the rocker arm's job much easier. Be sure to invest in a quality rocker stud.

Shaft rocker systems are also the latest news in high-end street engines. Jesel is the big dog in this playground with an affordable shaft system for the small block. Each different cylinder head requires is own pedestal system. Shaft rocker systems deliver less valvetrain deflection compared to stud-mounted rockers and eliminate the need for stud girdles for stability. These new affordable stud systems are only slightly more expensive than a high-end rocker stud system. Comp Cams has also just released a rocker shaft system using an individual shaft for each rocker. Power increases can be seen with higher-RPM engines or those requiring higher spring pressures, but there is power to be gained with more accurate rocker ratios and reduced rocker travel across the valve tip.

There is also rumor of a new Crane shaft rocker shaft system that employs a proprietary fulcrum bushing material instead of roller bearings. Crane claims that the bushing material makes less heat and therefore has a slight power advantage over roller bearings by reducing the bearing inertia. We've seen no testing to support these claims, but there may be merit to the claims since oil temperature is also reduced, which is an indicator of reduced friction.

Miscellaneous Components

Among the less celebrated valvetrain components are items like spring seats, lash caps, poly locks, rocker studs, and valveguide seals. We'll take a quick look at each of these since each can offer advantages to overall performance. Lash caps are those small caps that fit over the top of the valve stem. They were originally built to protect titanium valves from the abuse of drag race camshaft profiles, but they are now showing up in high-end street engines as well. Because

Valvetrains

Iskenderian offers an interesting adjustable pushrod guideplate that gives the engine builder the freedom to position the pushrod so that the rocker arm is centered over the valve tip. This does require welding the two halves together.

For years, factory iron heads used holes in the head to guide the pushrod and keep the rocker centered over the valve. For late model engines, the factory went to guided rocker arms that use rails on either side of the rocker pad to center the rocker over the valve. This is a Crane rail rocker. Never use a rail rocker with pushrod guideplates since that's guaranteed to cause a binding situation that will break parts.

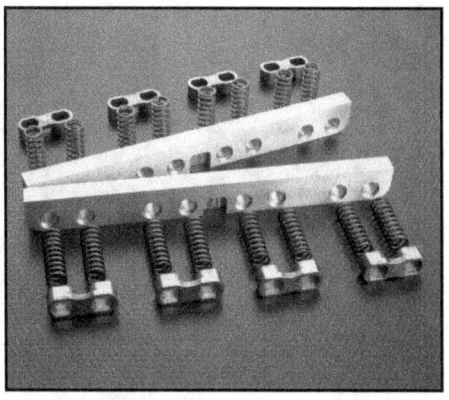

Heavy hydraulic roller lifters can be difficult to control at high RPM. Airflow Research developed the HydraRev to combat this problem by using spring pressure to control just the hydraulic roller lifter body, reducing the need for extra spring pressure that tends to pump the lifters down at high RPM. The jury is still out on whether this system delivers on its promise. A better idea would be to convert to solid roller lifters.

these caps are wider, they can often help with rocker tip travel over the top of the valve stem tip. If you choose to run lash caps, remember that the thickness of the cap will affect proper pushrod length.

Spring seats are essential items, not just because they protect aluminum heads from abuse by the valvespring, but also because they locate the spring on the head. At high RPM, valvesprings will dance or move about if not properly located. All valvetrain companies build both i.d. and o.d. spring seats and both do an equal job of locating the spring. Even stock heads locate the spring either with large valveguide bosses or spring seats that are cut into the head with a ridge around the outside of the spring. With performance heads using large dual springs, a spring seat is essential to locate the spring. Most companies recommend no more than 0.005-inch interference between the spring seat and the spring.

Rocker studs appear to be a simple product, but like everything else, don't overlook the importance of this component. Budget rocker studs are often not concentric to a centerline, which means the distance between the rocker stud and the valve can change, which will affect valvetrain geometry. We've seen budget rocker studs vary in concentricity by 0.030-inch! ARP makes an excellent rocker stud that most professional engine builders use. If your heads come assembled with a no-name rocker stud, do yourself a favor and donate them to a capital-challenged friend and use a set of ARP rocker studs.

Consider also the variable of the clearance between the roller rocker stud hole and the rocker stud. GM Performance Parts offers a Bow Tie roller rocker that is limited in lift capability to 0.570-inch, but improves stiffness by 30 percent through a shorter trunion slot. If nothing else, it makes for a great bench-racing topic. Poly locks are one of those overlooked items, but if you've got lots of them lying around, be sure to match the poly lock with the rocker. Do not allow the poly lock to contact the rocker body. Also, it's best not to tighten the lock against the stud by turning the poly lock body against the stud. Just use the Allen wrench to snug the lock against the stud.

Valveguide seals continue to improve almost yearly. What you don't want to use are those original white hard plastic seals. These were originally designed for race engines because they would fit inside a dual or even triple spring application. These hard plastic guides were then replaced often when the engine was torn down. For street engines, the hard plastic body is easily elongated by valveguide clearance, which allows oil to leak past into the chamber. If you have a set of these seals on a street engine, you've probably seen oil on the spark plug threads and have problems with oil usage. Swap these seals for a Viton rubber seal or other quality seal that is more flexible and heat resistant. You'll be glad you did. Remember that oil in the combustion chamber is an excellent way to promote high-speed detonation. Certainly not a situation you want to promote.

The key to building a solid, RPM-capable valvetrain is paying attention to the details. Using high-quality parts and really watching how the system is assembled will pay off with a great running engine that never gives you problems with bent pushrods or other nagging inconsistencies. The payoff is an engine that effortlessly sings through its entire power curve without fail. A little time spent on the valvetrain when assembling the engine will pay off with hundreds of hours of trouble-free engine time, no matter how hard you run the engine.

CHAPTER 9

CYLINDER HEADS

Now we get into the heart of small-block power. You can have a killer camshaft, valvetrain, intake manifold, carb, and headers, but if you bolt 'em to a weak set of heads, you won't make power. It's that simple. Conversely, spend your bucks on the best heads you can afford and your engine is destined to make excellent power. But this doesn't mean buying the most expensive, widest advertised, or even the biggest ports on the market. Always remember the engine is a system of interrelated components, and the one who makes the best power is the guy who figures out how to make all those parts sing in harmony. So let's dive into what makes cylinder heads so special.

IRON VS. ALUMINUM

This has almost become a moot point when it comes to making power.

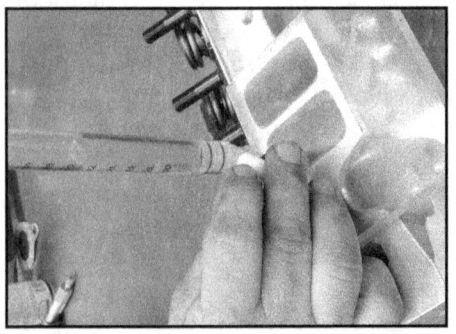

The best way to determine port volume is to measure them. Install a valve, place the cylinder head with the intake port in this orientation and fill the port from a graduated burette. Small-block heads measure between 160 and 240cc.

In the beginning, iron was all there was for the performance enthusiast. Today, there are more aluminum small-block performance heads on the market than anytime in the history of man. But recently there has been an explosion in iron performance heads that offer a budget alternative to the more expensive aluminum castings.

Strictly from an efficiency standpoint, iron heads should enjoy a slight performance advantage in that aluminum conducts heat much quicker than iron. This means that a certain amount of heat is lost through conduction, which also means a certain loss of cylinder pressure. While this appears to be reinforced by the fact that most aluminum-headed street engines can accommodate a little more static compression compared to otherwise similar iron-headed engines. However, when it comes to ultimate power, there appears to be no clear advantage to iron over aluminum.

While iron heads are usually less expensive than their aluminum-alloy cousins, there are also disadvantages to the cast iron route. Weight is the obvious penalty. You can expect a pair of aftermarket iron heads to weigh an additional 45 to 50 pounds over the front axle. In addition, cast iron is notoriously brittle, and cracks can occur that are difficult and costly to repair. Aluminum tends to crack less often and when it does it is much easier to repair. But don't let this dissuade you from defecting from the iron cause. If you get a great deal on a set of killer iron heads, go for it.

The question of iron versus aluminum is really more of a question of cost rather than performance. Iron heads generally are less expensive, but ultimately the price difference isn't significant enough to justify the weight penalty.

ANGLE OF ATTACK

All production small-block heads are based on a 23-degree valve angle that was established by Chevy engineers way back in the dark ages of the early 1950s. To maintain production engine interchangeability, that valve angle has only started to change in the last 10 years or so. Cylinder head porters will tell you that the more vertical (closer to zero) the valve angle, the better the airflow potential. This is due to several factors that include creating more uniform flow around the entire 360 degrees of valve circumference. Of course, this also demands that the port be made taller to take advantage of this taller valve angle.

Today, several companies offer taller valve angle heads, the most notably the 18-degree, 15-degree, and SB2.2 heads from GM Performance Parts, as well as

Cylinder Heads

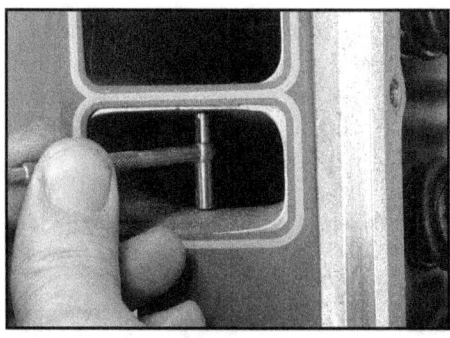

The smallest cross-sectional area for most small-block heads is usually located adjacent to the pushrod wall. The smaller the cross-section, the sooner a given engine will achieve its maximum inlet air speed.

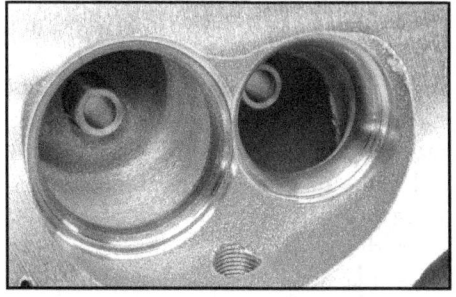

The combustion chamber shape can increase burn time if it is shaped properly. Current thinking leans toward a shallow kidney or heart-shaped chamber that lays the chamber walls back to unshroud the intake valve. This is the Brodix Track 1 chamber.

the 14-degree iron heads from Pro TopLine. But while alternate valve angle heads offer outstanding airflow, they come at a cost. Budget is not a word commonly used with these heads. The hidden costs are involved with pistons to accommodate the different valve angles along with specific valvetrain parts like rocker shafts that are necessary to make everything work. We only mention all this to get past all the hoopla and the interest in the major airflow these heads generate. It is also worth mentioning that Trick Flow Specialties (TFS) offers an 18-degree head that is more affordable than other heads, while still delivering excellent flow numbers for a small-block head. But we're still talking about a set of heads that will set you back all of $2000 and require a specialty intake manifold and custom headers.

Assuming that most street engine builders will opt for a set of 23-degree heads, there are dozens of heads to choose from. And within each of those heads are a myriad of options and ideas that are important to the overall engine combination.

PORTS O' CALL

The areas of most attention for any cylinder head are the intake and exhaust ports. Virtually the entire cylinder head world revolves around port volume numbers as an easy point of differentiation. Stock small-block heads vary in shape and size but hover generally at around a 170cc intake port volume. Before we get much further, however, we should quantify exactly what we're really discussing when we talk about port volume. The way port volume is determined is by simply stuffing a valve in the head, turning the head intake port face up, and measuring the volume with a calibrated burette. The problem with this measurement is that if we were to extend the length of the port, the volume will increase, but that would have negligible effect on power. In other words, the port would appear bigger when in fact it was really only longer.

The critical measurement that we should examine is the port's cross-sectional area. This is best described as the port's choke point where the flow area is the smallest. Imagine that our intake port is a simple tube. Increasing the length of the tube does nothing to improve flow. However, if we increase the diameter of the tube, flow will increase. Now, if we take that larger tube and constrict it slightly back to the original tube diameter, the flow will probably drop back to something close to the original tube's flow potential. Now if both tubes are the same length, measuring the volume might lead us to estimate that the larger volume tube would flow more because of its greater volume — mainly because it fits the simplistic "bigger is better" theory that permeates the performance world. As we've seen, the flow may not deliver on the bigger is better concept. This leads us back to the

A good indicator for power potential from a cylinder head is to use a flow bench. The most popular bench is the SuperFlow 600. There is more to a cylinder head than just intake and exhaust port flow, but for small-block heads, flow numbers are a great indicator of performance potential.

concept of port cross-sectional area.

A little experimentation with stock small-block heads reveals that stock heads measure in the neighborhood of 0.9-inch wide x 1.85-inches tall at the narrowest point of the port, which is where the pushrod wall intrudes into the port. This comes out to a relatively small area of 1.66 square inches. We'll use this as our baseline for comparison with other performance heads to see how they compare both with the port volumes of stock heads and other performance heads. As a point of reference, the original Brodix Track 1 intake port measured a much larger 2.3 square inches of cross-sectional area at the same point in the port. Port volumes tend to support the fact that the Brodix head is larger than the stock head, and this is why port volumes don't exactly lie to use in terms of small, medium, and large port heads. The cross-sectional areas of the smallest point in each of these ports tend to follow the volume numbers.

So why is port cross-sectional area so important? The answer goes back to our pipe analogy, but the reasons go much deeper. When the piston accelerates down the bore with the intake valve open, the pressure differential creates air movement in the port, which generates a velocity in the port as the air and fuel travel from the intake manifold into the cylinder. The smallest cross-sectional area in the head limits the volume of air

Chapter 9

If you are building a big-inch small block of at least 425 inches, the AFR 220 head is an excellent choice. It retains the 23-degree valve angle so it can use affordable valvetrain components, and it can produce big-time power from extremely good intake and exhaust ports.

If you're looking to make your big-inch small block all iron for the camouflage factor, the Dart Iron Eagle 230cc head is a good choice. This 23-degree head offers excellent flow from both the intake and exhaust, plus it's affordable.

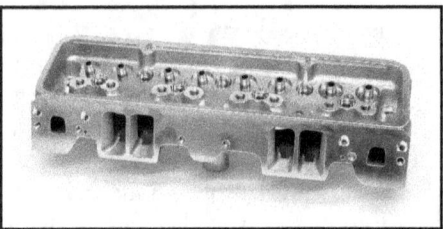

The Brodix Fast Burn head offers reputable flow potential with a medium port volume to promote outstanding torque for medium-displacement small blocks. With a 196cc intake port, the head employs up to 2.08/1.60-inch valves. An interesting feature is the head can accommodate both perimeter or center bolt valve covers as well as the Vortec or standard small-block intake-port bolt patterns.

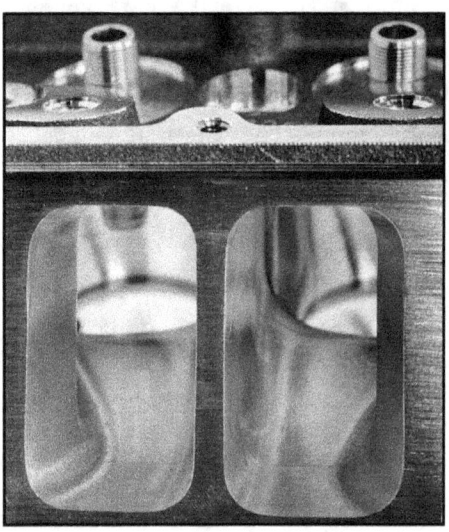

Many of the cylinder head manufacturers — AFR, Brodix, Dart, and others — offer CNC porting options that can step a cylinder head up in flow without having to radically increase port volume. This is a CNC-ported Dart Pro 1.

that can travel past this point. This minimal area also establishes the speed of the incoming air column.

Given this, a small port tends to create a given inlet air velocity sooner in the RPM curve, which can be equated to the peak efficiency point for the port. This also turns out to be the peak-torque RPM point. At engine speeds below this point, the air has not achieved sufficient speed to fill the cylinder entirely. At engine speeds above this max velocity point, the small cross-sectional area physically cannot supply the volume required by the cylinder to make more power. The engine still makes decent power, but once the peak torque point is established, most engines achieve peak horsepower within another 1,100 to 1,500 rpm.

We've just wrapped a bunch of variables that affect peak torque and horsepower (like cam timing, intake and header runner length, and a bunch of other stuff) all up in this intake port cross-section concept. The point is that intake port cross-sectional area is a major player in the torque and horsepower game. For example, a great example for this would be to test a series of intake ports (from 180cc to 230cc ports, for example) across the same engine, while all the other components remained the same. Plotting the torque curves on the same graph would reveal a distinctively progressive series of curves where peak torque increases in RPM. This is an excellent way to visualize the effect of bolting a larger intake port on an engine.

The higher-RPM peak torque figures also point to a better peak horsepower potential. But that does not mean that a larger intake port is always a good idea. Remember, the larger cross-sectional area of the port would require a higher RPM in order to achieve that peak inlet air velocity. Below that point, the slower inlet air velocity would not be insufficient to fill the cylinder. Therefore, torque would suffer. And that's exactly what happens with a street motor with the combination of a long duration cam and large port heads.

Another way to look at this is that with a given port cross-section, as displacement increases, the peak velocity point occurs at a lower RPM point. Taking this idea a step forward, a cylinder head with a larger cross-sectional area will make decent power without sacrificing a significant amount of torque. Since the non-ported volume of most 23-degree small-block intake ports is less than 230ccs, this occurs rather naturally. Early testing with a 454ci small-block by World Products has already generated 610 hp with a set of 220cc intake port Motown heads with an excellent torque curve that made 584 ft-lb at 4500 rpm and 559 ft-lb at 4000 rpm. Certainly this engine could make 475 to 500 ft-lb. even down at 2500 rpm.

The net effect of this is that the larger the engine's displacement, the smaller it makes the cylinder head look. Even though we are talking about displacements equaling a 454 rat motor, the largest small-block head is still tiny in comparison to a rectangle-port, big-block head. We measured the cross-sectional area of an intake port in an Edelbrock rectangle port Victor head and came up with 3.75-square inches. This is monstrously larger than any small-block head we've measured. This gives a larger cubic inch small-block a decided advantage in terms of torque, and based on the power created by World's 454ci small block, 600 hp is better than most rectangle port, big-block street engines equipped with a similar-sized cam. It's possible that there is something to this

Valve Seat Angles

This is an area that racers and internal combustion engineers have pored over for decades. Even with all the hype over intake port cross-sectional area, port-entry angles, and all the rest, the final determining factor is that all the air going in and out of the chamber must flow past a simple round poppet valve that opens and closes against a valve seat. Work continues to this day to determine the ideal combination of valve size and flow.

The most popular and time-tested valve seat angle combination is a three-angle valve job. This consists of a 45-degree main seat angle, a 30-degree top cut, and a 60-degree bottom cut. Often, this bottom cut can be enhanced with a 70-degree cut to blend into the port. In the past, the classic approach was to use grinding stones to establish this seat angle combination. First a 45-degree stone cut the seat, and then the top and bottom cuts established the 45-degree seat width. These angles were used for both the intake and exhaust valves with 45-degree angles machined into the valves. An increasing number of performance shops and product rebuild facilities now use the Serdi-style tool that machines all three angles simultaneously. This style of machine allows the cylinder head specialist to create a full radius seat on either side of the main seat angle instead of a series of specific angles. This approach also establishes a much more consistent valve job from cylinder to cylinder. If you are about to perform a cylinder head rebuild on a performance head, you might consider a machined valve job instead of the more traditional job performed by grinding.

Race engine builders will swear that the radius valve job is now the only way to go, but for a street engine virtually all aftermarket heads feature machined valve angles, but these will still be specific angles, rather than a full radius effort. The difficulty with the full radius valve jobs is that they tend to be very application specific. Furthermore, testing has revealed that each cylinder head tends to be very specific about what works best with that particular port. If you had the time and budget to do an extensive test of each port on your favorite head, there are probably significant gains to be made. This would have to be made on a specific port. Once you modify the port, the ideal valve angles would probably change. You can begin to see how complex this subject matter quickly becomes.

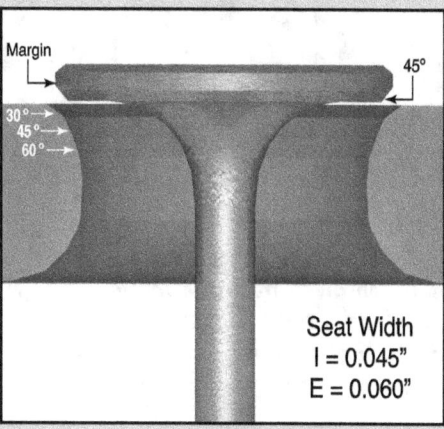

The standard seat angle of 30-45-60 degrees is the best place to start. This is the way most performance cylinder heads are configured.

Race and performance engine builders have known for years that one key to improved flow is with very narrow 45-degree seat angles. This is especially helpful on the intake valve when street engine seat widths can be as narrow as 0.045-inch. On the exhaust side, the main seat angle needs to be slightly wider, starting around 0.060-inch, both for durability and also to increase the surface area of the seat to conduct heat out of the valve and into the head.

On the valve side, consider the potential advantages of a 30 to 35-degree back cut on the inside of the 45-degree seat on the valve. Years of experimentation have shown that this simple operation generally benefits low and mid-lift flow with few trade-offs in high-lift flow. This can be an especially important addition to a head that has skewed its flow curve to enhance high-lift flow at the cost of reduced mid-lift flow. This back-cut can be somewhat application specific, so it would be best to experiment on a flow bench to determine the exact angle. We have seen tests where 33 to 35-degree angles tend to work better, but these tests were only performed on one head, so no general rule of application can be created from these limited tests.

You also want to move the actual position of seat angle as far out toward the top of the valve seat as possible since this also enhances airflow. A basic recommendation is to move the intake seat out to about 0.010-inch from the edge of the valve. Since exhaust valves operate at much higher temperatures, it's best to move the seat to the middle of the valve for durability. Just moving the intake seat from the middle of the valve to the outer edge can be worth as much as 8 to 10cfm. This does require equally careful attention to valve guide clearance to maintain this rather specific location. It certainly is worth mentioning that no performance valve job is worth much if the guides are loose. Intake valve guide clearance should be 0.0012-inch with a slightly larger 0.0018-inch for the exhaust for either bronze or cast-iron guides. This assumes no more than 0.0005-inch of taper or wear on the valves. A perfectly straight valve allows the machinist to create a more accurate clearance, which improves heat transfer and lubrication.

Paying close attention to valve angles will always pay off in improved airflow, better power, and a cylinder head that can continue to deliver excellent performance over a longer period of time.

Chapter 9

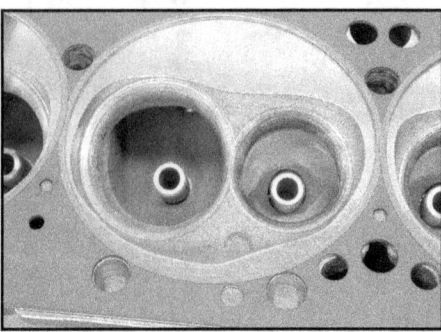

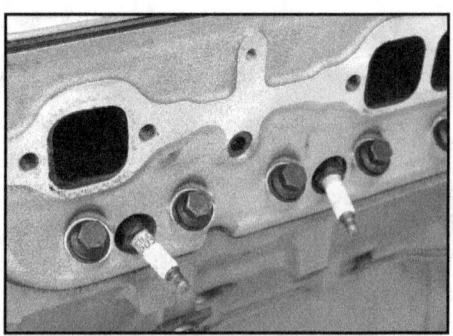

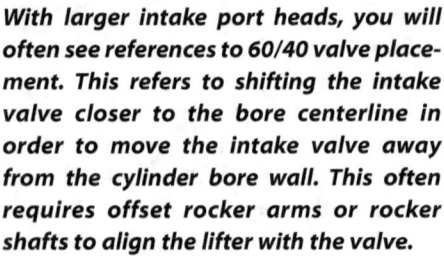

With larger intake port heads, you will often see references to 60/40 valve placement. This refers to shifting the intake valve closer to the bore centerline in order to move the intake valve away from the cylinder bore wall. This often requires offset rocker arms or rocker shafts to align the lifter with the valve.

A larger bore size will generally improve cylinder head flow by moving the cylinder wall away from the intake valve. A 4.185 or 4.200-inch bore offers major advantages over a 4.00-inch bore. A large bore also allows larger valves.

When Chevy first introduced the angle spark plug concept, much debate followed over the additional power it created. This is hard to quantify even today. The idea is to position the spark plug as close to the center of the chamber as possible to promote even combustion.

idea of improving inlet air speed with smaller ports that flow big numbers. A classic rule that has stood the test of time is the best port combines the highest flow with the smallest cross-sectional area.

Evaluating Flow

Before we get into looking at individual heads, it's important to know what to look for. The bigger is better approach demands going to the bottom of the flow bench chart picking the head with the biggest flow numbers. But all engines push the intake and exhaust valves run through a curve, which means the flow at 0.300 and 0.400-inch lift is also important. Let's say your camshaft can create a maximum of 0.600-inch lift. Let's assume the valve actually achieves that lift number (deflection aside). Even if it does, the valve will only do so once in the entire lift curve. The mid-lift numbers (0.200 through 0.500-inch) will be achieved both on the valve's way up to max lift and also on the way down. If you're smart, you'll begin by looking at a cylinder head's mid-lift flow numbers instead of the peak flow numbers, since these mid-lift numbers will probably contribute more to overall flow (and power) than the peak flow number.

This means you will need to have access to an entire flow chart in order to evaluate the performance of all these different heads. We have supplied a chart that offers flow numbers for a few of the more popular heads from several different manufacturers. The flow numbers were generated at Westech Performance, in Mira Loma, California, on a computerized SuperFlow 600 flow bench. All the flow numbers were achieved on the same flow bench run by the same operator using the same correction factors. All these flow numbers were tested at a test depression of 28-inches of water and corrected to standard temperature and pressure.

One thing that you might notice is that some heads appear to sacrifice mid-lift flow in order to achieve those greater high-lift flow numbers. This is the result of a complex combination of factors including port cross-sectional area, valve seat entry angles, valve seat angles, and dozens of other variables that make up the alchemy of cylinder head port flow. We don't want to minimize high-lift flow numbers, but it's important to note that the mid-lift numbers may contribute as much to overall cylinder filling as the high-lift numbers. It's important not to ignore the concept that the opening side of the cam lobe occurs at roughly the same time that the piston achieves maximum acceleration, which offers the maximum pressure differential between the cylinder and the intake plenum.

So far, we've focused on the intake side of the head, which is really only half the story. The exhaust ports are just as important, since no engine can make decent power if a sizeable percentage of the exhaust component remains in the cylinder. There are plenty of theories that surround the performance of exhaust port flow, especially in relationship to the intake side. The current accepted theory supports the idea that the exhaust port should flow at around 70 to 80 percent of the intake port flow at the same valve lift figure. As an example, if the intake port flows 220cfm at 0.400-inch valve lift, then the exhaust port should flow 176cfm if the exhaust flows 80 percent of the intake at 0.400-inch lift. Regardless of which percentage to which you decide to subscribe, it's important to remember that the key is to evacuate as much exhaust gas from the cylinder as possible.

Finally, it's important to give more than passing credit to combustion chamber shape and the effect of the chamber on the combustion process. If you look at the gradual progression of small-block chambers from the 1960s to today, you can see that the early chambers were bathtub-shaped with deep walls that tended to shroud airflow both from the intake as well as out the exhaust. Today, current chamber shapes favor a more shallow kidney shape intended to improve airflow while also encouraging improved mixture motion. This is difficult to quantify, but the idea is to encourage the mixture to move toward the exhaust side of the chamber so that once combustion is complete, piston movement encourages the residual gas to move in that direction.

Cylinder Heads

It's also worthy of mention that many of the heads mentioned in this book employ a tight, 64cc chamber. Since large cylinder bores are part of the big-inch equation, you might want to consider opening up the chamber slightly to unshroud the intake and exhaust valves up to the bore diameter to maximize port flow. Cylinder head companies have not started building heads and chambers to specific bore size, so most must assume the smallest, 4.030-inch bore size for chamber wall position. But plug in a 4.155 or 4.200-inch bore and there are measurable flow increases available to the enterprising hot rodder who is willing to take advantage of a bigger bore, beyond just displacement.

Iron Heads

We'll start our look at performance heads oddly with a stock casting that deserves attention. The production iron GM head for the early Vortec engines is an outstanding example of a 170cc intake port that offers excellent low and mid-lift flow that is perfect for a mild 383 or torquey 406ci small block. With the right small cam, a 406 could easily make well over 520 ft-lb of torque with a set of these heads while still being capable of 465 hp. This head is a derivative of the iron LT1 cylinder head used in the Impala SS, and it was also found on '96 Chevy pickups. Perhaps this head's best feature is the price. Since it is still built on a GM assembly line, you can purchase a complete pair of these heads from a GM Performance Parts dealer for well under $500.

The head does have limitations. The valvesprings won't accept more than 0.470-inch lift and the guide boss is very large, which limits some springs. Comp now makes a beehive spring that will work, but you should machine the guide boss down for more retainer-to-seal clearance. Or, you can purchase a modified set of these heads from Scoggin-Dickey or one of several other GM Performance Parts dealers that offer modified heads. The Vortec has a 64cc chamber and requires the use of a center bolt valve cover as well. Perhaps its biggest drawback is its unique 8-bolt intake manifold bolt pattern that requires Vortec-specific manifolds. In comparison with other GM iron small-block heads, the Vortec is superior to them all, including the cast iron Bow Tie head, which means there's no reason to run the Bow Tie unless the rules dictate its use.

World Products' Sportsman II head still enjoys some popularity, which is the result of its position as one of the earliest aftermarket performance iron heads. Unfortunately, it's past its prime and not really up to today's cotemporary flow standards, despite its 200cc intake port volume. Ironically, a properly set up Vortec head would probably out-power the Sportsman II and do it for less money. World Products also offers a relatively new 220cc Motown iron head that appears to be a decent flowing head with good power potential. This head is offered only with a 64cc chamber, 2.055/1.60-inch valves,

Exhaust to Intake

One way to evaluate a cylinder head is to look at both the intake and the exhaust. In regards to the exhaust port, you can use the exhaust-to-intake (I/E) port flow relationship to judge the efficiency of the exhaust side. This is accomplished by dividing the exhaust port flow by the intake port flow at a specific valve lift. By way of example, if a head flows 250cfm at 0.500-inch lift and 125cfm at the same valve lift on the exhaust side, the I/E would be 50 percent. Conventional wisdom contends that an I/E of between 75 and 80 percent encourages efficient scavenging of the cylinder during the exhaust stroke. Numbers lower than this indicate a poor exhaust port, while numbers exceeding 85 percent can point to either an excellent exhaust port or an inefficient intake.

It's best to plot the I/E across the entire flow curve from 0.100-inch to peak valve lift and evaluate the entire curve in order to get an idea of how well the exhaust port works. This is just another indicator of how well the head performs. This is not the only concept, but rather a tool used to point to the head's overall potential. It's also worth noting that a weak I/E percentage does not mean that the head will be an underachiever. The cam timing can also be used to help exhaust port flow with additional duration or lift. This is another way to look at the systems approach to engine building where the entire package must be considered, rather than individual parts. However, the performance of individual parts is still critical to total power.

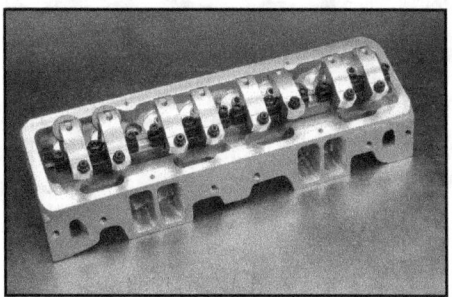

Looking for a great bolt-on head that still offers excellent throttle response but is still fairly large? The AFR 210 is a good choice that falls in great for 400 to 430ci small blocks.

Chamber size has a direct effect on compression ratio. The difference between a 76cc chamber and a 64cc chamber can be worth as much as 1.5 points of compression on a 4.155-inch bore, 4-inch stroke engine.

Chapter 9

Cool Holes

If your next 400-based engine will employ a production block, you should know that these engines used cooling holes drilled between the cylinders. For street engines, this required drilling matching cooling holes in the heads to prevent forming steam pockets in the top of the block. Aftermarket heads do not include these holes, which means you'll have to drill them yourself. This requires careful positioning of the holes and angle drilling three of these holes to tap into the cooling passage in the head.

Place the cylinder head with the combustion chambers facing up with the intake face away from you (left). Place a 400 head gasket over the deck surface and carefully mark the six holes with a starting punch. The holes on the exhaust side should be drilled straight into the head. The holes on the intake side must be drilled at a 30-degree angle toward the exhaust side as shown in the illustration. You can use an inexpensive protractor to help establish the 30-degree angle.

Fel-Pro has also changed its performance head gasket line to incorporate restrictions in the head gasket to increase coolant flow between the two center cylinders while restricting flow between the two outboard cylinders. Note that the center hole has been increased to 7/16-inch while the two outboard cylinder holes have been restricted to 3/16-inch. This is done to improve cooling efficiency at the point where the two adjacent exhaust ports tend to concentrate heat. This is only the case on the high-performance Fel-Pro gaskets. The stock replacement head gaskets do not employ these modifications.

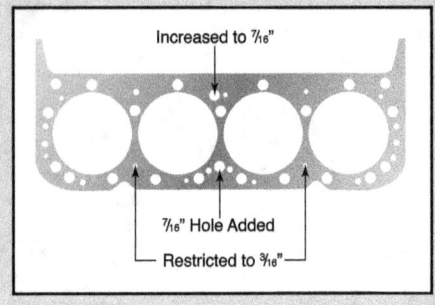
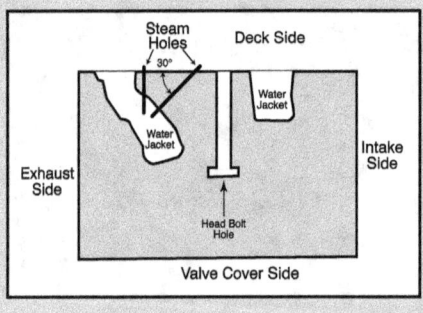

and either angle plug or straight plug configurations. As with most cylinder head companies, you can purchase these heads either bare and equip them with your own valves and springs, or purchase them complete. There are also two spring options, either 1.437-inch or 1.550-inch duals, with the larger spring offering more spring pressure.

The newest cylinder head company is a New Zealand operation called Pro TopLine. Pro TopLine offers a staggering array of different small-block cylinder heads, including some wild 14-degree valve angle castings intended for circle track racing classes that dictate the use of an iron cylinder head. Among the more streetable iron stuff is a line of heads called the Pro Lightning heads featuring 180, 200, 220, 228, 235, and even some large by huge 243cc intake port volume designs. Most the heads come with either 64 or 72cc chambers. The 180 to 220cc heads are relatively affordable priced between $900 and $1000 per set with good springs and stainless valves. These are virtual clones of TopLine's aluminum Pro Lightning heads that we'll get into in more detail in the aluminum head section.

Dart also offers an excellent lineup of Iron Eagle castings ranging from 165, 180, 200, 215, and even 230cc intake port volumes. Like the TopLine heads, Darts' iron heads are very close cousins to the Pro 1 series of aluminum heads, but with a wider selection of port volumes. The Dart iron heads that look the most appealing are the 200 and 220cc intake port versions that offer the best potential for a big-inch street engine based on their flow potential. The largest 235cc head could also be good for larger engines displacing more than 420ci. These heads are less expensive than Dart's aluminum versions, but have the potential to flow just as much air.

The downside to any iron head is of course the weight penalty. In addition,

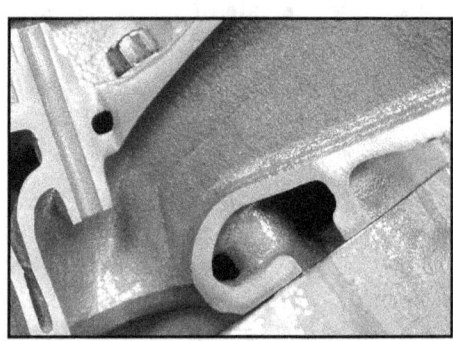

The best place to concentrate on port work is the area 1-inch below the valve seat. Stock iron heads respond well to work in this area, but when you get to higher-flowing aftermarket heads you need to work carefully. It is easy to reduce flow even though the work looks better. The only way to know for sure is by testing on a flow bench.

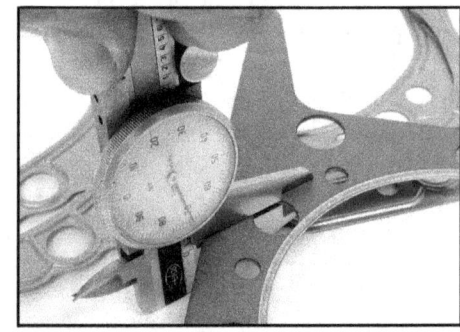

Head gaskets can affect compression as well as piston-to-head clearance. Keep in mind that adding a thicker head gasket to reduce compression also reduces the effectiveness of the quench area. Gasket thickness ranges from steel shims at around 0.15-inch, to 0.051-inch for the new multi-layer gaskets.

Cylinder Heads

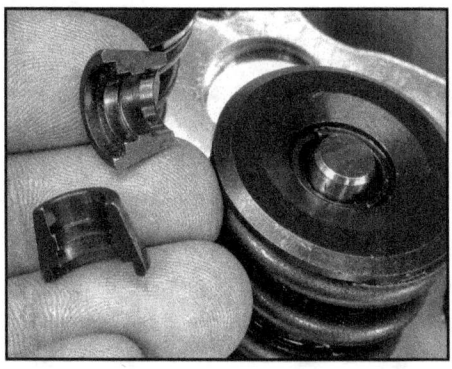

Most large-port heads use the beefier 10-degree locks and retainers, which are intended for use with high-rate valvesprings. These locks are heavier, but offer increased strength and durability.

Often a simple 30-degree back cut on the intake and/or exhaust valve can improve low-lift flow with only slight trade-offs of lost flow at higher valve lifts. The effect of the back cut is application specific so it may not work on all heads.

Reducing stem diameter at the transition to the valve head is difficult to see on the flow bench, despite major claims by the valve manufacturers. This does reduce valve weight, which is always a good idea.

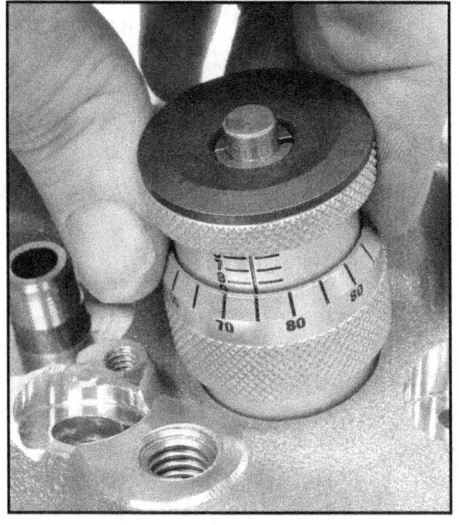

You must always check installed height when assembling heads or new valvesprings. Subtract installed coil bind height from installed height to ensure sufficient clearance. Also take this time to measure retainer-to-seal clearance.

iron is more time-consuming to modify and is much more difficult to repair should one crack or be damaged. This also means iron heads will cost more to repair compared to aluminum. Generally speaking, assembled Dart iron heads save around $200 per pair, depending upon which head you choose. With an overall cost of roughly $1,100 for a pair of assembled aluminum heads, it appears the aluminum castings would be the smarter buy, if only for the weight savings.

This leads us directly to the fillet mignon of this chapter, which is the aluminum castings. Since there are so many heads on the market, we'll focus on only the most popular and best flowing heads for the street. We'll remain with 23-degree heads since they offer the best performance for their cost.

ALUMINUM HEADS

AirFlow Research

Both alphabetically and from a pure performance standpoint, AirFlow Research (AFR) heads are among the best performing street heads on the market today. Among the street heads that would fill the bill for a big small block include the 180, 190, 195, 200, 210, 220, and 227cc heads in the standard 23-degree valve angle, standard-port configuration. There's also a 215cc Raised Runner head that retains the 23-degree valve angle but raises the entry point of the intake port to straighten the runner for superior port flow.

The newest of the AFR head family is the 180cc head which has excellent flow for its rather small port size and is rumored to actually out-flow its older but well-established 190/195cc cousins. This head would be perfect for a big torque application on a 383 or 406ci small block aimed at a truck or towing application. The larger 190/195cc heads are grouped together here since they are identical except for the port entry size. The smaller 190 is designed to be used with smaller intake manifold applications like an Edelbrock Performer while the 195cc head employs a larger port entry that is intended for use with larger, single-plane intakes like the Victor Jr. or Super Victor style manifolds.

The 210 and 220cc port heads would be best used with a larger displacement small-block such as a 420, 427, 434, or 454ci small block, since the larger intake port would be able to feed these larger displacements. Flow numbers on the 220cc AFR head are on the order of over 280 cfm at 0.600-inch lift while maintaining excellent flow numbers even at the mid-lift positions. Of course, the exhaust side is also important, and all the AFR heads match an excellent exhaust port with the intakes, which create a great opportunity to make power.

The only reason you wouldn't seriously consider the AFR heads would be because of budget constraints. The AFR heads consistently deliver outstanding performance and torque for excellent street power. As an example, we have tested a 383ci small-block with 9.5:1 compression using a set of 190cc AFR heads, a set of 1 3/4-inch headers, a dual-plane intake, and a Comp Cams hydraulic roller camshaft (236/242 degrees of duration @ 0.050-ich tappet lift with 0.520/0.540-inch valve lift). This particular 383 made 517 ft-lb of torque and 503 hp at 6000 rpm. This engine also made well over 450 ft-lb of torque at 2500 rpm.

Brodix

This Mena, Arkansas, facility created by J.V. Brotherton started out building exotic aluminum heads for circle track racing. Over time, Brodix has created what might just be the widest selection of small-block Chevy aluminum castings of any manufacturer. Brodix has recently fired up its small-block cylinder head machine with a series of new heads. The newest is the Fast Burn 1000 series of 23-degree heads that features a 196cc intake port with 2.02, 2.05, and 2.08-inch intake valve options, each with a 1.60-inch exhaust. The heads offer a dual intake bolt pattern to handle either the standard or Vortec intake manifolds. They also use the standard exhaust port configuration. This casting will also accommodate either the perimeter style or center bolt valve cover arrangements. With such a new head, there is no "book" on this head as yet, but it looks promising with flow numbers in the 240cfm range at 0.500-inch lift.

Brodix has also redesigned the original Track 1 head using a 221cc intake port volume with 2.08/1.60-inch stainless steel valves and a 67cc combustion chamber. As with all the Brodix heads, there are CNC options available, as well as selections for valvesprings, and other optional valvetrain equipment. Brodix claims the new Track 1 will flow over 260cfm at 0.500-inch intake valve lift. Also, the Track 1 utilizes an exhaust port that can create around 70 percent exhaust to intake flow ratio at 0.500-inch valve lift. In addition, Brodix also has built a series of 23-degree small-block heads that include the -8 Pro (185cc), -8 STD (194cc), -10 STD (210cc), and -11 STD (221cc) plus a -11X that pushes port volume to 225cc. These heads all come fully assembled with straight or angled plug options and excellent flow potential.

One of Brodix's strengths is that virtually any head is available in very specific configurations. It's possible to obtain a head prepared anywhere from a pure, as-cast, ready to assemble state, all the way up to fully CNC-machined with prepped chambers, hand-blended valve bowls, or in any combination you wish. All you have to do is tell them what you want and they'll build it for you.

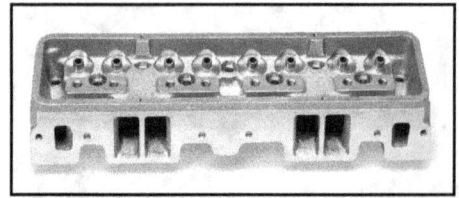

Edelbrock's Victor Jr. head is one of their more popular 23-degree head with a high-flow 215cc intake port, 2.08/1.60 valves, and a 70cc chamber.

Dart

This is Pro Stock master Richard Maskin's Detroit-based company that has slowly created a solid reputation in the industry for high-quality products that perform as advertised. Dart's Pro 1 series of aluminum heads are the street-oriented castings that combine excellent intake and exhaust port designs to create some of the best small-block heads in the business. The lineup includes 200, 215, and 230cc intake port heads in the standard 23-degree valve angle. In addition to the as-cast heads, Dart also offers a fully CNC-ported version of the 215cc head the ends up with a 227cc intake port and an 85cc exhaust port. This head promises serious flow of over 300 cfm and would be an outstanding head on a large cubic inch small block like a 434 or 454ci mouse motor. This particular head sells for over $2,300 per pair complete. But considering that it offers such incredible airflow for a 23-degree head, while accepting all standard 23-degree valvetrain components, it is hard to ignore. All these Dart heads are available with either 64 or 72cc chambers and also offer the options of 1.437- or 1.550-inch diameter valvesprings to be compatible with hydraulic or mechanical roller camshafts. Dart also offers a line of both single-plane and dual-plane intakes to go along with this selection of heads.

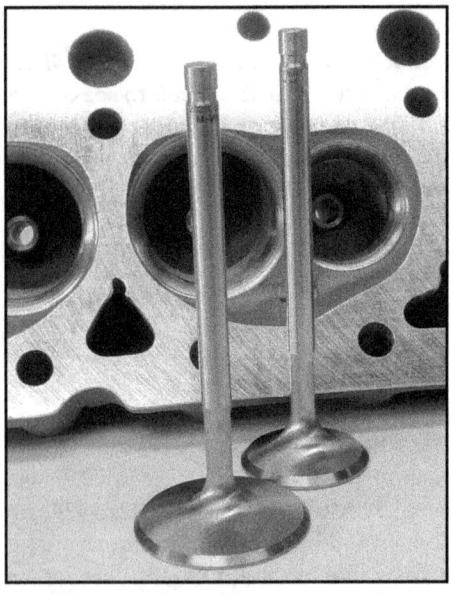

High-quality stainless steel valves are a virtual necessity with any strong small-block head. These valves also flow better than stock equivalents and weigh less too. Reducing valve weight is a great way to reduce the tendency toward valve float, along with lighter retainers.

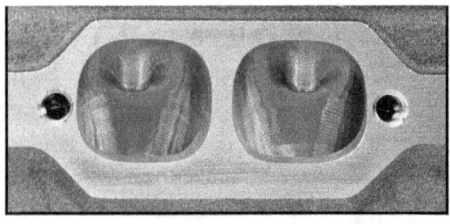

Don't forget the exhaust port when considering cylinder heads. Generally a wide exhaust port floor improves flow. When evaluating port flow numbers, consider that just adding a pipe to the end of the port will improve flow significantly.

Raising the entire exhaust port will increase flow, but also affects header fitment. Consider this when choosing a cylinder head since this can make fitting headers difficult, possibly requiring custom headers.

Cylinder Heads

Standing Tall

For the over-the-top crowd who really want to move some air, there has never been a wider selection of race-oriented cylinder heads for the small-block Chevy. When Chevrolet decided to really get serious with NASCAR Winston Cup racing a few years back, a series of race-only heads came streaming out of GM's Warren, Michigan engineering building — these heads changed the face of Chevrolet racing forever. At first there was an 18-degree head, then a 15-degree head, and most recently the SB2 and 2.2 version heads. These heads all aim at standing the valve more vertically and raising the intake port entry angle. The intake valve angle on the latest race head the SB2.2 is 11 degrees with a 4-degree tilt while the exhaust aims at an almost vertical 8 degrees. Actually, this head has very little in common with what is currently considered to be a typical small-block head, since about the only thing it has retained is the head bolt pattern. Virtually everything else has changed. This represents perhaps the state of the art of small-block head development — at least as far as NASCAR is willing to let it go.

So where does that lead us? Since those floodgates have opened, several companies have begun casting cylinder heads in the alternative valve-angle arena. Keep in mind that all of these heads require significant changes over a typical 23-degree setup. You'll need specific valvetrain components — usually an offset rocker shaft system with offset roller lifters, as well as longer, larger, and more expensive valves. You'll need new pistons with valve reliefs for the taller valve angle, along with a set of custom headers and intake manifold. Did we mention the fabricated valve covers, intake and exhaust gaskets, and specialty fasteners? All of those additional pieces could easily cost another $2500 to $4000 — and that's after you've bought the heads.

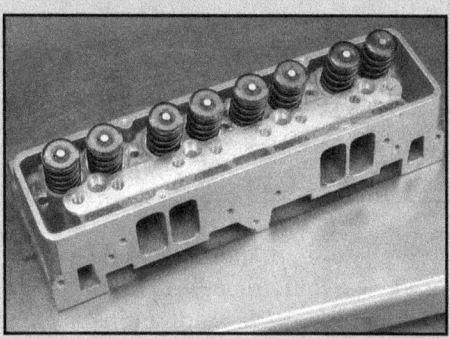

The TFS 18-degree head is another "affordable" 18-degree head that offers a 250cc intake port, a 56cc chamber, and 2.15/1.60-inch valves. This head uses the Jesel rocker shaft system, but promises serious airflow and power.

If all that hasn't scared you off, we'll take a quick glance at a few of these heads. Let's start with the GM Performance Parts 18-degree head with 256cc intake ports. It cranks a killer 327cfm at 0.500-inch lift with 2.18/1.62-inch valves and an intake cross-sectional area of a massive 2.75 square inches. This head is recommended for bores of around 4.155-inch or larger to take advantage of the big valves and additional flow. Of course, GMPP also offers the symmetrical-port, splayed-valve head that features 240cc intake ports with 16-degree intake-valve angles, and an 11-degree exhaust with a 4-degree tilt. This head can accommodate a 2.20-inch intake and a 1.65-inch exhaust valve.

Finally, there's the SB2.2 that uses mirror-image ports pointed toward the center of the engine with an 11.4-degree angle on the intakes and an 8-degree exhaust. Plus the intake centerlines have been moved 0.250-inch closer to the intake centerline and 0.080-inch closer to the bore centerline. GM recommends a 2.15-inch intake valve and uses an extremely shallow 48cc chamber that would make 12:1 compression with a flat-top piston. The advantage here is big-block-like 349cfm at 0.500-inch intake port flow from a port with a massive 3.06 square-inch area.

Brodix has an interesting twist with their 18X head, which incorporates a 245cc intake port with 2.14/1.60-inch valves and yet will accept a budget Jesel or T&D rocker shaft system that is designed for a 40/60 valve spacing. With a 68cc chamber, you could keep the compression down on a big-inch small block. This head will need a dedicated Brodix 10-degree intake manifold. The airflow numbers are impressive with Brodix claiming just over 300cfm at a mere 0.500-inch valve lift with flow numbers as much as 320cfm at 0.650-inch lift. This isn't as strong as a dedicated 18-degree head, but also cuts several corners that keep the cost down. If you are contemplating an 18-degree head, then this might be the one to price out to see how much all this would cost versus a big 23-degree head.

Edelbrock and Chapman heads has almost a full page of 18-degree Victor heads. These heads feature between 236cc and 266cc intake ports, monstrous 2.15/1.625-inch valves, and cross sectional areas between 2.5 and 2.7 square inches. The intake flange is drilled for both 1 and 2-piece intake manifolds and includes a center water outlet for auxiliary cooling systems. Their chamber sizes vary from 65cc to a very shallow 47cc.

The TFS 18-degree head sports a massive 250cc intake port, a set of 2.15/1.625-inch valves, and can accept up to a 2.20-inch intake valve. TFS claims that airflow will run up to 325cfm, which can be worth well over 650 horsepower for a large cubic-inch small block with a big camshaft. The heads will require a Jesel shaft offset-rocker system, along with a set of 0.180-inch offset roller lifters on the intake side. Of course, these heads will also require custom, 18-degree headers.

There are certainly many more exotic heads, but this will certainly open some doors into what it takes if you are considering a set of exotic heads to bolt on to your big-inch small block.

Most aftermarket heads use a 3/4-inch, long-reach, gasketed plug, such as the upper Bosch plug. This is also an extended-tip plug where the center electrode projects into the chamber. Most OEM and stock replacement small-block heads use a shorter threaded plug that relies on a tapered seat to seal the plug to the head (lower plug). Be careful not to mix plugs with gaskets or tapered seats

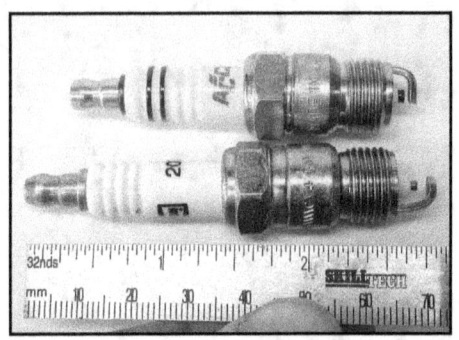

ACCEL makes a shorter overall length spark plug that just may make the difference between constantly burning plug wire boots and a long service life. This particular plug is an ACCEL 576S. The "S" suffix stands for short.

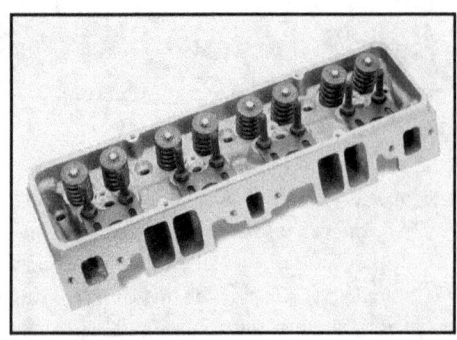

One of Dart's best heads is the CNC-ported 220cc Pro 1. This head offers excellent flow and a strong intake to exhaust balance. You can run a single pattern cam and make great power.

This is a typical Serdi machine that machines all three (or more) seat angles simultaneously. Most cylinder head pros feel that this machine offers significant advantages over seat grinders.

Edelbrock

Edelbrock offers a relatively wide range of heads that spans the entire range of applications from conservative small-block Performer and Performer RPM heads to fully ported High-Port CNC Chapman heads that deliver serious flow for a more competition-oriented small block. The Performer RPM head makes for great, torque-enhancing cylinder head for 383ci street engines with its 170cc intake port. Next up the ladder is the Edelbrock Victor Jr. 23 degree head that increases the intake port volume to 215cc with CNC-ported entries and 0.400-inch raised exhaust ports. The heads come with 2.08/1.60-inch valves and a 70cc chamber. Edelbrock offers this head with several different valvespring applications, or you can purchase the head bare. There's even an as-cast head ready for professional porting. This head still works with 23-degree valvetrain pieces and intake manifolds.

Another excellent head that Edelbrock offers is the new E-Tec 200cc head. The larger intake port generates an excellent intake port flow that peaks around 280 cfm and can still generate excellent flow numbers at 0.300 and 0.400-inch valve lift on the intake side. The exhaust port is no slouch either. This head certainly has 500 hp-plus capability and would be an excellent choice on a mid-sized small block around the 383 or 406ci.

The largest Edelbrock head series includes the Edelbrock/Chapman Victor 23 degree High-Port CNC heads. These heads come in port volumes of 238cc, 243cc, and up to a monstrous 247cc volume. These heads require custom offset rocker arms because of the 0.350-inch intake offset and zero offset on the exhaust side. This high-port design also necessitates 0.200 or 0.300-inch longer 2.100/1.625-inch valves to accommodate the ports. The smaller 238 and 243cc heads could be used on a large displacement engine of 420ci or larger. These tend to be on the exotic side of the street cylinder head market, but could be considered if for no other reason than the fact that large displacement small blocks were also considered exotic no more than a few years ago.

TFS

Trick Flow Specialties (TFS) is a Summit Racing-owned company that began by specializing in small-block Ford heads. They have also branched out with several excellent small-block Chevy castings that produce great results for the money. The basic 23-degree TFS head is actually a superb medium-port, 195cc small-block head employing standard 23-degree valvetrain pieces and 2.02/1.60-inch valves. The exhaust port generates a good 70 to 80 percent exhaust-to-intake relationship with a standard 64cc chamber size. TFS does offer a CNC-machined 72cc chamber, but that comes at an additional cost. Flow numbers on this head are excellent, which makes it easy to create 415 hp from a basic 350, offering the advantages of excellent torque from a 383 or even a 406ci small-block. This should be enough to support a solid 450 to 475 hp with around 520 ft-lb of torque with excellent power just off idle.

If this is a little too small for your liking, TFS also offers an outstanding 215cc intake port 23-degree head that offers an aggressive intake port that is worth some serious power, especially with a larger inch engine like a 420-434ci mouse. The heads run a 67cc chamber fitted with 2.08/1.60-inch stainless steel valves. You also have the option of heads with either 1.520 or 1.550-inch diameter valvesprings, depending upon the cam you intend to run. The valve seats are ductile iron with bronze guides and beefy ten-degree retainers and locks.

World Products

The Motown 220 Lite is World's entry into the larger port small-block head market. This head features 2.055/1.600-inch stainless steel valves enclosed in a 64cc chamber. The head will accept all the normal 23-degree small-block valvetrain pieces. The Motown 220 Lite assembled head uses Manley Race Master stainless steel valves, PC seals, and Manley 10-degree retainers and keepers encompassing either 1.440 or 1.550-inch springs. Airflow numbers for these heads are not quite up to the point of other heads of the same port volume, but they are affordable both in bare or complete form. The combustion chambers are completely CNC machined, which is the major difference between the iron and aluminum versions of this head.

CONCLUSION

With all the opportunities today, choosing a cylinder head is not an easy task. Even with the information presented here, this only narrows the field slightly. The one advantage of the larger displacement engines is that choosing a head with larger port volume is probably a good idea, especially with engines displacing over 420 cubic inches. At the same time, if your new engine is going to be a mostly street driven, don't be afraid to bolt on a decent flowing set of heads at around 200ccs. This will deliver outstanding torque and still produce horsepower in the 1.25 to 1.3 hp/ci range. Your biggest problem then will figuring out how to hook all the power to the ground!

Cross Sectional Area

Intake ports are always a subject of much discussion among engine builders and tuners. The SA Design Desktop Dyno book by Larry Atherton offers a rough rule of thumb for creating an induction system cross-sectional area that may help create balanced intake-runner inlet air velocities. His ideal cross-sectional area lies somewhere on the conservative side of optimal flow potential. A large cross-section intake port size that is overly efficient will always look better on the flow bench, but may not do well in the engine. This simple formula offers an introduction into the cross-sectional area that will at least point in a direction toward selecting a cylinder head. The formula looks like this:

Minimum Port Area = (RPM x Stroke x Bore x Bore) / 190,000

We have computed a couple different big-inch combinations using this formula that may be of some interest. All results are in square inches of cross-sectional area.

Engine A	Engine B
406ci	**440ci**
4.155-inch bore	4.185-inch bore
3.75-inch stroke	4.00-inch stroke
@ 5500 rpm = 1.87	@ 5000 rpm = 1.84
@ 6000 rpm = 2.04	@ 5500 rpm = 2.02
@ 6500 rpm = 2.21	@ 6000 rpm = 2.21
@ 7000 rpm = 2.38	@ 6500 rpm = 2.39

As you can see, if we used the same port cross-section in both of these engines, it forces a higher peak engine speed with the smaller engine or the lower RPM with the larger engine. This is a common result of using the same heads or intake on two different displacement engines.

This formula tends to be conservative, which may be beneficial for street engines since you want to be conservative in order to maintain inlet air speed for decent mid-range torque. Compare this to the cross-sectional areas of some performance cylinder heads and you might have a way to help you choose the right head and intake system for your next engine.

We've included a list of the minimum cross-sectional areas for several popular small-block cylinder heads as a reference tool. All these heads were measured in the center of the intake port at the pushrod wall restriction. These measurements may change due to production tolerances and casting variations, but they should give some type of comparison between different heads.

Cylinder Head	Cross-Sectional Area (sq in)	Port Volume (cubic centimeters)
Edelbrock Performer RPM	1.43	170
GM Vortec iron	1.66	170
TFS 195	1.93	195
AFR 180	1.93	180
AFR 195	1.98	195
AFR 210	2.05	210
Dart Pro 1 200	2.06	200
Dart Pro 1 215	2.14	215
Brodix Track 1	2.30	221
Dart Pro 1 230	2.40	230
Edelbrock 23 High Port	2.53	238
Edelbrock 18 Degree	2.71	266
TFS 18 Degree	2.80	250

CHAPTER 10

EXHAUST SYSTEMS

We're going to approach the engine a little differently in this book. Most books approach engine building and the explanation of engine operation by starting with the induction side. But in numerous discussions with engine builders and designers, it's clear that it's best to start with the exhaust side. If you look at the camshaft degree diagrams and pressure versus crank angle diagrams, they all start with the exhaust event. So that's what we will do here.

The reason for this is because much of what occurs in the cylinder is a direct result of pressure pulsations that occur while the exhaust valve is open. Again, we will start with quite a bit of exhaust system theory because that's the only way to really understand what's going on inside the engine.

EXHAUST OPENING

Let's begin the exhaust side of things with the opening of the exhaust valve. Combustion has already occurred and somewhere around bottom dead center, the exhaust valve opens. At this point, there is tremendous pressure in the cylinder and evacuating or reducing the pressure is important so that the engine does not have to expend power to pump the exhaust gas out of the cylinder. When the exhaust valve first opens, there is a pressure pulse that is sent out the exhaust header pipe along with the particles of exhaust gas residue or remnants of the combustion process.

It is important to evacuate as much of this residual exhaust gas as possible during the exhaust cycle. While purging 100 percent of the exhaust gas is probably not realistic, the greater amount of exhaust that is scavenged from the cylinder will result in less residual exhaust mixing with the next incoming intake charge. This mixing of exhaust gas with the fresh incoming air and fuel will reduce the potential cylinder pressure since the exhaust component will not burn a second time. So you can see that no matter how well you design and execute an induction system, the engine won't make good power unless you do an equally good job of evacuating the exhaust from the cylinder. That's another reason why the exhaust side of the engine is so critical. Again, this supports the system approach engine building.

It's obvious that there is no reason to consider running cast iron manifolds on any big cubic-inch small block, since their poor flow characteristics virtually eliminate the advantages of building a big-inch engine in the first place. Headers are the only real choice when building a big-inch small block.

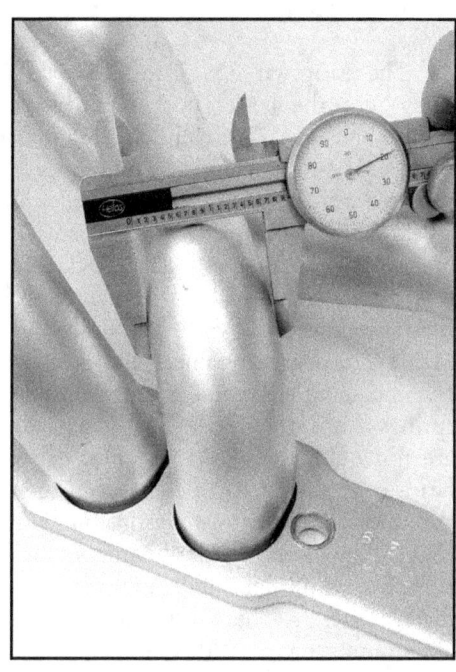

Primary pipe diameter is perhaps the biggest concern with choosing a header. For big-inch small blocks, a 383 to 420ci small-block will work great with a 1 3/4-inch header. Larger engines or ones intended for high-RPM power at or above 7000 rpm would be better served with a 1 7/8-inch primary pipe diameter.

Early production engines did a poor job of addressing the exhaust side of the engine, using inexpensive, log-style cast-iron manifolds to duct the exhaust gas into the exhaust system, perhaps through a pair of mufflers and then out the tailpipes. This restrictive system allowed the exhaust gas to stack up, creating pressure in the system. This required the engine to use power from

Exhaust Systems

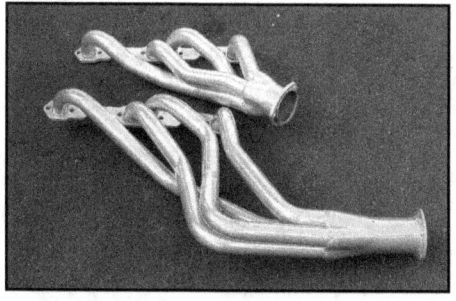

Most street headers have primary pipes that are between 26 and 34 inches long. When searching for headers, it's generally a good idea to always go with the long-tube style headers. Look for headers with a gentle radius leaving the exhaust port. Tight turns right off the port restrict flow.

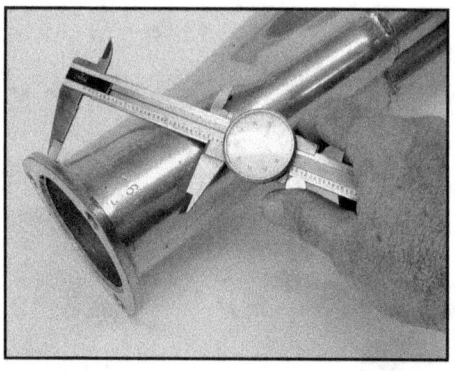

A collector will generally improve power below peak torque with very little, if any, loss of top-end power. This can be helpful especially with long duration cams that sacrifice some low-speed torque with late-closing intake valves.

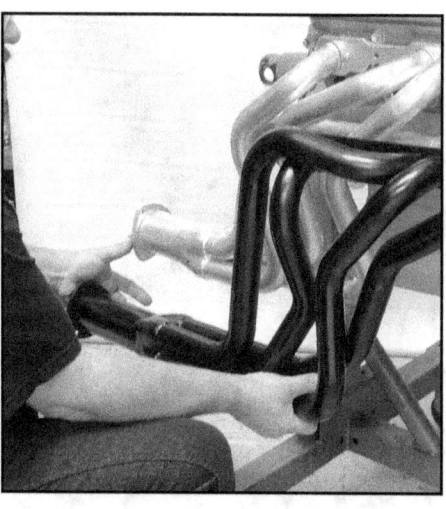

"Equal length" is a relative term, since the primary tubes on most street headers are not truly equal length. However, the bargain basement headers can be off much more than the higher-quality tubes. We measure length using a length of string and a tape measure to determine tube length. This isn't the most accurate, but it does get the job done.

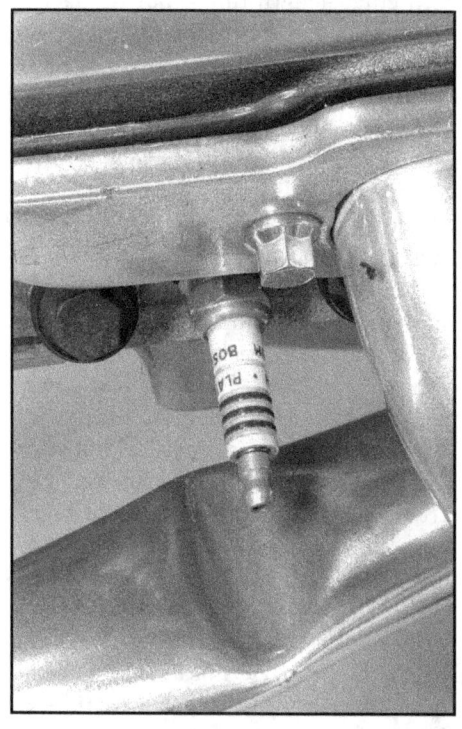

It's best to double-check the clearance between all the spark plugs, boots, and the headers on both sides before bolting the engine in the car. It's a whole lot easier to make changes to the header before you try putting them on the car.

the other cylinders to push the exhaust gas out of the cylinder. Because of this residual exhaust pressure, more exhaust gas remained in the cylinder. Reducing backpressure is a great way to increase horsepower and torque, merely by creating a less restrictive path for the exhaust to escape.

We will concentrate most of our attention on headers, but it is critical to emphasize that the entire exhaust system is crucial to overall engine performance. Since we are focusing on street engines, mufflers and full exhaust systems are required on most cars. This means the exhaust system must be sized accordingly with the engine. Large diameter systems tend to be louder, attracting the wrong kind of attention from the local representatives of the law. Large diameter exhaust pipes are also difficult to route past suspension and body pieces as well. It is possible to construct an efficient exhaust system in the 2 1/2 to 3-inch range that is quiet, high flowing, and efficient.

Primary Pipe Diameter

The best way to help understand how an engine creates its power curve is to think in terms of gas velocity. The engine is an air pump, ingesting air, mixing it with fuel, squeezing and combusting the mixture, and then dumping the residual exhaust gas out of the cylinder. The velocity at which this air moves through the engine is critical to performance. As a way of understanding this, take a deep breath and then try to exhale the entire contents of your lungs through a small drinking straw. Exhaling all that air through that small straw is difficult and requires significant effort on your part to do so. Now increase the diameter of that straw and you'll notice that it is much easier to exhale. This is exactly what the engine experiences except on a much grander scale.

Header tube diameter dictates much of this exhaust velocity. Exhaling through that small straw created a certain maximum gas velocity that is dictated by several factors, but the most important is the diameter of the pipe. Smaller pipes create higher gas velocities, but are limited to reduced volume by their small size. Larger pipes increase the volume of airflow, but suffer from reduced velocity. Neither situation is ideal. Compound this dilemma by operating the engine over a wide RPM band, and no single header pipe diameter is ideal. But we can come up with a few compromises that can improve overall power. In essence, we are compromising velocity with mass flow to create an exhaust pipe combination that will do both adequately.

Engine RPM directly relates to maximum exhaust gas velocity. That's why small primary pipe diameters improve low and mid-range torque but cannot support adequate mass flow at higher engine speeds. Larger diameter pipes do

Look for a header that creates a gentle radius exiting the exhaust port. Block hugger headers, for example, create a very tight radius that restricts flow due to the tight radius bend coming off the exhaust port.

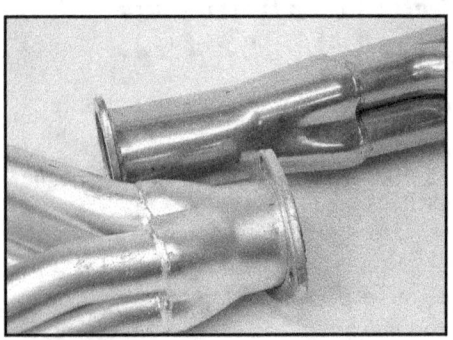

There is torque to be made by experimenting with collector length and diameter. Not all headers use the same collector diameter or length. These shorty headers use a very abbreviated collector that probably sacrifices torque because of its shorter length.

When running larger 1 7/8-inch headers on a small block, you will need spacer plates to bolt the headers to the head. These spacer plates relocate the mounting holes for the larger headers since there is insufficient room for the bolts with these larger diameter pipes.

a better job of supporting good exhaust gas speed and mass flow at higher engine speeds, but suffer from slow exhaust gas speed at lower engine speeds, creating a loss of torque. The accompanying sidebar on the effect of primary pipe diameter on an engine's torque curve will help you see how this works.

PRIMARY PIPE LENGTH

The second half of the header equation is primary pipe length. If timing is everything, then that is also true when it comes to header pipe length. If you've read the sidebar on wave tuning, then you know that a reflected wave occurs after the exhaust pulse has traveled out the end of the header tube. This reflected wave can be used to help induction tuning if it arrives at the proper time. One factor affecting the timing of this wave is the length of the header primary pipe. Longer primary pipe lengths require more time for the reflected wave to travel back up the pipe to arrive during the overlap cycle when both the intake and exhaust valves are open. This reflected wave can be used to increase power, but it only works within a very narrow RPM range. A shorter header pipe length tends to improve power at higher engine speeds because the reflected wave has a shorter distance to travel. Longer header pipes tend to improve power at lower engine speeds because there is more time to allow the reflected wave to travel the length of the pipe. This is where the term tuned-length headers originated.

One other point worth discussing is actual primary pipe length. Many header companies claim to offer headers with equal-length tubes, but the fact is that with a few exceptions, you need to go to a custom-fabricated set of headers in order to truly achieve equal length. The idea behind equal-length headers is simple. With various primary pipe lengths, the additive effect of each cylinder enhancing power within the same narrow RPM band should improve torque at that point. If the pipe lengths vary, this will diminish the cumulative effect, but also spread the torque out over a broader RPM range. Most racers will also choose a set of headers with true equal-length primaries, but this may not necessarily be the answer. For street engines, equal-length primary pipes are not nearly as important as the pipe diameter and overall average length.

What does appear to be important is that the primary pipes are somewhat equal. It's not good when one tube is eight or ten inches shorter than it's longest cousin. The better quality headers tend to minimize the difference in length, but again, they are rarely equal. As far as length is concerned, the best street headers even for big cubic-inch small blocks tend to be around 25 to 32 inches in length. Shorter headers, as you might expect, are easier to fit in the car, but generally give up torque in favor of slightly better horsepower numbers. Header primary pipe diameters for a big cubic inch small-block will likely start at 1 3/4-inches and perhaps go to 1 7/8-inch on some of the larger engines of over 430 cubic inches.

Exhaust Systems

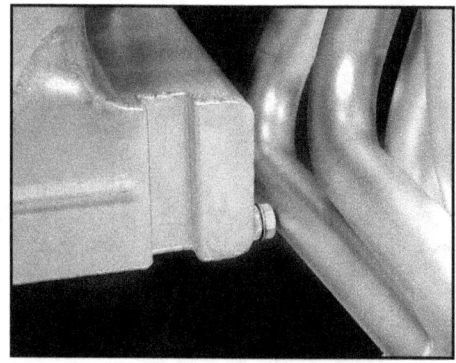

Some headers may need to be modified in order to clear a kick-out oil pan. Or you could choose a different header that will offer excellent flow without interference with the oil pan.

Burns Stainless is the leading champion of merge collectors. The idea is to change the pressure by increasing velocity through a converging/diverging collector. For open-header engines, there is power to be gained here.

Careful matching of the collector adapter to the exhaust pipe can help exhaust efficiency. Cut the collector extension at the place where it matches the size of the exhaust pipe. Do not merely slip the pipe over the collector extension and then weld it in place. This creates a restrictive cone inside the exhaust pipe.

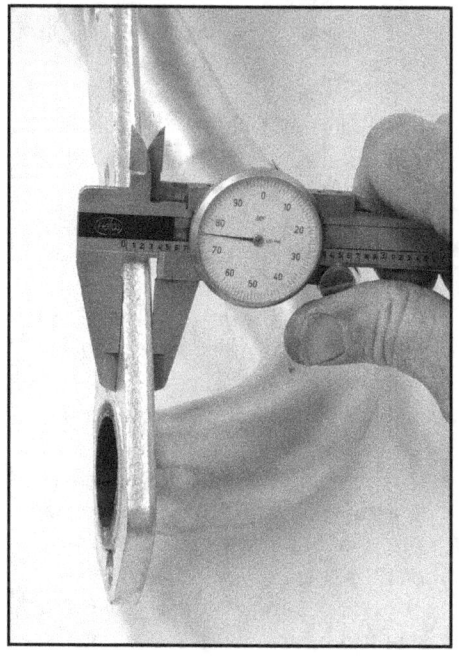

High-quality headers come with thick header flanges to reduce the chance of a gasket failure. Most of the better headers use a flange that's at least 3/8-inch thick.

There is some discussion and there have been tests performed on engines equipped not only with various length tubes but also ones of varying diameters. The idea is based on creating a family of four, two-cylinder engines that merely combine their power over a greater RPM range. This can create a broader torque curve in which you might actually see two distinctly separate torque peaks with a slight dip in between. The idea is more power across a wider RPM range for a circle track application where the engine can pull off the corner better. This has never gained major acceptance in the racing community and perhaps never will, since this also requires a rather complex camshaft with four different intake lobes and four different induction and exhaust pipe cross-sectional areas! It's an interesting idea, however, and might have possibilities in the street market.

Collector Effects

The collector was originally developed just to connect the four pipes into a common single pipe. But racers soon learned that by changing the shape, diameter, and length of the header collector, there was hidden power to be found. The collector, it turns out, is also a collector of additional power, if you know how to reap its rewards.

For standard-diameter primary pipes arriving at the collector, this is the first large area increase that the pipe experiences. This area increase also sends an expansion wave back to the cylinder. Individual pipes create a strong but short returning expansion wave back to the cylinder. But add a collector around the four pipes, and the expansion wave becomes less intense but stretches out over a longer period of time. The net effect is generally a boost in low and mid-range torque, with no negative effects at higher engine speeds. The torque increase is directly attributed to both the diameter and the length of the collector itself. Length plays the biggest part in developing when the torque increase is felt. Racers have known this for years as based on the results of lengthening the collector. Most often, there is a sweet spot at which additional length does not increase torque gains.

The net result of idealizing the collector is that power is increased below peak torque with no negative affects to top-end horsepower. Most collector diameters come in around 3 to as much as 4 inches in diameter for large cubic-inch big blocks, but the most common collectors are 3 and 3 1/2 inch.

There is also considerable work on what are called merge collectors. The Burns Stainless company has probably done the most amount of work in this area and claims significant success with most open-header configurations. What is unusual is that the diameters of these merge collectors are generally much smaller than conventional collector sizes, as small as 1 3/8-inch in diameter for a small block. The gains are attributable to the converging/diverging collector design that enhances exhaust gas velocity while also increasing the net effect of the reflected wave back into the cylinder.

Chapter 10

Wave Tuning

This short discussion of wave tuning that occurs within an engine must be aggressively abbreviated in order to get the ideas across in a reasonable amount of space. Simulation designer Curt Leaverton introduced this information into the performance engine building community quite a few years ago as part of his engine simulation program called Dynomation. This is probably the best way to look at the very complex interactions of physical pressure excursions that occur through completion of an entire four-stroke cycle.

Let's begin with a few definitions. Sound waves are pressure pulses that offer very small amplitudes and yet even these tiny pressures can inflict hearing damage. Pressure waves that create much greater energy than acoustic waves are called finite-amplitude waves. These waves are created inside an engine and offer pressure spikes almost 10,000 times greater than acoustic waves. It is the actions of these finite-amplitude waves that dictate engine operation — good or bad.

Let's start with the exhaust stroke and exhaust valve opening (EVO). Directly after EVO, a large finite-amplitude compression wave travels down the exhaust pipe towards the atmosphere. As illustration A indicates, a positive compression wave travels down the pipe from left to right, propelling the exhaust gas in the same direction but at a much slower rate. We'll assume that this direction of travel is from the cylinder towards the atmosphere. As the compression wave exits the end of the pipe into the atmosphere, a reflected wave is created that is called an expansion wave. Expansion waves create a negative pressure wave that travels from right to left, or back toward the cylinder as in illustration B. The interesting phenomenon is that this expansion wave propels the exhaust gas particles in the opposite direction, or away from the cylinder. This has an additive effect of assisting movement of the exhaust gas particles out of the cylinder.

This is important to know because of what occurs as the reflected wave arrives back at the exhaust valve. All of this wave action takes time to occur, even though it might be in hundredths of a second. With a given length of header pipe at a given RPM, this reflected wave arrives back at the cylinder at the point where both the intake and exhaust valves are open during overlap. Because this is a reflected or expansion wave, it's component is a significant negative pressure. This negative pressure is employed to pull on the induction side of the engine to increase cylinder filling before the piston has really started down to create its own negative pressure.

This wave analysis technique explains how it is possible for the engine to overfill a naturally aspirated cylinder. In addition, there are intake pressure waves also reflecting back and forth within the induction side. This sounds very simple because of this extremely basic explanation; but in reality, variables like cam timing (especially intake and exhaust valve closing), intake port cross-sectional area, header pipe diameter, port flow characteristics, intake port length, and perhaps a dozen or so other factors that all contribute to the power curve. This is why it is so difficult to not only create a powerful engine combination, but also to predict the power that will occur.

In the old days, engine builders had to rely on trying dozens if not hundreds of engine combinations in search of that elusive, all-powerful combination. But Curt Leaverton's work with the Dynomation program allows the engine builder to simulate these various engine combinations and weed out the ones that don't look promising and concentrate on those that do. The program is not simple and does require both computer power and some time to master its intricacies. However, the Dynomation program is a great way to learn more about the incredibly complex internal combustion engine without having to spend thousands of dollars on parts. It is no replacement for actual engine experience, but it is a great tool to be used both to learn and to help make more power.

A

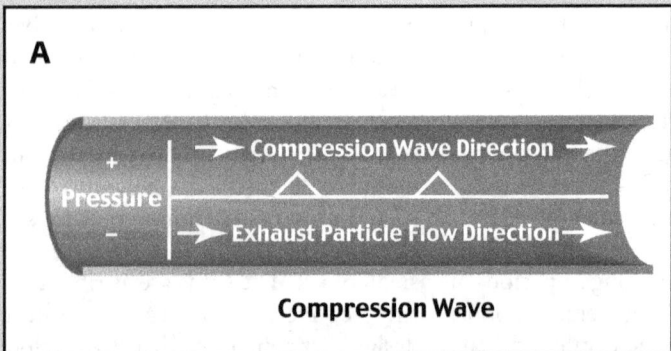

Compression Wave

B

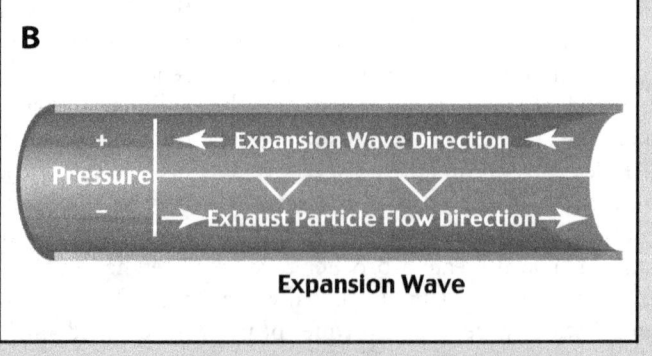

Expansion Wave

Exhaust Systems

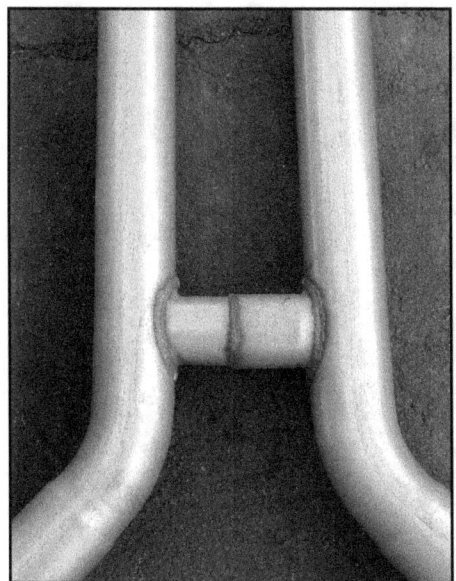

This is an H-pipe exhaust system modification that ties the two separate exhaust pipes. In some applications, the larger H-pipes can be worth small torque increases. This result varies with the application.

Sizing the exhaust system is critical to ensure that it does not choke the engine. For the largest small block, you may have to increase the pipe diameter from 2 1/2-inch to 3-inch pipes.

Smaller pipes will increase velocity, but may create backpressure. Tapping into the exhaust system ahead of the mufflers and reading the pressure with a 0 to 10 psi pressure gauge will indicate the backpressure. Readings of 2 psi or less indicate a quality system. At 10 psi or more you have a serious problem!

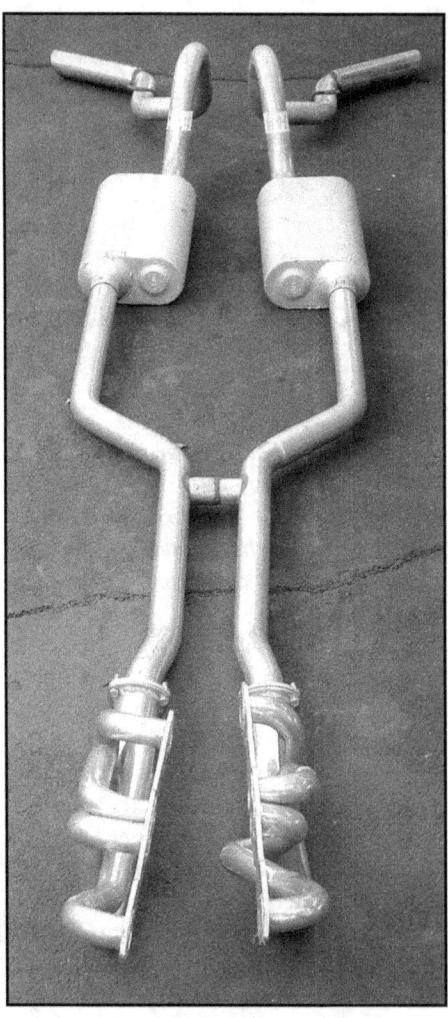

Companies like Flowmaster and Torque Technologies both build quality, mandrel-bent systems that fit very well. Both companies now offer 3-inch systems for some applications, like Chevelles.

What has not been documented is the overall power gain that could be realized by using these merge collectors in conjunction with a muffled exhaust system. The merge collector relies on a major area change at the end of the collector for open-header applications. In a muffled exhaust system, this does not occur in as dramatic a fashion, so the positive horsepower effects of the merge collector may not be present. A series of dedicated tests on muffled street engines would be necessary to underscore their importance.

Header Variables

The most common style of header is the four-into-one style header where each of the four primary pipes join at the collector. A variation of that theme is the 180-degree header where cylinders firing 180-degrees apart from each other are joined at each collector. This means that two pipes from each bank must cross over under (or over) the engine to join the collector from the opposite bank. As you can image, this creates a very complex header system that eats up a lot of room. For a street car, this is impractical and is generally used only on competition engines. These header designs tend to maximize power within a very narrow RPM band, which is probably another reason why they're not as highly prized, except perhaps for their distinctive high-pitched screaming exhaust note.

Another variation in the header routine is the Tri-Y design where the four primary pipes are joined roughly halfway down the header length into one larger secondary pipe. The two secondary pipes are then joined to a smaller collector creating a four-into-two-into-one system. This header design has some slight torque advantages over the four-into-one design, but sacrifices top-end power in the process. Generally, for a big-inch street engine that enjoys a torque advantage through displacement, the Tri-Y would not appear to be a primary choice.

Stepped headers are another variable that became popular with race engines in the late 1980's. The idea was to create a small exhaust pipe at the connection between the exhaust port size where it is an extension of the port. Then 8-10 inches later you step the pipe size up. Be careful here, because this is very application specific. While the idea has merit, and several companies offer these headers in street configurations, the advantages have never been proven consistent.

Chapter 10

Mufflers don't make power, but a quality muffler will prevent losing power to backpressure. The higher-flow mufflers also tend to be the loudest, so be prepared to deal with a loud exhaust note to get the power out.

Unusual gains in power could probably be duplicated with a larger primary pipe header with a larger collector.

Another consideration for large displacement small blocks, is the concern that a 454ci small block may need to go to a header with 1 7/8-inch primary pipes. This size header is not beyond the realm of race-style small blocks, but for a street car, it does mean that you will need to invest in a set of custom or race-style headers. Hooker, for example, does make a 1 7/8-inch and a 2-inch header for a small-block Camaro or Chevelle applications. These headers generally come with an adapter plate that fits between the head and the header. This is used to position new attachment bolts since the larger tubes do not allow using the stock bolt holes. These headers can be adapted to fit a full exhaust system without having to weld the collector directly to the exhaust lead-down pipes. Another advantage to these headers is that they often offer adjustments to the primary pipe length if you wish to experiment with longer primary lengths. These adapter flanges are also available from Hooker and other header companies to allow you to adapt headers to other specialty heads such as 18-degree heads.

H and X-Pipes

Racers and enthusiasts are also inveterate tinkerers, creating some unusual

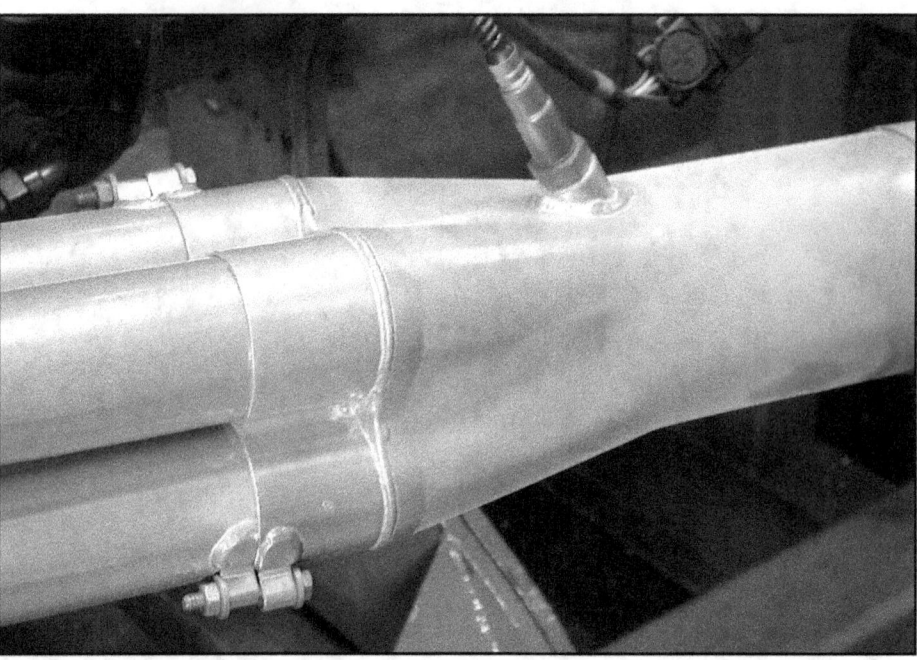

This is a Dynatech merge collector that gradually tapers the exhaust gas into a long collector; it should be worth some torque and horsepower. There's much to be learned from these collectors and some of it may be very application specific.

designs that can lead to small power gains. Downstream of the header collector, H-pipes were created to increase the volume and equalize the pressure imbalance on each side of the engine during the entire 720-degree firing cycle. The closer you move the H-pipe to the collector, the greater gains are possible. These H-pipes merely connect the left and right-bank pipes with a short, equal, or larger-diameter pipe. Tests have shown this idea to be worth some additional torque, but not all H-pipes work as advertised. The gain may be in found in the additional volume in the cylinders or perhaps in some reflected wave excursions, but the results are not consistent.

Another popular revision of the H-pipe idea is the X-pipe, where the two exhaust systems are merged in the shape of an X sharing a common area at the convergence of the two pipes. This system enjoyed some notoriety when used on Terry LaBonte's Daytona 500-win-

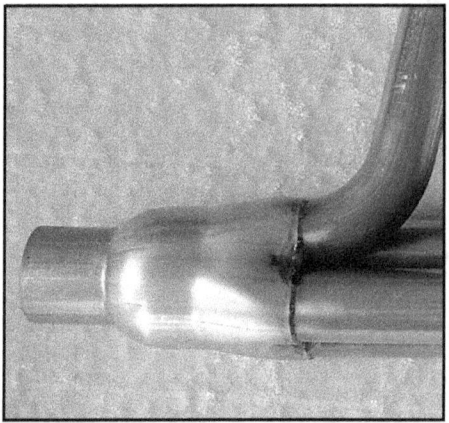
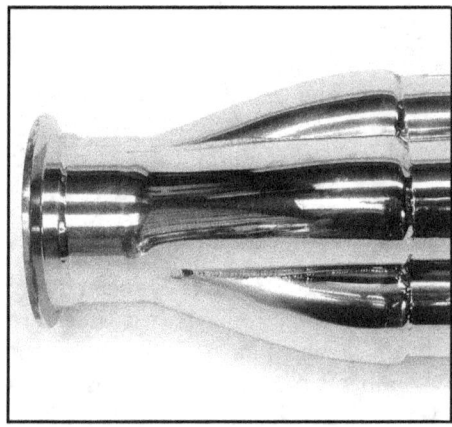

Here is an example of a poor collector design (left) that places an abrupt, almost square edge to the transition to the smaller exhaust pipe connection. Collector (right) employs a merge collector design to taper the collector down to its tailpipe connection. The merge collector's small diameter also enhances exhaust gas velocity.

Exhaust Systems

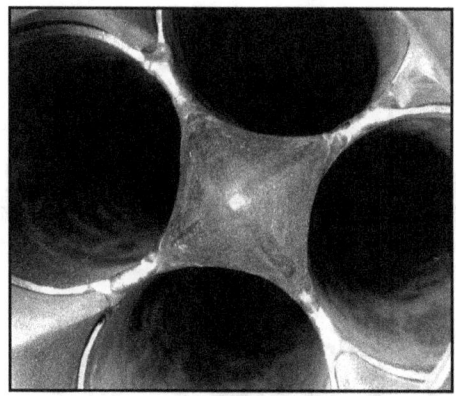

This is the view from the collector end of the Steve Watt header using a custom built stainless merge design. This looks exotic but it merely tapers the exhaust gas into the collector from the four individual tubes. This concept works, but is expensive to build.

ning NASCAR car for a couple of years, but this system has yet to really prove itself on the street, although in certain applications or combinations of parts it may be found to create power in a limited RPM band.

Making Everything Fit

Ensuring that whatever combination of parts you choose fit properly is more than just a small concern. One of the biggest problems with headers is fitting them in the chassis and making sure they will clear the spark plugs. The biggest problem is that each head manufacturer places his spark plug in slightly different locations and angles. This is a nightmare for header manufacturers who can't possibly offer a header for each cylinder head and chassis combination. This leaves it up to the end user to ensure that the headers will clear the spark plugs and spark plug boots. Sometimes this requires some minor header tube dimpling in order to create the necessary clearance. The best way to dimple a header is to heat the tube first with an oxy-acetylene torch, or even a hand-held propane torch, until the pipe is red hot. Then place a mandrel or large socket on the tube and strike the mandrel with the hammer. Do not hit the tube directly with a hammer. This will most likely split the

Header Pipe Diameter

Often a chart or illustration is better than hundreds of words. While many enthusiasts don't realize it, header primary-pipe diameter has a major effect on the engine power curve. If we employ one of those dangerous rules-of-thumb, we can state that as primary pipe-diameter increases, this tends to move or shift the peak-torque RPM point higher in the power curve. This is great for making maximum peak horsepower. But, like most things in life, there is no free lunch. As you increase primary-pipe diameter, this shifting of the torque curve higher means that you now are sacrificing torque at lower engine speeds. Depending upon your application, this may work to your advantage. For street cars, there is a point where larger pipes only hurt the torque curve and do nothing to improve peak horsepower, because the rest of the engine combination cannot support that tuned engine speed.

So the key is again a combination that will create the best overall power curve within a wide RPM band. This generally means that conservative header tube diameters will create this overall best curve. To illustrate this point, let's image we've run five different primary-pipe sizes across the same engine. If the diameter of the primary header pipes is the only thing we changed, a plot of all five torque curves would look something like the accompanying chart. Note that the smallest primary pipe creates excellent low-speed torque but quickly falls off. Each larger pipe establishes peak torque at a slightly higher engine speed. These larger headers create better horsepower numbers but sacrifice torque to get there. For a street engine, selecting a header somewhere in the middle would be a good choice in an attempt to maximize both horsepower and torque.

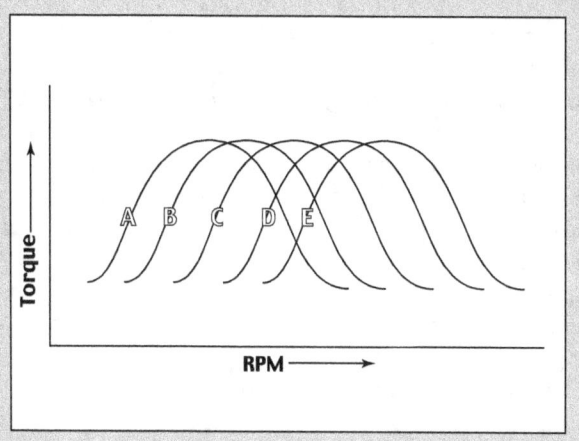

tube, which will require welding to repair. Generally, a few whacks with a hammer on the mandrel will create the clearance you need.

Another trick that will help create spark plug and boot clearance is to use one of several shorty spark plugs that are now on the market. Most aftermarket heads use a long reach, gasketed spark plug. ACCEL offers a shorter version of this spark plug whose overall length is reduced to help with clearance problems. Depending upon the model and the manufacturer, there are several companies that build spark plugs that

are slightly shorter and could offer clearance advantages.

The overall goal of the exhaust system is to carefully match the headers to the engine combination so that the exhaust does not present a restriction and also does an excellent job of scavenging as much of the residual exhaust gas out of the cylinder as possible. Do that, and your engine will reward you not only with excellent peak power numbers, but will also make great torque. This creates an excellent street engine that does everything well. That's when you know you've done it right.

CHAPTER 11

INDUCTION SYSTEMS

An intake manifold is about as simple as it gets, right? They have no moving parts and merely have to connect the carburetor or throttle body with the intake ports. Do that in a non-restrictive manner, and you have a good intake manifold. What could be easier?

As it turns out, there's much more happening with intake manifolds than merely connecting the dots. The physics of pressure excursions, finite pressure waves, and reversion pulses are just some of what occurs inside an intake manifold. The results of these actions are powerful, complex, intriguing, frustrating, and fun, all wrapped up in an aluminum spider-like package of runner length, plenum volume, approach angles, port cross-sectional areas, and a host of other actors. It's kinda like a good Tom Clancy novel with protagonists, antagonists, plot twists, conflict, unexpected endings, intrigue, and a rousing good time.

INDUCTION THEORY

There's that word again. We always start here because it's important to know the why before we can get into how manifolds do what they do. Another good reason to start with theory is that this information applies to all engines, regardless of displacement or whose name is stamped into the valve covers.

We will concentrate our discussion on carbureted intake manifolds, but we'll also touch on a few fuel-injected varieties as well. There are basically three types of intake manifolds — individual runner, single plane, and dual plane. Individual-runner manifolds are essentially like the old Hilborn or Enderle mechanical fuel-injection manifolds. These manifolds do not employ a common plenum between each intake runner, choosing instead to allow each port to operate independently and without interference from the other intake ports.

Dual-plane, or divided-plenum manifolds do employ a plenum, or common area between the ports. They use a divider that splits the plenum and the carburetor down the middle to the left and right. The two left-side barrels feed one half of the engine while the carb's opposite half feeds the remaining cylinders. It's not a left vs. right bank thing either. The main reason for dual-plane intakes is to create 180-degree phasing, giving the plenum time to rest between pulses. If you look carefully at a typical dual-plane intake, the runners end up feeding cylinders on both banks. This also increases the number of twists and turns the runner must make, which is not the best thing when working with air and fuel, but is a necessary evil that can't be avoided.

The third type of intake is what is called a single-plane or open-plenum manifold. In this configuration, all eight intake port runners feed into one large area directly underneath the carburetor, called the plenum. This arrangement reduces the length of each runner and by design, some runners end up longer than

It's easy to spot a single-plane intake versus a dual plane. The dual plane looks like a couple of snakes all tangled up (left) while a single plane (right) employs a large, open plenum area.

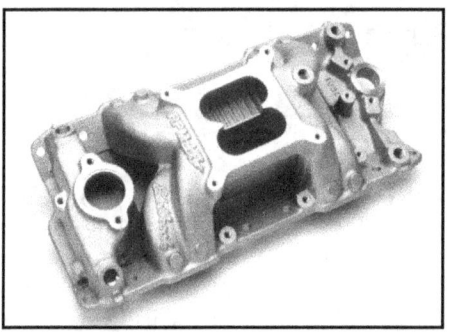

Dual planes often use runners with smaller cross-sectional areas to help speed up the inlet flow. This helps promote low-speed torque at the expense of high-speed horsepower. The Edelbrock Performer RPM Air Gap is an excellent compromise manifold that can make both excellent torque and horsepower, especially for 377 through 406ci small blocks.

Induction Systems

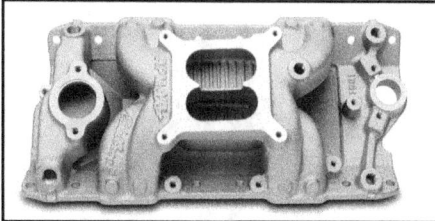

The Edelbrock Performer RPM Air Gap is perhaps the best dual-plane intake on the market today. It combines excellent torque capability with sufficient airflow for 480 to perhaps 500 hp.

others. This has important ramifications that we will discover later. Generally, this manifold configuration also allows the designer to increase the cross-sectional size of each of the runners.

It is possible to build a single-plane intake, for example, that offers the additional runner length of a dual plane. But in order to achieve the length without the bends, this intake manifold must become very tall. This is how the tunnel ram came about. For street engines, especially in later model cars with low hood lines, this is impractical for all but the most outlandish Pro-Street-style machines. It is possible to create a longer runner length manifold in a twin four-barrel crossram configuration, but this too is often impractical. Here is where the practical limitations of the vehicle also play a part in designing manifolds.

Port Length

This leads us into the meat of basic manifold design. One of the critical elements in determining how a manifold works is the runner length. Ideally, we need to take into account the entire length of the port from the centerline of the intake valve all the way up to the radius entry into the manifold plenum. Length is critical in helping shape the engine's power curve. It's best to think of the air entering into the cylinder as like a column of air, or perhaps even an invisible freight train carrying the air into the cylinder. When the intake valve opens as the piston is moving downward in the cylinder, there is a pressure differential created between the atmospheric pressure on top of the carburetor and the pressure inside the cylinder. This vacuum in the cylinder is actually very low pressure created by the increasing volume, which means the greater pressure on top of the carburetor pushes the air through the carb and manifold and into the cylinder. This doesn't happen instantaneously. It takes time for that column of air to get moving, just like a heavy freight train takes time to gain speed.

Once our freight train of air begins to move, however, it gains velocity and picks up momentum. Even though air is very light, it also has fuel in with it and together, this column of air and fuel has a mass. With a longer port, this column of air becomes longer with additional momentum, much like a freight train with additional cars attached increases its momentum. But this greater column of air requires more time to get moving, basically because it is being pushed into the cylinder by atmospheric pressure above the carburetor. This column must start at the intake valve and then extend all the way up the port to the carburetor. This requires time, just like a long freight train, which accelerates very slowly at first.

Given this, longer runners tend to increase cylinder filling at lower engine speeds when there is sufficient time for this column of air to get moving and to fill the cylinder. Peak torque is the RPM at which the engine is most efficient, when there is sufficient time to fill the cylinder before the intake valve closes. Obviously, cam timing plays a big part in this as well. Below peak torque, the column of air and fuel has not achieved the ideal air speed to move quickly into the cylinder. Above peak torque, the inlet column of air and fuel has insufficient time to completely fill the cylinder because as RPM increases, the intake valve is open for a shorter period of actual time.

If the engine is tuned properly with intake, cylinder-head ports, cam timing, and exhaust components that work well together, it is entirely possible to achieve more than 100 percent volumetric efficiency (VE). This means that the column of air can actually fill the cylinder to

Carburetor spacers seem to work best on single-plane intakes. Open spacers usually increase top-end power at the sacrifice of low-end torque. The four-hole spacers trend toward doing the opposite, but each of these changes are minimal.

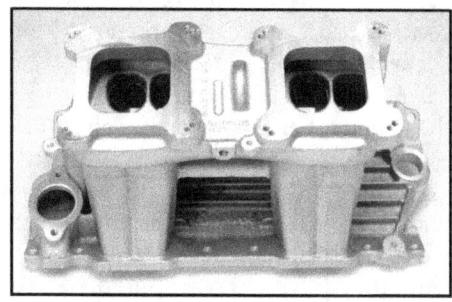

Tunnel-ram manifolds have received a bad rap, perhaps due to their over-use during the heyday of Pro Street. A tunnel ram is really a long-runner, single-plane intake, which can be a beneficial combination. Avoid the flat-bottom manifolds. A better design are the V-bottom intakes, since they suffer less mixture distribution problems.

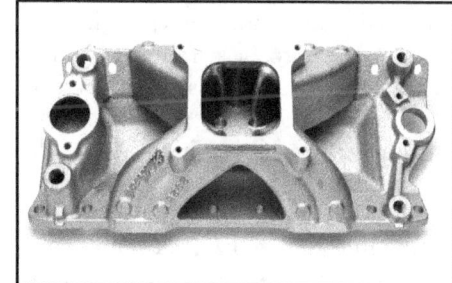

Edelbrock's 2925 Super Victor is a great manifold that would work best on big-inch small blocks with more than 420ci. It is probably a better choice over a Victor Jr., unless you get a screamin' deal on a Jr.

How To Build Big-Inch Chevy Small-Blocks

Chapter 11

Tall-deck engines will require either a dedicated tall-deck manifold or the use of spacer plates between the heads and the intake. Using these plates requires two sets of intake gaskets, but it does allow you to run your favorite short-deck manifold.

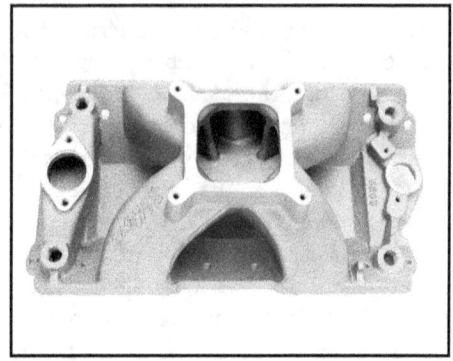

Specialty heads like the 14, 15, and 18-degree heads also require dedicated intake manifolds. Before you invest in a set of 18-degree heads, you should also know what intake manifold choices exist.

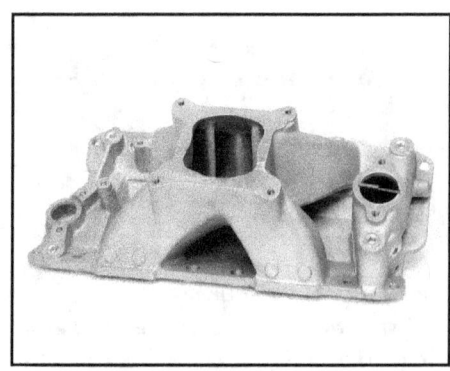

The Professional Products Hurricane single-plane intake is an excellent intake that holds its own against the Victor Jr., GM Bow Tie, and others. The best part is that this manifold is one of the least expensive single planes that make good power.

more than the amount of air it would contain with standard pressure. This occurs because our freight train of air has momentum and can actually overfill the cylinder before the intake valve closes. We've seen highly-tuned, normally-aspirated race engines achieve VE numbers of 110 to 115 percent. We've seen numbers approaching 130 percent with four-valve engines, but these are very peaky engines that only make power in a very narrow RPM band.

Port Size

It would seem that if eliminating restrictions in the induction system is beneficial, then a very large port would be the best way to make power. While that seems logical, the internal combustion engine does not always act in what would appear to be a rational manner. Inlet air velocity plays a big part in engine operation. The speed at which the inlet gas travels is critical. If the inlet gas speed is too slow as a result of a port that is too large, the incoming column of air and fuel will not have the momentum necessary to overcome the increasing pressure in the cylinder. When this happens, increasing in-cylinder pressure will force the air and fuel back into the port before the intake valve closes. In addition, the pressure waves created within the engine will be reduced due to the larger cross-sectional area of the port. This reduces the intensity of the waves and therefore particle flow will be reduced. Conversely, a port that is too small is simply a restriction that reduces cylinder filling at higher engine speeds, killing power. So much like the fairy tale with Goldilocks and the three bears, the porridge has to be just right, or the engine just won't be happy.

Dual-Plane Intakes

Edelbrock

The best dual planes right now seem to be the intakes stamped with the big red E for Edelbrock. The top dog for most of our testing is the Performer RPM Air Gap. While the initial thought was that the Air Gap series was just the RPM manifold with a gap under the floor of the manifold, comparison testing quickly revealed that Edelbrock redesigned the Air Gap series adding about 10 ft-lb and 5 to 10 hp to the manifold over its regular RPM cousins. Thankfully, Edelbrock also deemed it necessary to build the Air Gap for the 8-bolt Vortec intake bolt pattern as well as the standard 12-bolt small-block intake pattern. This is an outstanding manifold for medium displacement small blocks looking for a great compromise between torque and horsepower.

We've even seen dyno comparisons pitting the RPM Air Gap against the much-vaunted Edelbrock Super Victor single plane. In this test, the 383ci small-block was fitted with an excellent set of Dart Pro1 CNC heads and making over 500 hp. The 2925 Super Victor made the most peak power, but the Performer RPM Air Gap generated significantly more torque throughout most of the power curve. With a typical street car with a limited gear ratio of 3.55 or lower gears, this combination would be quicker in the quarter, especially with a heavier car that needs torque to help it accelerate. The 2925 manifold would be best in a lighter car with a 4 or 5-speed and deeper gears that could take advantage of the upper-end horsepower created by the single plane.

This is not always the case. For larger displacement small blocks, like those above 420 cubic inches, for example, would usually benefit from a good single-plane intake. While shorter runners reduce lower-end torque, in the case of a 427 to 454ci small block, these engines make so much torque anyway that you can afford to sacrifice some low-end torque in order to make more top-end power. The key would be to choose a high-flow intake with relatively long runners. Here is where an electronic fuel injection intake could be of benefit since this may open up intake runner options.

Induction Systems

Professional Products

Another excellent dual plane is the Professional Products Cross Wind intake, which can generally stick with the Edelbrock Performer RPM Air Gap. These manifolds have not received a lot of attention, but recent tests seem to indicate they can make excellent power and are generally priced a little better than the Edelbrock, mainly because they are made in China. Despite some bias against their origins, these appear to be high-quality intakes that fit right. Both Dart and Brodix also offer dual-plane intakes that perform well and are worth it if you can get a deal on them. Because they don't enjoy the popularity of the Edelbrock intakes, they are slightly more expensive, due to their lower production volume. If you are considering a dual plane, look for the tallest manifold possible. This indicates not only larger runners, but also larger plenum volumes that can help the transition from the plenum to the runners. This can create hood clearance problems, so be aware of that before making your final decision.

SINGLE-PLANE INTAKES

Here is the major market for the big cubic-inch small-block. There are numerous players that can all get the job done, so you have dozens of options. Among single planes, cross-sectional area of the ports and runner length make up the two biggest variables. Large plenum areas tend to make the manifold lazy at lower engine speeds, but they do help at higher RPM. Manifold height is another important criteria since this tends to stand the runners up, giving them a straighter shot at the port. There are also manifolds designed specifically for use with tall-deck engines. Let's take a look at some of the better single planes.

ACCEL

Ironically, one of the better single-plane intakes that we've run across is from a company that you don't normally think of as an induction manifold source. ACCEL built a single-plane intake manifold a couple of years ago for its ACCEL/DFI fuel-injection program. This manifold is fitted with fuel injector bungs and is part of ACCEL's new GEN VII EFI program as a package complete with single-plane intake, throttle body, injectors, and fuel rail. We've tested this intake against a couple of the better single planes out there and we've yet to find an out-of-the-box single-plane intake that beats this casting. According to ACCEL, this manifold was designed by John Lingenfelter, which would explain its excellent mixture distribution and combined torque and horsepower capabilities. You don't even have to buy the entire fuel injection system in order to get this intake. You can get the bare manifold separately under part number (PN) 74140 or with

---

Wave Dynamics

As we saw in Chapter 10 on exhaust tuning, there are very powerful pressure waves that exist inside an engine. As an example, we've witnessed a thin sheet metal dam hastily constructed inside an intake manifold plenum literally ripped apart and destroyed in a matter of seconds after the engine was started. These pressure waves are exerting serious control over the induction system and the better we understand how they work, the better tuners we will become.

In the exhaust chapter, we saw how a positive pressure compression wave in a pipe creates a negative pressure wave as it hits the atmosphere. As we will see, there are equal pressure waves that act upon the intake side as well. Let's start with the intake valve opening just as the piston begins to pull down, creating a negative pressure based on the increasing volume in the cylinder. This significant drop in pressure creates a strong suction wave moving toward the open (plenum) end of the intake port and intake manifold runner. When the suction wave exits the port, it creates a reflected negative pressure wave back down the intake runner.

Now add the variables of engine speed and the length of the intake runner and port, and it is possible that at the right speed, this reflected wave will arrive at the open intake valve just before it closes. When this reflected wave enters the cylinder it tends to push particle flow inward, helping to fill the cylinder. This positive pressure wave also helps to overcome the building pressure in the cylinder that is created both by cylinder filling and the fact that the piston is now moving upward, reducing the volume in the cylinder. This pressure wave prevents reverse flow back into the intake port. This is often called reversion.

When an engine builder comes across a combination of parts that seem to make more power than other combinations, he has probably run across this phenomenon. It depends upon a complicated series of interrelated parts that include cam timing, port flow, intake port restrictions, intake port cross-sectional area, and probably a dozen other variables. There's much more to this phenomenon than we're able to touch on here, but it is a fascinating subject that the more adventuresome engine builders might want to investigate. If you are interested, there is a book published by CarTech under the SA Design series of performance books written by Larry Atherton with technical consulting by Curt Leaverton called *Desktop Dynos* (ISBN 1-884089-23-2). It goes into far more detail than we can in this short sidebar. Check it out.

There are literally dozens of different boosters, but one of the best is the dogleg style (top) that creates a better signal to the main jet than straight-style boosters (bottom).

fuel rails under (PN) 74139. This is not a budget intake, but if you were looking for serious power, this would be an excellent choice.

Brodix

The intake manifold pages in the Brodix catalog are filled with 40 different single and dual-plane intakes, but most are manifolds intended for specific race cylinder head applications. Perhaps the most common Brodix single plane is the HV1000 for 4150 style carburetors. Like most single planes, the manifold comes with four-corner water outlets as well as dual distributor hold-downs. The carb mounting pad is located 6.5 inches off the china wall, giving carb position an excellent shot at the ports. The china wall is the vertical portion of the lifter valley at the front and rear of the block that seals the manifold. The china wall gets its name because the curved shape looks like the Great Wall of China. This manifold is intended for use with -8, -10, -11 and Track 1 heads.

Dart

Dart actually builds 13 different single planes designed for either the 4150 or 4500 Dominator style carburetors. They also make the same pieces for tall-deck engines. The ports are raised up above the manifold base to direct cool air underneath the plenum to help minimize manifold heating. One area to concentrate on when looking at any single plane is the divider wall between the ports. Since the top of the port is longer than the bottom, often the divider walls will be tapered upward so that this tends to increase the length of the port at the bottom, making the port appear straighter to the air. Dart also offers small-block spacers that allow you to use 18 or 23-degree manifolds on a tall-deck block.

Edelbrock

The most popular and versatile Edelbrock single plane has to be the Victor Jr. This manifold is available for both the standard small block and the Vortec head intake pattern and also comes in a couple of carburetor height configurations. The 2975 is the low profile manifold and can be optioned with a 1 or 2-inch carb spacer if height permits. There's even a CNC port-matched manifold (PN 2900) that is blended out to the Fel-Pro PN 1205 intake gasket size. The Victor 4+4 PN2976 intake is an interesting manifold that utilizes two port cross-sectional areas that tends to spread the torque curve out over a longer RPM band. This intake doesn't get much attention, but offers an interesting idea, especially for street engines.

The Super Victor (PN 2925) is one of the newest single planes. It features a 2.80 square-inch cross-sectional port area and is designed to be used with the new flat floor 23-degree heads. This manifold also sports a one-inch taller carb height, which should improve top-end power. This Super Victor is also available for the Vortec style bolt pattern and sports a slightly smaller 2.60 square inch port cross-section. There are also Victor High-Port intakes for the raised runner Chevrolet heads as well as Victor

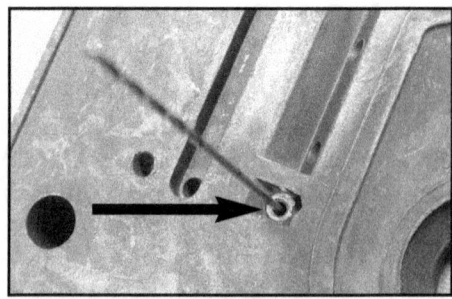

All performance Holley carbs are universal, which means they will not be idealized for your combination of displacement, camshaft, and induction package. Optimizing your carburetor may entail reducing or enlarging this idle feed restrictor (arrow) to match the fuel requirements of your engine — the smaller the cam, the less idle fuel.

18-degree manifolds with huge 3.2 square-inch cross-sectional areas that would be mostly intended for high-RPM race engines.

Holley

Perhaps the most successful Holley single-plane, small-block manifold is the Strip Dominator. It enjoys continued success to this day. This tall manifold offers excellent runner length that works especially good with automatic transmission equipped cars to spread out the torque curve. Lately, the Holley lineup has been bolstered by the addition of a series of Keith Dorton-designed single planes that are intended for either standard or raised port heads. The 300-110 is intended for classes with unported heads, but also offers excellent velocity along with good mixture distribution with a 2.4 square inch cross-sectional area. The raised runner version employs a slightly greater 2.5 square inch area aimed at higher-RPM operation.

Professional Products

We mentioned this company in the dual-plane section and they also offer a couple of single-plane intakes that also perform well. In fact, we recently looked over the results of an intake shootout that pitted the Power+Plus Hurricane single plane against four of the better single

Induction Systems

The Barry Grant Demon line of carburetors seems to have a superior fuel curve compared to most Holleys. The Speed Demon line of carburetors is a great match for a big displacement small block.

The Barry Grant Mighty Demon offers much of the fuel curve adjustability of a Race Demon without the expensive replaceable venturis. This is an excellent step-up from a Holley 4150 style carburetor, with an excellent out-of-the-box fuel curve.

of this intake as well. Both manifolds offers dual distributor hold-downs, four-corner water outlets, and even nitrous bosses if you want to do a little squeezing.

Carburetors

The other half of the induction side of the engine is the carburetor. Its job is also simple — throttle the air into the engine and mix fuel with the air in the right proportions. While carburetors have mystified enthusiasts for generations, it's relatively simple if you learn how all the circuits work. There are plenty of books on this subject and we're not going to add to that impressive list of books with this chapter. Instead, we'll touch on some of the highlights of different carburetors, their good and bad points, and the fuel mixers we've had the best luck with. This should point you in the right direction and save time, money, and grief.

Let's just touch on some basics and then we'll get into a few specific evaluations. All carburetors are rated in cubic feet per minute of airflow (cfm). However, not everyone rates its carburetors in the same fashion. Holley, for example, rates their carburetors at 1.5 inches of mercury (Hg) in wet flow. This means that fuel is introduced through the carburetor while it is being measured. Edelbrock rates its carburetors in a dry flow condition, which makes them appear larger in flow capacity because there is no fuel in the air stream to displace air. Barry Grant rates his carburetors in a wet flow cfm condition, which like Holley, is a more conservative and perhaps accurate way to measure actual airflow.

While it may not appear to be that important, the difference between dual-feed and single fuel inlet carburetors can make a big difference in power production. Most needle-and-seat assemblies

planes on the market. When pitted against a Victor Jr., a Weiand, and a Bow Tie single plane intake, the Hurricane not only made the most horsepower, but it generated excellent overall power as well. The Hurricane showed exceptional promise and is designed around the Fel-Pro 1205 intake gasket.

Not only is this intake a great power producer but it also is a decent deal for the money. It should go for around $150 in the satin finish but is also available in a polished version for about $50 more. Professional Products has also recently released a Vortec head version

Spacers

There's a significant amount of voodoo surrounding carburetor spacers. Generally, most of the claims of major power increases are inflated and difficult to duplicate, but the subject still bears investigating. If there are power increases to be made, four-hole spacers tend to improve low-speed torque, while open spacers tend to increase top-end power.

There are basically two types of spacers, the four-hole and single-hole designs. The four-hole spacers are often used to maintain velocity out of the carburetor before entering a single-plane intake. The most recent versions offer CNC radius milling that transitions the incoming air and fuel into the intake. There may be some slight advantages to a spacer of this type. Less significant are the straight, four-hole spacers with sharp edges ending at the bottom of the spacer. If you are experiencing problems mixture distribution problems, a cleverly machined spacer could bias fuel flow toward the lean cylinder when combined with some staggered carburetor jetting.

Single hole, or open spacers, are most often used to increase plenum volume for a single-plane intake manifold. Spacers taller than 1-inch are less popular for hood clearance reasons, but also because radical changes in plenum volume usually don't help power. Keep in mind that when adding a spacer, this tends to alter the signal to the carburetor, often leaning the fuel delivery curve slightly. Adding a spacer that instantly creates a power increase can often be credited more to reducing the fuel curve than to the effect of increasing plenum volume.

Open spacer can be of benefit with small carburetors where the mixture velocity is very high coming out of the carburetor. Here, a spacer can create volume and slow the mixture down sufficiently to prevent the heavier fuel particles from separating from the air and puddling on the floor of the manifold.

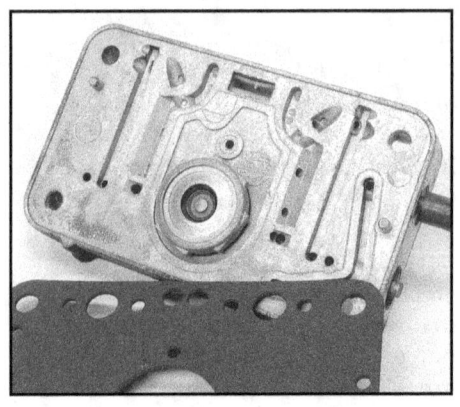

Power valves allow running a leaner primary main jet for leaner part-throttle operation. Yet when the vacuum drops, the valve opens and (depending upon the size of the power valve channel restrictors) adds another 5 to 8 jet sizes to the primary-side fuel delivery.

are sized around 0.110-inch. With engine power on the rise, it becomes difficult for a carburetor with only a single inlet, like a typical Carter, Edelbrock, Quadrajet, or Holley single inlet to feed upwards of 400 horsepower, but only the Q-jet is a true single needle-and-seat design. The others all have a single-feed inlet but with twin needles and seats and dual float bowl areas. Edelbrock has just released the Performer, dual-inlet, 800 cfm carburetor that addresses that point and may work well. But for those other single-inlet carbs, the best plan is to limit their use to 425 or less horsepower, since it is difficult for the carburetor to bring sufficient fuel in, especially with a limit of around 4 to 5 psi of fuel pressure.

The aforementioned Q-jet and Carter-style carburetors do offer excellent part-throttle mixture metering characteristics, however, which make them an excellent choice for a mild street motor. This is based on the Q-jet and Carter method of using a metering rod placed inside a jet. At light throttle, the tapered metering rod displaces a majority of area of the jet, creating minimal fuel flow. As the throttle opens and more fuel is required, the metering rod is pulled out of the jet, creating greater fuel flow. The position, taper, and overall size of the jet and the metering rod create a broad spectrum of opportunities for part-throttle metering. The Holley metering system (which the Barry Grant carburetors also emulate) is a much more simplified system using merely a fixed jet. Part-throttle metering is limited by using a power valve, which introduces more fuel into the main metering circuit under high-load conditions, which is also adjustable by changing the power valve.

The success and popularity of the Holley and later with the Barry Grant carburetors is their simplicity and modular design. Remove the four bowl screws, drain the fuel, and you can access the main jets in a less than 90 seconds. Swap them out and you can be up and running in just a few minutes. Improvements in booster design have led to the use of increasingly larger carburetors on the street without serious drivability problems. If the user does a little intelligent tuning, he can create an exceptionally responsive carburetor that gets decent gas mileage yet can still deliver amazing power. All of this can be done with a simple carburetor, but that rarely occurs without some tuning skills and a willingness to experiment.

For years, the performance magazines have preached conservative carburetor sizing for street cars for good reason. The majority of enthusiasts drive mild 350ci displacement engines that rarely make more than 300 to 350 hp. A 600 cfm Holley or even a 750 cfm Q-jet could actually work very well on these engines delivering excellent throttle response and fuel mileage. But the problem is that most of these same car guys believe their engine makes more like 450 hp and they have to have a 750 cfm or, better yet, an 850 cfm double pumper.

When it comes to big-inch small blocks, this is one time where a larger carburetor is probably a good idea. The very common 0-1850 600 cfm single inlet Holley vacuum secondary carburetor is just out-classed when it comes to feeding a 450 hp 383 with a roller cam and a single-plane intake. For most large-displacement small blocks, the 750 cfm Holley or equivalent is the entry-level carburetor with sizing increasing

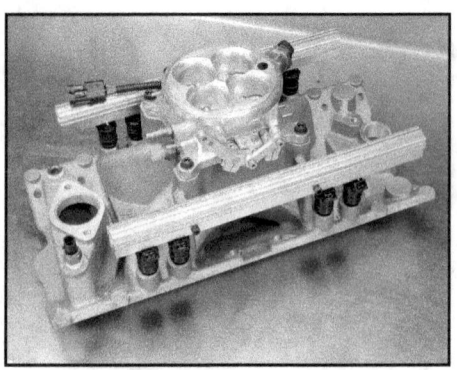

One of the best single-plane intakes is actually intended for EFI operation. The ACCEL ProRam small-block single plane was designed by John Lingenfelter and it rocks when it comes to overall torque and horsepower. There's no reason this manifold could not be used with a carburetor, all you'd have to do is plug the injector holes.

when we get to engines displacing more than 420ci. But there's a bunch more to this story than just bolting a 750 cfm carburetor on top of your engine and calling it a day. Let's take a look at what Holley offers and then we'll get into the fuel mixers from Barry Grant.

Holley

Before we get into specifics, let's run through a few basics with Holley's numerical references just so we're all on the same page. The standard square-flange Holley four-barrel carburetor is referred to in several different forms. The standard performance style is the 4150-style carburetor that is equipped with dual-feed fuel inlets and a metering block with removable jets on both the primary and secondary sides. A less expensive version is referred to as a 4160-style carburetor. This can be either a single or dual-inlet carb and uses a metering plate instead of a metering block on the secondary side. The entire plate must be replaced to change the secondary metering on these carburetors. This plate is also thinner, which shortens the length between the fuel bowls for a dual inlet fuel line. Of course, the 4160 can be converted to 4150 status by adding a secondary metering block that accepts removable jets.

Induction Systems

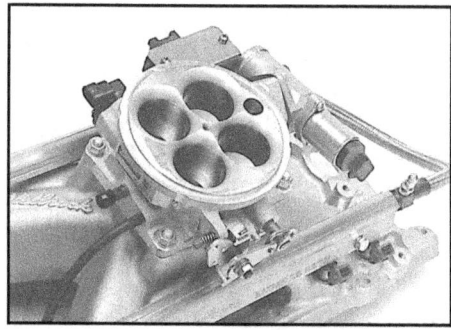

Those 1000 cfm throttle bodies aren't any bigger than a typical 750 carburetor in venturi size. The reason for the increase in airflow is that there are no boosters to impede flow. You can use a much larger throttle body with no loss of throttle response because you're not trying to move fuel with a booster.

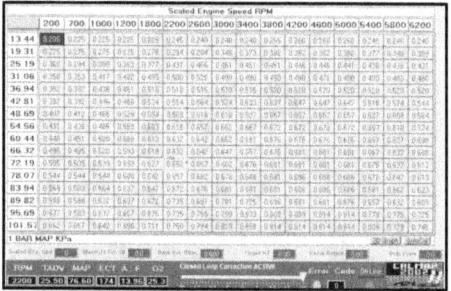

This is a base fuel map from the ACCEL/DFI Gen VII fuel injection system. This illustrates the incredible control over the fuel you have. This screen allows you to make changes to the fuel curve that are impossible with a carburetor.

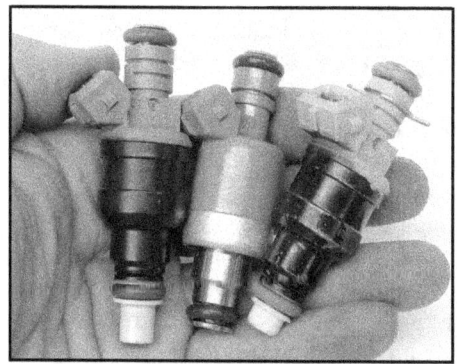

It's important to match the injector size to your engine. ACCEL offers a simple formula for determining injector size in their catalog. Also keep in mind that you may want to add injector size to accommodate up to a three-stage nitrous system, using the injectors for fuel enrichment.

There is also a 4500 series of carburetors known as the Dominator series. These carburetors were originally designed strictly for high-RPM, drag, and circle-track competition where the engine spends very little time at idle and part throttle. These carburetors use a much larger throttle body bolt pattern that require their own specific carb mounting pad on the manifold. Holley does make a 750 cfm Dominator carburetor, but the majority of these Dominators are either 1050 or 1150 cfm monsters that are not really intended for street use. While it is certainly possible to make these massive carburetors work on a street engine, there's very little reason except for rare, high-end street machines to do so.

Within the 4150/4160-style, square-flange carburetors, these fuel mixers are also differentiated by secondary actuation. The mechanical secondary or double pumper carburetors are the older and more sought after carburetors. Here, the secondaries are actuated after the primary throttle achieves roughly half open. This is called a staged throttle opening, and is necessary to produce some semblance of fuel economy on the street. There is also a vacuum secondary carburetor that uses air velocity through the primary side of the carburetor to signal when the secondaries should start to open using a vacuum diaphragm located on the passenger side rear of the carburetor. Unfortunately, these vacuum secondary style carbs don't always fully open, which can cost power. For this reason, most serious street runners run mechanical secondary carburetors almost exclusively. Certainly, you can make a vacuum secondary carb very well if you're willing to get into it and optimize it for your application.

The most popular 750 cfm Holley carburetor has to be the 0-3310. There are at least seven different versions of this vacuum secondary carburetor currently listed in Holley's numerical carburetor listing. Most of these carburetors are 4160-style carbs and can do a decent job, especially if converted over to 4150-style with a secondary metering block. Stock primary jetting for these carbs is usually a 72 jet. Earlier 3310's used a

There are plenty of fuel injection systems out there, the ones we've worked with include the new ACCEL Gen VII, F.A.S.T., and Electromotive's Tec3, among others. The best systems like the ACCEL or F.A.S.T. systems offer multi-stage nitrous control as well. This is the main screen for the new Gen VII ACCEL system.

dog-leg style booster that droops down into the venturi and offers slightly better fuel distribution and throttle response. Newer 3310's now use a straight leg booster that is not quite as responsive.

The double-pumper version of the 750 cfm Holley is most often referred to as a 0-4779 and there have been 9 different versions of this configuration. Despite the different models, little has changed with this carburetor and it remains one of the classic square-bore performance carburetors. The latest versions now come with 4-corner idle circuits and built-in blowout protection for the power valves that have also been seriously redesigned to make them more durable. Standard jetting for this carburetor is 70 or 71 (primary) and an 80 secondary jet, unless the carb came with a rear power valve, in which case the jet dropped to a 73. If you get confused with jetting your combination, a smart move is to always return to the stock jetting and retest. Often that works the best.

Beyond the 0-4779, Holley has produced several variations on the basic 4150-style carburetor. The most popular of these is the HP series of carbs. The HP series offers a high-flow version of this same venturi size, using a specific radius air inlet design that eliminates the choke horn and improves airflow into the carburetor. These carbs also feature more accurately located boosters for more even fuel flow between all four

How To Build Big-Inch Chevy Small-Blocks 103

Chapter 11

Manifold Shootout

This comparison of these four manifolds was performed on a 355ci small block on the SuperFlow dyno at Westech Performance in Mira Loma, California. Despite the 355ci displacement, this test reveals some interesting information. Had the test been performed on a larger engine, the differentials would probably remain the same, but the power levels would be achieved at a lower engine speed. The manifolds are all big single planes including the Professional Products Hurricane, the GM Performance Parts Bow Tie, the Edelbrock Super Victor, and Holley's Strip Dominator. This comparison points out just how close all four of these manifolds are with power differences of as little as 3 to 5 horsepower.

Note the differences. For example, the Holley is down as much as 24 ft-lb of torque at 4000 to the Super Victor, but then storms back at the top end to make the most peak horsepower by as much as 21 hp over the Super Victor. The Hurricane makes decent power throughout the entire curve, as does the Bow Tie, although it's slightly down to the Holley at peak horsepower. This is where the manifold can have a slight affect on the power curve. When you dial the price into this comparison, the Super Victor and the Hurricane would appear to the best buys for the money.

Manifolds

RPM	Hurricane TQ	Hurricane HP	Bow Tie TQ	Bow Tie HP	Super Victor TQ	Super Victor HP	Strip Dominator TQ	Strip Dominator HP
4000	401	306	400	305	404	308	380	290
4400	421	353	419	351	421	353	405	340
4800	446	407	443	405	443*	405	438	401
5200	444	440	443	439	442	437	446	442
5600	445	475	444*	473	442	471	444	474
5800	450*	497	442	505	442	495	449*	496
6200	440	519	436	515	432	510	439	518
6600	419	527*	414	520*	413	519*	421	530*
7000	382	509	378	504	381	507	387	516

boosters, as well as adjustable idle and high-speed air bleeds and notched floats with jet extensions in the secondary side. These carburetors tend to offer a much more even fuel flow throughout the carburetor's entire flow curve and can often be found to improve power over a standard 4150-style Holley, while also using less fuel. There is power in these carburetors over a standard 4150 and the price reflects this ability. However, these are still affordable carburetors and would work very well on a large cubic-inch small-block street engine. These carbs come in sizes ranging from 650 cfm through monster 950 cfm applications using Dominator fuel bowls. There are even methanol-calibrated HP carburetors for those crazies that choose to mess with alcohol.

Demon

Several years ago, Barry Grant decided to take a run at Holley and has parlayed that competition into a big-time business success. Grant started out modifying Holley carburetors and decided it was cheaper and easier to build his own. The Demon line of carburetors is modular like a Holley, but with his lines of Road Demon, Race Demon, and King Demon carbs, there is something for every application.

It really isn't fair to Holley to compare the Race Demon line of general competition carburetors with the straight Holleys like the 750 cfm double pumper. The Race Demons are actually similar to Holley's HP lineup, but offer some interesting upgrades. The base plate is a billet material rather than a casting and the metering blocks are constructed of a more accurate die-casting method rather than the older sand castings. Another important point about the Demon lineup is that the company spends a significant amount of time positioning the boosters in the venturi and ensuring that each of the boosters are matched. In many production-line carburetors, the boosters tend to migrate around inside the venturi, creating inconsistent signals and fuel flow from the four boosters. This is one point that the HP line of Holleys also addressed.

Each carburetor manufacturer matches the airflow through the carburetor with fuel flow for the mass flow of air through the carburetor. After experiencing dozens of dyno tests with these carburetors, it seems that the Demon line of carburetors does an excellent job of making great power with less fuel. This is created both by efficient boosters, and also excellent integration of the main fuel well and the air bleeds to create this fuel curve. We have seen several tests where a Demon carburetor made the same or more power than a competitive carburetor and usually used less fuel.

A great addition to an excellent single-plane intake like an Edelbrock Victor Jr. or a Professional Products Hurricane for a big-inch small block would be a 825 cfm Race Demon with a solid fuel delivery system to back it up. Or if a milder small-block like a 383 with a Performer RPM Air Gap is more your cup of hydrocarbons, then we'd top it off with a Holley 0-4779, or perhaps even a Road Demon of around 750 cfm.

EFI

Let's get right into this. Everyone wants to know if electronic fuel injection (EFI) makes more horsepower than a carburetor. With everything else being equal, generally a carburetor will make a

Induction Systems

One way to have tunnel-ram-like torque and horsepower potential might be with the Holley Stealth Ram intake. Combined with the Holley Commander 950 software system, this makes a strong EFI system. The Commander's only limitation is that it does not offer nitrous control within the EFI system.

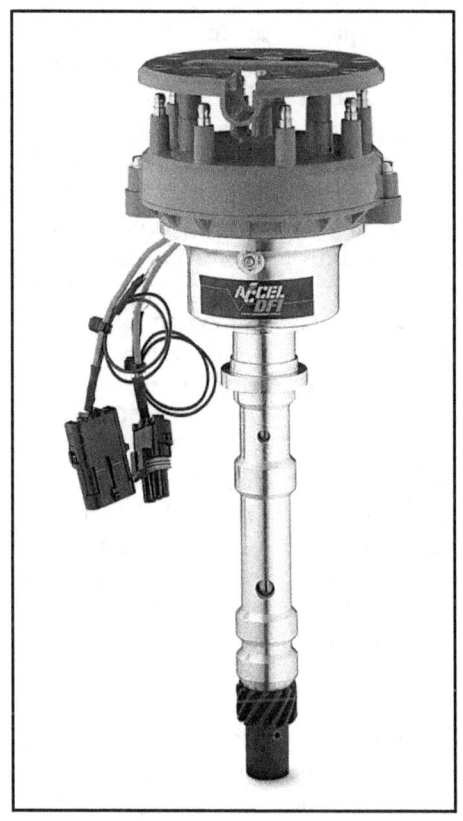

Sequential EFI requires some kind of cam sensor to tell the computer where the number-1 cylinder is in the firing order. ACCEL's dual-synch distributor does that with no external sensors or wiring leads. This makes it really easy.

Holley vs. Holley

How good is the Holley HP over the standard 4150-style carburetor? We decided to find out. We used a 425hp 406ci small block equipped with an Edelbrock Performer RPM Air Gap intake as our test bed. We ran a 4150-style 0-4779 750cfm double pumper carb against one of Holley's HP series 0-80528-1 750cfm carburetors. This motor made excellent torque and decent horsepower and served as a repeatable engine for this test. Note that the HP carb made as much as 20 ft-lb of torque more power at 3200 rpm with roughly the same amount of fuel. Throughout most of the curve, the HP carb made more torque with less fuel! When we added fuel to the 0-4779 carb, power dropped. This is a case where how the fuel is delivered made more power than just more of it. The decision then becomes whether the power increase justifies the greater cost of the HP carburetor.

RPM	0-4779 750cfm TQ	HP	0-80528-1 750cfm TQ	HP	Difference TQ	HP
2600	465	230	483	239	18	9
2800	476	254	488	260	12	6
3000	483	276	493	282	10	6
3200	491	299	511	311	20	12
3400	506	328	521	337	15	9
3600	513	351	525	360	12	9
3800	509	368	522	377	13	9
4000	504	384	515	392	9	8
4200	498	398	508	406	10	8
4400	488	408	499	418	11	10
4600	473	414	480	421	7	7
4800	456	417	464	424	8	7
5000	441	420	449	427	8	7
5200	423	419	430	426	7	7
5400	402	413	410	422	8	9

How To Build Big-Inch Chevy Small-Blocks

Don't scrimp on the plug wires. ACCEL, MSD, Moroso, and others offer high-quality spiral-wound wires that feature low resistance. Any wire with 100 ohms per foot or less resistance will do a great job.

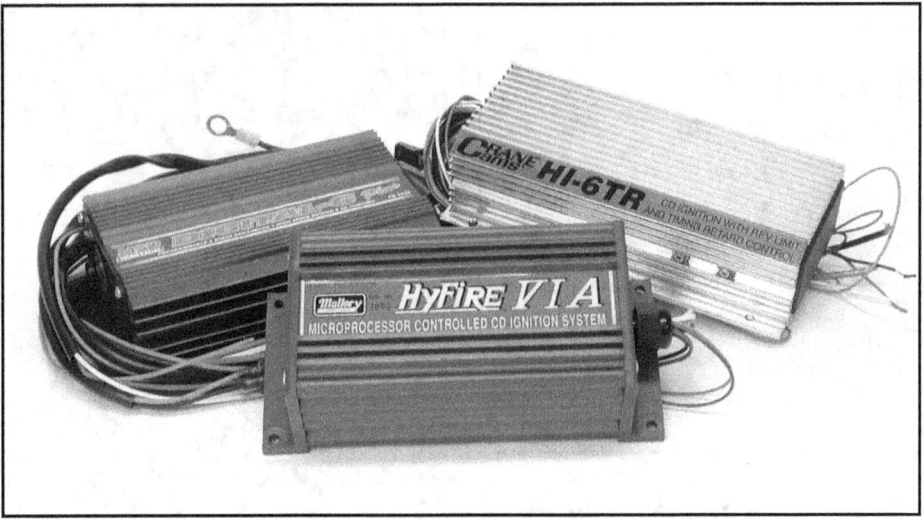

We're only touching on ignition in this book, but a high-quality capacitive discharge (CD) ignition system like those available from MSD, Mallory, Jacobs, or ACCEL are excellent choices.

slight amount more power, usually due to what is called latent heat of vaporization. This means that when fuel is introduced into the air stream, the fuel begins the process of changing from a liquid to a gas. This vaporization of the fuel pulls heat out of the incoming air, making it more dense. Because a carburetor introduces fuel further upstream than a multi-point fuel injection system, it has a longer period of time to chill the air. This is usually why a carburetor can make more peak horsepower than EFI.

It should also come as no surprise that a even a simple single-plane intake manifold-type, multi-point fuel-injection system will cost roughly two to three times what you can expect to invest in a new intake, carburetor, and fuel delivery system. This certainly begs the question as to why you would want to go with EFI over a carburetor. We will venture the notion that the decision to run with EFI over a carburetor has less to do with horsepower and more to do with whether or not you are a believer in technology.

The carbureted guys will probably never buy into the aftermarket EFI, no matter how many bells and whistles are added to these stand-alone systems. We're not going to waste anybody's time here by trying to convince you one way or the other. But if you're willing to look into the advantages of EFI, there is much to learn about the increased manipulation over the spark and fuel curves, which control the power output.

Perhaps one of the most salient points contributing to the success of EFI is its ability to handle otherwise rather balky, high-output street engines. Systems like the ACCEL/DFI version VII, the F.A.S.T. system, Electromotive's TEC3, and Holly's Commander 950 system offer significant advantages in part-throttle operation and ultimate control over fuel and spark that make these systems far superior to a carburetor.

The newer systems like the F.A.S.T. and ACCEL/DFI version VII systems also offer wide-band oxygen sensors that can give the user closed-loop feedback control over wide open throttle operation. You can even set the air-fuel ratio you want and then let the computer work with the oxygen sensor to maintain it. Not too long ago, this technology was virtually unheard of, and now you can get this kind of accurate control over the fuel with a street fuel injection system!

Want more? You can also step up from batch or bank-to-bank firing of the injectors to a more sophisticated sequential system. With sequential EFI, the injector fires only when the intake valve is open, offering yet even more specific control over the fuel. This has proven to be worth some power. This is especially important with thumper engines that demand very specific air-fuel requirements, especially at part throttle. Closed-loop control, even with the factory-style oxygen sensors, allows the computer the ability to accurately maintain a 14.7:1 air fuel ratio at part throttle that not only reduces emissions but also produces fairly decent fuel mileage — much more than you could expect from a carburetor.

These EFI systems also control the spark side of the engine as well. This is really helpful at part throttle where a little bit of tuning can offer big drivability improvements. Where this electronic spark control is especially important if you decide to use nitrous. Most of the EFI systems (except for the Holley Commander system) offer one to three-stage of nitrous control where both spark and fuel controls can be carefully maintained. The EFI system can trigger the nitrous based on various control parameters like throttle position, RPM, and also on a time delay. Once the nitrous is triggered, the EFI system will pull back the timing the exact amount specified as well as richen the mixture via the fuel injectors — you don't even need a fuel solenoid. The EFI computer can also shut the nitrous off at the designated engine speed, ahead of the rev limiter so you don't encounter problems. The one thing you never want to do is hit the rev limiter under nitrous. This will cause all kinds of expensive problems!

This has been just a rough overview of the advantages of EFI. There is a ton more information on these systems and we urge you to look more closely into the advantages of EFI before you just blow it off as an expensive gadget. EFI and a large cubic-inch small block could be a powerful combination.

Chart 1: Intakes to Go

The following is short list of some of the better intake manifolds from the companies we've listed in this chapter.

Manifold	Company	Part Number
Single plane	ACCEL	74140
Dual plane	Brodix	HP1016
Single plane	Brodix	HV1000
Single plane	Brodix	HV1014
Dual plane, Kool Can	Dart	4281100
Single plane, std. port	Dart	42411000
Single plane, large port	Dart	42311000
Dual plane, RPM Air Gap	Edelbrock	7501
Dual plane, RPM Air Gap Vortec	Edelbrock	7516
Single plane, Victor Jr.	Edelbrock	2975
Single plane, Victor 4+4	Edelbrock	2976
Single plane, Super Victor	Edelbrock	2925
Single plane, Strip Dominator	Holley	300-25
Single plane, Keith Dorton	Holley	300-110
Dual plane, Crosswind	Professional Products	52020
Single plane, Hurricane	Professional Products	52031

Chart 2: Carb Loading

The following is a short list of 4150-style, square-flange carburetors that we've found to work well both on the street and on the drag strip.

Carburetor	CFM	Company	Part Number
Vac. secondary, 4160	750	Holley	0-3310C
Vac. secondary, 4150	750	Holley	0-80573S
Mech. secondary, 4150	750	Holley	0-4779C
Vac. secondary, 4150	750	Holley	0-80529-1
Mech. secondary, 4150	750	Holley	0-80528-1
Mech. secondary, 4150	830	Holley	0-80509-1
Mech. secondary, 4150	850	Holley	0-9380
Mech. secondary, 4150	950	Holley	0-80496-1
Vac. secondary, 4150	750	Barry Grant	1402010VE
Mech. secondary, Race	750	Barry Grant	2402010GC
Mech. secondary, Race	825	Barry Grant	2423010GC
Mech. secondary, Race	1000	Barry Grant	2563010GC

CHAPTER 12

LUBRICATION SYSTEM

The oiling system for the small-block Chevy is almost legendary for its durability and out-of-the-box performance. Here is one area where being conservative is a smart move and can also save you a bunch of money. Dry sump systems are exotic, they look cool, and for a road-race endurance engine or a circle track left-turn specialist, there is good reason to step up to this kind of system. But for a street-driven, big-inch small block, the time-tested wet-sump oiling system works wonderfully. Perhaps the biggest dilemma is squeezing in the largest pan you can fit in your chassis with sufficient ground clearance.

By now you should know the drill — we're going to jump into a little theory first before we start talking about all those oily parts. The small-block Chevy uses a simple spur gear oil pump driven off the camshaft by a shaft. Oil is stored in the pan and squeezed between two gears to create both pressure and volume. The oil is then pushed through a filter, and then up into an oil galley where it feeds both lifter rows, then travels around the cam bearings and down to the main bearings where it also finds its way to the rods. On the top end, the lifters transmit oil through the pushrods to the rocker arms where the oil splashes over the valvesprings to ensure that they remain cool. The oil then drains back from the heads and the lifter valley back over the camshaft into the pan where the process starts all over again.

As we mentioned, this all starts with the oil pump creating both pressure and volume. You can't have volume without pressure since it is the pressure that pushes the oil where it needs to go. In the performance community, the more is better theory is a constant, goading companion even with something as simple as oil pressure. Wives' tales encourage the belief that high oil pressure is better for engine performance. In reality, most street small-blocks require only 45 to 55 psi of oil pressure to maintain that film of oil between the bearings and the crankshaft, for example. This is true even for engines up to 600 hp. This oil film, which the engineers call a hydro-dynamic wedge, supports the crank and keeps it away from the engine bearings. When everything works properly, engine bearings can look almost brand new even when subjected to 700 to 1000 hp levels.

As engine speed increases, the oil pump must be capable of sustaining suf-

No need to get trick when it comes to oil pumps. The standard small-block 4-bolt pump works in almost all cases. The deeper 5-bolt, rat-motor pump will bolt to a small block but there's little need for that additional volume. Plus, there is a certain amount of horsepower lost to running a larger pump.

Melling makes an excellent high-performance version of its standard M-55 pump that uses 10-percent larger gears for a slight volume increase, a bolt-on pickup, and a larger pickup tube. It also comes with its own 4150 chrome-moly steel oil pump shaft.

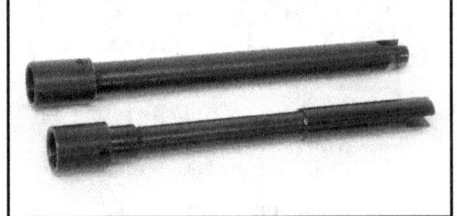

All big-inch small blocks will need to run the reduced diameter oil pump drive shaft to prevent binding around the larger 400ci diameter crank journal. This is an ARP driveshaft for the 400ci small block compared to a stock 350ci-style shaft.

Lubrication System

ARP also makes an excellent oil pump stud to replace the stock bolt. This prevents damage to the threads in the number-5 main cap.

The only right way to install a press-in small-block pickup screen is with a special installation tool. The tool drives the pickup into the pump without distorting the pump body. According to Melling, if you mount the pickup in a vise and drive the pump onto the pickup with a steel hammer, this could distort the pump body and cause the gears to lock. Both Melling and Federal-Mogul make an installation tool. This is the Federal-Mogul tool for the 5/8 and 3/4-inch pickup tubes.

Always remove the oil pressure relief spring when welding the pickup into the pump cover. The heat generated by welding could weaken the spring.

ficient volume to replace the increased amount of oil thrown off the bearings from the centrifugal force. If the pump volume is not sufficient to supply the demand, pressure may drop as a result. This rarely occurs with the small block since the standard pump is capable of sufficient volume as long as clearances are not excessive. Large main and/or rod bearing clearances place a greater load on the oil pump since this larger area creates an easier path for the oil to escape from the bearings. This additional volume can be compensated for with a high-volume oil pump, but this creates other problems that can all be traced back to the larger bearing clearances.

The increased oil volume created by excessive bearing clearances also creates a greater amount of oil thrown off the bearings. This oil creates a heavy mist inside the crankcase that the crankshaft must work its way through. This requires horsepower to drive the crank through this oily maelstrom, eating power. This additional oil also finds its way to the cylinder walls where it places an additional load on the oil rings to scrape the oil away, increasing the chance that some of that oil will find its way into the combustion chamber. In addition, there is a horsepower price to pay for pumping that greater volume of oil with the pump. This is also an internal parasitic power loss. Add in a thick viscosity oil to help oil pressure at high engine speeds and you have a recipe for lost power. Let's look at some ways to improve the performance and efficiency of the small-block Chevy lubrication system so that

If you plan on extended high-RPM use like road racing or top speed competition, it's essential you employ an oil-pump pickup with a separate support to prevent the pickup from vibrating. Vibration could cause the screen to break off even when the pickup tube is welded into the pump.

we can recover some of that lost power and push it out the crankshaft where we can use it to go faster!

Oil Pumps

The lowly stock small-block Chevy four-bolt oil pump may not be pretty and may not be fancy, but it does a great job. This pump has performed the task of lubricating small-block Chevys for almost 50 years and continues to do so today. Rather than buy into some slick, expensive, heavily modified oiling system, most small blocks are better off with a few simple modifications that can help the stock pump do its job more efficiently.

Perhaps the most popular standard replacement small-block Chevy pump is the Melling M-55 that accommodates a stock 5/8-inch inlet pickup tube. For street engines that rarely see the high side of 6000 rpm, this pump works just fine. The typical modification is to install the pickup on the pump and bolt it on the engine. Then measure the distance between the pickup and the bottom of the oil pan for clearance. This is generally between 1/4 to 3/8-inch. This places the pickup near the bottom of the pan so it is always submerged in oil, but not so close that the pickup is restricted. Next, remove the pump cover and drive out the roll pin that retains the pressure relief spring. With the spring removed, you can now spot weld or braze the pickup directly to the pump cover. There's no

Chapter 12

The Melling pump makes access to the oil pressure relief spring easier with a Allen head pipe plug instead of the hassle of driving the roll pin out with a very small punch.

Moroso's performance oil pump uses anti-cavitation slots and pressure-balance grooves cut in the cover to create an excellent pump in a standard volume container. Be aware that this pump causes pressure fluctuations at idle as a result of the grooves.

reason to completely weld this all the way around the tube. This prevents the pressed-in pickup from falling out. Removing the pressure relief spring prevents heat damage from the welding.

While some enthusiasts will place a small AN washer behind the stock spring to increase the oil pressure, a smarter move is to just buy the high-performance white pressure relief valvespring from GM Performance Parts (PN 3848911) that will produce

It's important to check the clearance between the oil pump pickup and the bottom of the oil pan, especially when mixing and matching an aftermarket system of pump, pickup, and oil pan. The low-tech clay method works in most applications, but be sure to include the oil pan gasket you will be using. Cover the inlet screen with tape so that the clay doesn't push into the screen.

between 65 and 70 psi, even with a remote oil filter and cooler. But frankly, even this small modification isn't really necessary. Once the pump cover has cooled, you should also check to ensure it has not warped. If so, gently sand the cover on a flat surface until the gear side of the cover is flat.

High-volume pumps have become popular items for street-driven small blocks for no apparent reason other than the typical street engine builder thinks he needs the additional volume. As we mentioned above, if you've built the engine with conservative bearing clearances, then there's no real reason to include a high-volume pump. Even the addition of an externally-mounted oil filter and perhaps even an oil cooler would not necessarily demand a larger pump. This would probably depend upon the pressure drop across both of these items, but a slightly higher operating pressure would probably cure this as well.

A good idea, especially for large displacement small-blocks, is a high-quality, standard-volume oil pump. Melling, Moroso, and others build excellent oil pumps. The Moroso pump comes with pressure balancing slots cut in the cover that balance the forces inside the pump. These feeder grooves and anti-cavitation slots cut in the bottom of the pump place

If you decide on a block with a wide oil pan rail for stroker crank clearance, remember that you will need a wide-rail oil pan as well. Notice how the Fel-Pro one-piece gasket sits far inside the Dart block with the wide pan-rail. Moroso offers a deep-sump oil pan for Rocket blocks that uses an 8 1/4-inch deep sump with a windage tray and 7-quart capacity.

a more even demand on the pump drive shaft, which reduces the load on the shaft and extends the pump life. Moroso offers this pump in both a standard volume configuration (PN 22100) or in a high-volume design (PN 22110). At low engine speeds, this does create erratic and fluctuating oil pressure readings however, which some may find disturbing. This is a function of the pressure balance grooves so be aware of this fact before you invest in one of these pumps.

Melling offers a redesigned small-block pump that now uses a bolt-on pickup that does not require welding, uses a larger, more efficient 3/4-inch inlet tube, and comes with its own oil-pump drive shaft. This pump is offered in several different configurations so check the Melling catalog or web site for more information on this pump.

Don't overlook the oil-pump drive shaft, either. The stock shaft uses a plastic collar for the connection between the shaft and the oil pump that is a little too cheesy for our taste. Be careful when selecting an oil-pump shaft, however. The 400 small block requires a reduced diameter shaft to clear the main cap. Several companies, including ARP, sell a performance shaft (PN 134-7901) that is reduced in size to fit without having to machine the main cap.

Lubrication System

Synthetic oil is a great addition to any high-performance engine. The thinner-weight oils reduce pumping losses and can actually be worth some horsepower. We've seen tests on the Royal Purple synthetics that show increases of 5 to 6 hp at 500 hp levels. Synthetics also offer excellent high-pressure lubricants that can be helpful with high valvespring pressures.

Wide, solid windage trays like this '69 Z28 tray help keep the oil in the pan, but they also trap oil between the crank and the tray. If you are thinking about using a windage tray like this one, it isn't necessarily bad, but there are better ways to go.

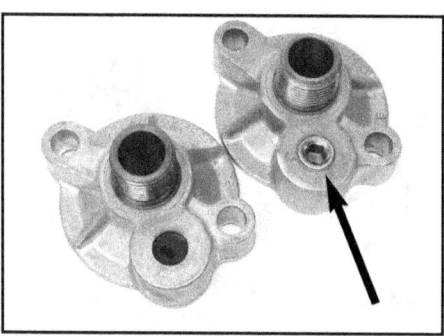

The oil bypass valve in the filter adapter probably doesn't bypass much oil since it relies on a pressure differential in the filter to open. However, it doesn't hurt to ensure that all the oil that enters this area runs through the filter first by plugging this bypass by tapping the hole for a pipe plug (arrow). Do not rev the engine until the oil temperature comes up and keep up your filter maintenance effort, since a plugged filter is death for your engine.

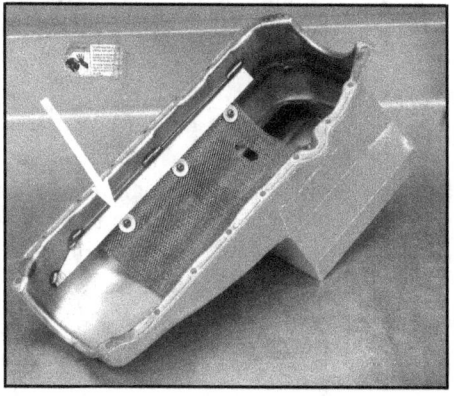

A simple 1/2-inch deep scraper like this one (arrow) can be worth some significant power in a long-stroke small block where the pan is tight to the crankshaft. If your pan doesn't have one of these, add one.

Oil Pans

It would take a book this size just to list all the aftermarket oil pans available for the small block Chevy. The variables involved with an oil-pan selection make this choice somewhat difficult. The variables include the chassis, ride height, header clearance, sump depth, room for an oil pan kick-out, starter motor clearance, oil capacity, and the style of windage tray you wish to run. Aviaid, Billet Specialties, Moroso, Milodon, and Hamburger Oil Pans, now owned by TD Performance, have the widest selection of small-block pans. We're only going to hit the high points in favor of brevity.

Ultimately, the ideal wet sump oil pan is one with a very large kick-out on the passenger side that extends the length of the pan combined with a very deep sump that allows for maximum oil capacity along with clearance away from the crankshaft. This is a Comp Eliminator style pan that all the tube-chassied drag cars run. Unfortunately, this is impractical for the street, so we must endure a few compromises. The passenger side kick-out is important because at high RPM, the crankshaft wants to sling the oil laterally away from the crank aimed directly at the passenger side crankcase and oil pan vertical walls. The kick-out merely catches the oil farther away from the crank, reducing windage losses.

For the street, small kick-outs are possible, but are often difficult to package in the car because the starter and headers are in the way. The next best approach is to incorporate an angled scraper built into the oil pan on the passenger side that will help peel the oil away and direct it back to the pan. While those custom-built, tight-clearance scrapers get lots of press from the magazines, the reality is that these scrapers can actually cost horsepower in high-RPM situations by creating drag on the crankshaft. According to several professional engine builders including Ken Duttweiler, a simple, angled length of tin roughly 1/2-inch deep and running the length of the crankshaft attached to the passenger side of the oil pan will do the most good of anything else you can do in the oil pan.

This brings us to the subject of windage trays. Again, most professional engine builders shy away from the solid style windage trays such as the classic, '69 Camaro Z28 tray. While this tray does a good job of helping keep the oil in the sump, it unfortunately also traps oil between the crank and tray, increasing windage losses. While diamond scrapers seem to enjoy some popularity, the jury is still out as to the extent of their effectiveness. These do a better job of scraping oil with larger displacement engines due to the longer stroke. However, much of the discussion of the advantages of scrapers and windage is all tied to engine speed. With a large displacement engine spinning at 6500 rpm or less, the advantages may be minimal.

More important is controlling the oil that is already in the pan during high-g acceleration, braking, and lateral-g maneuvering. This is where a deep sump is advantageous, but must be compromised in favor of ground clearance. A 6-1/2-inch to 8 1/2-inch sump depth (measured from the oil pan rail) is about as deep as you can go with a typical street car oil pan, especially for early muscle cars like the '67-'69 Camaro and '64-'72

Chapter 12

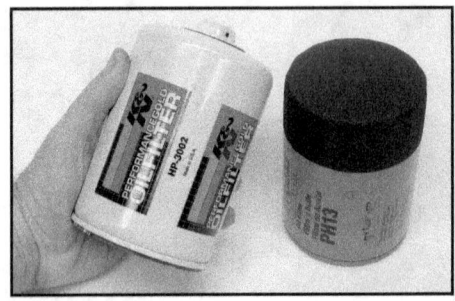

Cheap, stock oil filters can grow by 0.050-inch in diameter when hit with even mild oil pressure of 50 psi. Performance filters use thicker cans to contain the pressure and employ a better O-ring seal. These filters are probably worth the investment. A Filter Magnet is also a good insurance idea as well.

Fel-Pro's one-piece oil pan gasket makes installing an oil pan an absolute breeze. No silicone is required and there are even built-in torque limiters to prevent overtightening the bolts. We'll never build another small block without these gaskets.

Chevelles. Moroso makes a slick, stock-appearing, 4-quart "claimer" pan that is 7 1/2-inches deep and looks like a production oil pan (PN 21804 for pre-'80 blocks). On the inside, it is fitted with a crank-length scraper along with two trap doors designed to retain oil in the sump. This is an excellent street pan and is also very stealthy. Milodon also makes a claimer-style pan that works well.

Milodon also makes more than a few performance oil pans, including its Pro Competition steel pan (PN 31167) that is designed to clear those early Camaro and Chevelle chassis with an 8 1/4-inch deep sump, a kick-out on the passenger side, and a louvered, full-length tray assembly. There's also a double trap door assembly in the sump that helps prevent uncovering the pickup on hard deceleration.

If hiding your performance intentions is not important, Moroso and Milodon also make street/strip pans with a kicked-out sump that increases the pan capacity to 7 quarts by increasing the depth to 8 1/2 inches. This decreases the ground clearance, but also moves the sump away from the crank. Keep in mind that all deep pans will require a custom oil pickup designed to properly position the pickup in the pan.

Another useful item is an anti-slosh plate that can be bolted between the oil pump and the rear portion of the oil pan. This prevents the oil from climbing the rear wall of the oil pan and potentially uncovering the oil pump pickup tube. This is a simple plate that can be installed during engine assembly that further helps control the oil. The antithesis of this is the inexpensive aftermarket oil pan with absolutely no baffles of any kind in the pan. Even on the street in panic stop situations, all the oil migrates to the front of the pan and uncovers the pickup, pushing the oil pressure to zero for what seems an eternity. The lesson here is not to cheap out on an oil pan, but it's not necessary to spend thousands of dollars on a wild-side, trick-of-the-week oil-pan setup either. And leave the dry sumps to the circle track racers.

Synthetics

If there is a buzz word in the world of lubrication, it has to be synthetic oil. To be sure, there are definite advantages to synthetics over petroleum-based oil, so that means we should investigate the differences. Petroleum-based oil, as you've probably guessed, is dead-dinosaur based and over the years has become an excellent lubricant. The Society of Automotive Engineers (SAE) has developed a rating system for all gasoline-style, internal combustion engines that determines viscosity of the oil for both straight-weight and multi-grade oils. When you see a 30 on a bottle of oil (remember when they used to be metal cans?), this means the oil is a straight-weight oil with a viscosity rating of 30. Higher numbers (between 30 and 50) are intended for summer driving when oil is subjected to serious heat. As little as 40 years ago, multi-grade oils had not made a name for themselves yet and people in cold weather climates used lightweight 10w in the cold months and 30w oil for the warmer summer months.

Today, multi-grade oils do away with that hassle, allowing you to run a 10w40 oil for example that at 0 degrees F acts like a thinner 10-weight oil while at much warmer temperatures, the oil's viscosity index improvers increase the thickness of the oil to the equivalent of a 40-weight oil. Man-made synthetics are rated in the same fashion, but offer certain advantages over petroleum-based oil.

The big improvement in performance with synthetic oil is its ability to withstand higher temperatures. You may remember the Mobil 1 commercials where they placed petroleum-based and Mobil 1 in a frying pan to illustrate what happens under extremely high temperatures. Conventional oil begins to break down at temperatures above 250 degrees F while most synthetics are able to withstand oil temperatures of 300 degrees F for short periods of time.

This may seem like extreme temperatures, but a typical street car in the daily grind of slow-moving traffic will often generate oil temperatures of 220 to 230 degrees F. Add more horsepower to the equation and perhaps a 20-minute stint through the canyon twisties and oil temperatures of 250 to 260 degrees F are not uncommon. This is especially true with engines not equipped with oil coolers. Few street engines are equipped with oil temperature gauges, but if they were, the temperatures might scare you. This is the reason for using a high-quality synthetic. And don't be misled by water temperatures that may hover at 180 or 190 degrees. Oil temperatures generally run 20 to 30 degrees higher than water temperatures, which is all the more reason to run a synthetic in your big-inch small block.

Drag strip applications rarely run long enough to generate excessive oil temperatures, but road race, circle track,

Lubrication System

Don't forget to install this small press-in plug underneath the driver's side of the number-5 main cap. If you leave this plug out, all the oil will bypass the oil filter completely. That's not a good thing for any engine.

These oil restrictors used to be the hot ticket to reduce the oil to the top end of the engine. What this did was overheat the valvesprings, quickly destroying valvespring pressure. Don't run these in any small block.

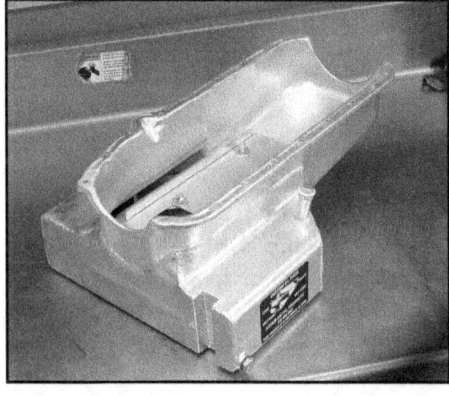

This Aviaid oil pan is designed for road racing with plenty of trap doors to keep the oil in the sump, especially during those high-g turns when the oil tries to climb the vertical walls of the oil pan.

and even the occasional street car track day can skyrocket oil temperatures. This is the reason that all TPI L98 Corvette engines all came with small water-to-oil coolers. These coolers duct engine coolant through a small sandwich cooler located between the oil filter and the engine block. Though these coolers were small, the idea was to mediate the oil temperature to prevent damaging the engine. In '92 and later Corvette engines specified Mobil 1 synthetic oil and eliminated the oil cooler. This doesn't mean the engine doesn't heat up the oil, it's just that the synthetic oil can handle the additional temperature. If you shoot for an oil temperature of around 220 degrees F, this may be roughly ideal for performance. Cooler oil temperatures increase viscosity and increase pumping losses while excessively high oil temperatures can limit the oil's ability to both cool and lubricate. Once an oil breaks down, it ability to create that hydrodynamic wedge in the bearings breaks down and internal engine damage is only moments away. If it sounds like a reputable oil temperature gauge should be a part of your gauge complement, you'd be right.

Oil Coolers

While we're on the subject of high oil temperature, aftermarket coolers are becoming increasingly important especially with the emphasis now on Pro Touring and G-Machine style of cars. With a high-output small block and high g-load capabilities, it's easy now to push a car like these for extended periods of time at high horsepower levels. This kind of performance driving demands a decent oil cooler to keep the oil temperature in line. Earl's, Setrab, Fluidyne, and several other companies build dozens of different oil coolers. The most common are the air-to-oil coolers using a remote mount generally in a high-pressure area at the front of the car.

Plumbing these coolers is critical since adding unnecessary 90-degre fittings and bends only increases the pressure drop through the system. The most common way of plumbing an oil cooler for a small block is to use a billet oil fil-

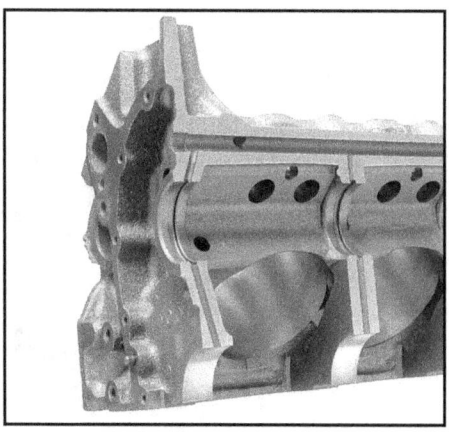

This production block cutaway shows how the oil travels down the horizontal main oil passage in the middle of the lifter valley, around each of the cam bearings, and down to each main bearing saddle. Despite this lengthy passage to get to the main bearings, small-block Chevys rarely experience lubrication problems.

ter adapter that bolts to the stock oil filter mount on the block. These adapters allow you to connect -10 or -12 AN braided high-pressure line from the engine to an external oil filter and then to the cooler. This configuration helps protect the cooler in case of engine damage, the metal particles are blocked by the filter before they reach the cooler. If the cooler becomes contaminated with metal debris, it's best to trash it, since coolers are notoriously difficult to clean thoroughly. If you are using a Bow Tie, Dart, or World Products block, you can reduce the length of the AN return line by routing the oil to the front of the engine just above the timing-chain cover.

Conclusion

Unlike the trick 4340 steel cranks and romantic stroker rotating assemblies we discussed earlier in this book, the oiling system should generally be more conservative and traditional, especially for a street engine where exotic parts often fall prey to problems. The smart move is to protect those expensive rotating parts with a well-designed and thoroughly thought-out lubrication system that will work forever and allow you to concentrate on more important things — like how to make more power!

CHAPTER 13

BUILDING AND BLUEPRINTING

Bolting an engine together is easy. It's much more time-consuming and demanding to custom-build and blueprint an engine. The term blueprinting is an often over-used and misused term that has probably lost much of its meaning in the world of high-performance engines. It was originally intended to mean that you would go further to ensure that the clearances were what you wanted (not just measure how they came out).

Actually, blueprinting is as much art as it is science. It's about putting effort into the engine rather than just slapping it together. This is more a state of mind than a process. The payoff is with an engine that not only makes great power, but is also one of those engines that seems to run forever. You know you've got a good engine when you can buzz the wee out of it for an afternoon at the track, run the valves afterward (assuming you're running a mechanical cam) and discover that the valve lash has

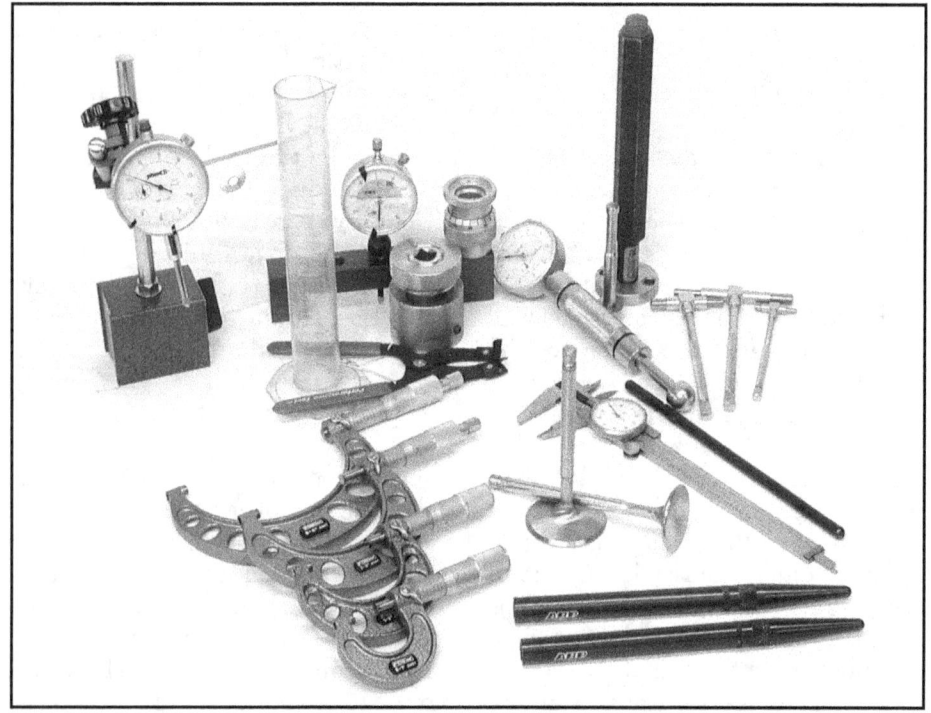

In order to perform measurements, you have to have specialty tools. These include quality micrometers, dial indicators, piston stops, degree wheels, height mics, and dozens of other tools, some of which you may end up making yourself. This is a sizeable investment, but if you are committed to building engines, these are must-have tools.

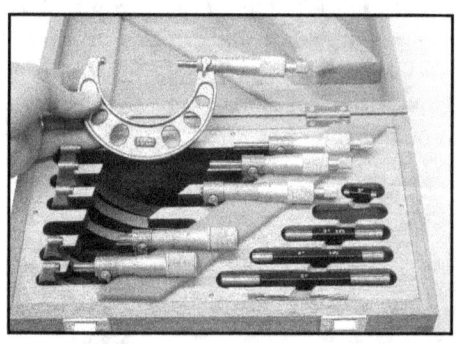

Micrometers are sensitive measuring instruments and a high-quality mic is always sold with a standard that is used to ensure the mic is accurate. The mic should be checked against its standard every time you use it. Shop temperature is another big variable. All the measuring tools and the component to be measured should be the same temperature. Measure a crank main-journal at 110 degrees F and at 60 degrees F and the diameter will be different.

Building and Blueprinting

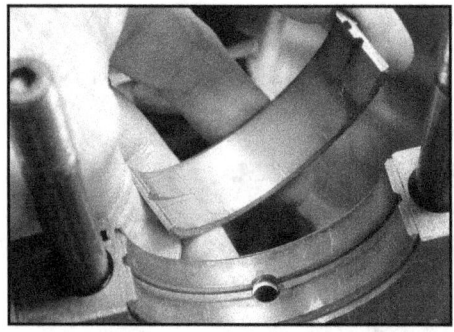

It's perfectly acceptable to mix and match bearing shell halves to create the clearance you require. For example, if you need roughly 0.0005-inch additional rod bearing clearance, you can use one bearing shell from a +0.001 rod bearing set to achieve this additional clearance. You must always use the bearing half from the same manufacturer.

Most ring manufacturers will tell you that the best way to install rings is to use a ring spreader like this K-D tool. There is no hard evidence to indicate that spiraling rings on a piston damages them but this minimizes the risk.

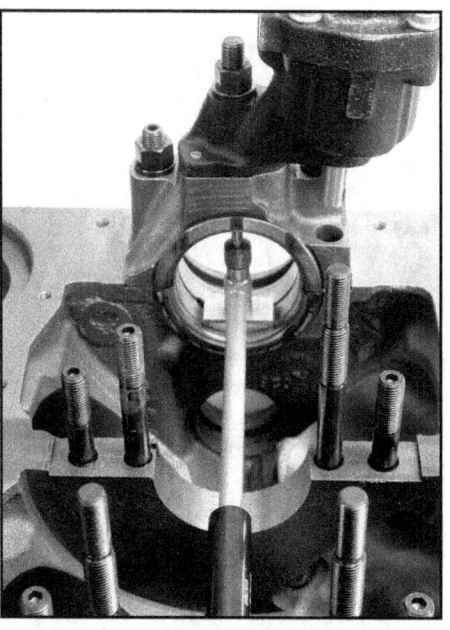

Always torque the oil pump in place on the number-5 main cap using the actual fastener before checking that main bearing's clearance. The oil pump will distort the cap and change the bearing clearance. You will find a difference in bearing clearance even between an oil pump stud and a bolt. Quality machine shops also do this when they align hone a block.

changed perhaps a couple of thousandth's on one or two cylinders.

An important rule when assembling an engine for the first time is to not be in a hurry. You have to be willing to pre-assemble portions of the engine perhaps four or five times in order to get all the clearances correct. The more aftermarket parts and exotic stuff you've added to the engine, the more time you can expect to spend on pre-assembly clearancing. For example, a long-stroke crank and a new block will need to go together several times before they are happy. Add in rod clearance to the cam (which means you need to degree the cam first to ensure it's installed correctly) and you have plenty to do. The last thing you want is for a connecting rod to run into a cam lobe during final assembly. That will ruin your whole day.

The cardinal rule for engine assembly after you've learned patience is very simple — trust no one. Even if your mother did the machine work, it's the engine builder's responsibility to ensure that the clearances are right. If you slap the engine together and only discover the mistake after the engine begins to eat itself, you will find no sympathy from the machine shop. If a clearance is wrong and you catch it, most machine shops will take the parts back and do the job right, especially if you approach them from the standpoint that you'd like them to re-measure and tell you if they get the same results. If they do, there will be no problem.

However, if you allow the mistake to get past you until after the engine fires, that's when all bets are off. The machine shop will, and rightfully so, inform you that you probably didn't assemble the engine correctly, and that's why the pistons scuffed or the bearings were wiped out. The whole effort of double-checking your work and ensuring all the clearances are correct is

Always install the camshaft in the block after installing new cam bearings. Often a bearing will crush slightly small, which will prevent installation of the cam. It's better to discover this with a bare block rather than with the entire short block assembled.

How To Build Big-Inch Chevy Small-Blocks

Chapter 13

How to Degree a Cam

This is one procedure that every engine builder should know how to do. This ensures that the cam is actually where the engine builder thinks it is. If you are going to spend a lot of time choosing the right cam, you should spend a little more time to ensure it's installed properly.

There are only a few specialty tools that you need to degree a cam. You'll need a degree wheel, a piston stop, a pointer, and a dial indicator with a magnetic base. It's also good to have a specialty cam follower, but these aren't essential. The larger degree wheels offer more accuracy, but you can certainly accomplish the task with a standard size wheel. All the cam companies offer complete kits if you'd rather buy everything at once. To do this procedure, you'll need the crank and number 1 piston and rod assembly in place, along with the cam, cam drive gear, and timing chain installed. We'll assume the heads are not installed on the engine.

The first task is to establish the exact location of top dead center (TDC). This is the most important step in the process because if TDC is not accurate, all the rest of the effort will be in error. To do this, you need to mount the degree wheel on the end of the crank. There are several ways to do this. The quickest way is to merely bolt the degree wheel to the end of the crank, but you will need a separate way to turn the engine over that does not disturb the degree wheel. Tool companies like Powerhouse sell a large hex crank nut that fits over the crank snout. This allows you to turn the crank with the hex without disturbing the bolt that attaches the degree wheel to the crank. This hex also requires a very large wrench, usually one that is adjustable. A better approach is to use a professional-style degree-wheel mount unit that fits over the end of the

The easiest way to mount the degree wheel on the crank snout is with this professional-style hub that positions the wheel and allows easy movement of the crank with the 1/2-inch drive arrangement. You will also need an indicator — in this case, a simple length of coat hanger wire. This is one of Comp Cams' professional degree wheels. The larger the wheel, the more accurate it will be.

crank and is splined to the keyway. This piece also mounts the degree wheel with a large threaded opening that allows you to position the degree wheel and then lock it down. You turn the crank with this same device without disturbing the relative position of the degree wheel. This professional tool requires a larger hole in the degree wheel that not all wheels have, so be sure to match them up.

Turn the engine over until the number-1 piston is at TDC. Now bolt the degree wheel in place. We usually make a pointer out of a length of coat hanger wire and bolt it to the block. Move the degree wheel to indicate TDC on the indicator. This is just an estimate. Now turn the engine counterclockwise roughly 45 degrees and bolt on a piston stop on the top of the number 1 cylinder. With the stop in place, slowly turn the engine clockwise until the piston contacts the stop. Record the number indicated on the degree wheel. Now turn the engine counterclockwise all the way around until the piston again hits the stop. Record that number and then compare the two. The numbers will be on either side of TDC.

This specialty tool mounts the dial indicator on one end and offers either a flat or roller tipped end on the other for checking both types of cams. This is a fast and easy way to set up the dial indicator.

Building and Blueprinting

The time-tested way to set up a dial indicator to check lobe lift is to use an old lifter along with a magnetic base that mounts the dial indicator. Be sure to locate the dial indicator on a flat portion of the lifter. Do not use the pushrod cup.

There are several commercially available piston stops that can be used to mount over the top of the number-1 bore. Or you can just make your own.

If you are degreeing the engine with the heads on, an old spark plug with a bolt through it or one of these specialty piston stops work well. Be aware that some heads, like AFR castings, point the spark plug uphill so that a spark plug style piston stop cannot be used.

When the degree wheel indicates true TDC, both numbers will be the same. Let's say you recorded 20 degrees after top dead center (ATDC) and 24 degrees before top dead center (BTDC). This means the degree wheel is not at true TDC. The wheel needs to be moved two degrees closer to the ATDC position (half the difference). In this case, you would move the degree wheel to indicate 22 degrees on both sides of TDC and then you'd be set. Always recheck your work by moving the degree wheel back the other way to ensure that both sides indicate the same number on the wheel. Since this is the most important step in the entire process, double-check your work before moving to the next step. Once you've established TDC, do not move the degree wheel or the indicator. If you do, you'll have to go back and redo the TDC step to ensure accuracy.

Now we can place a lifter in the second lifter bore back from the front, which is the intake lobe for the number-1 cylinder on a small-block Chevy. You must use the same style lifter as the cam. Do not use a roller-style lifter on a flat-tappet cam or vise versa. The tool companies sell a specific lifter/follower tool that fits in the lifter bore and connects to a dial indicator. If you don't have one of these tools, you can just as easily use an existing lifter and place the dial indicator on the body of the lifter. For flat-tappet cams, we often use an old hydraulic lifter with the pushrod cup glued in upside down, using the oil hole in the middle of the flat portion of the inverted cup to locate the dial indicator rod. Do not use the lifter's radiused pushrod cup since the dial indicator rod will move around inside the radius of the cup and produce false readings.

Position the dial indicator so that it is parallel to lifter travel. Also make sure the lifter travels easily over the lobe and in the lifter bore. A sticky lifter will fool you if you're not paying attention. Test your setup by rotating the engine several times, watching to see that the dial indicator returns to zero each time. If not, make sure the dial indicator is not limiting lifter travel or that the lifter is not sticking.

Once the system works smoothly, rotate the engine slowly watching the dial indicator until you see 0.050-inch tappet lift. Compare the number on the cam timing card with your reading. If the lifter is opening too soon, the cam is advanced. If the opening point occurs later than the specified point, the cam is retarded. Since intake closing is the most important of the four points, it's best to check the cam at the 0.050-inch intake closing point. If your readings are within one degree, it's probably not worth trying to move the cam. If the measured numbers are two degrees or more, you should certainly move the cam. Always double-check your information, especially after moving the cam. Just like in carpentry, measure twice and cut once.

How to Degree a Cam *Continued*

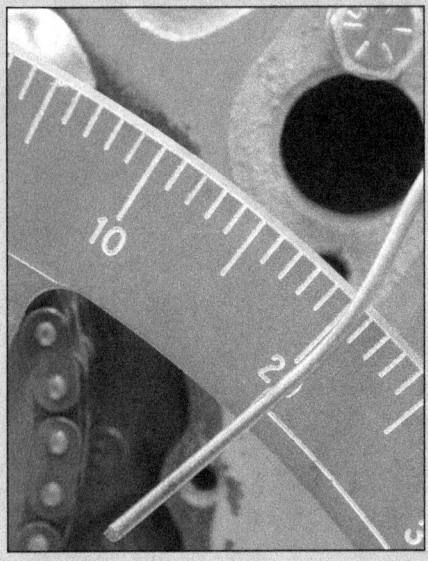

You will have an accurate TDC mark when the degree wheel reads the same number of degrees on either side of the piston stop. In this case, it's 20 degrees on either side of TDC.

If the cam needs to be moved, the easiest way is to pull the crank gear and reposition it on the crank keyway. Take care to compare the mark on the keyway with the same mark on one of the gear teeth. After repositioning the cam, always recheck your work.

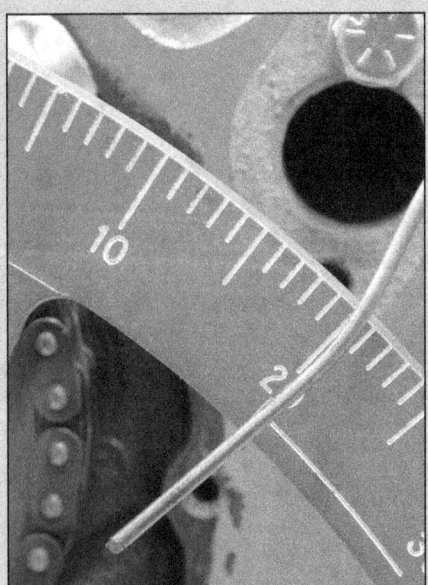

If your cam card gives opening and closing points at 0.050-inch tappet lift, it's a simple matter to crank the engine until the dial indicator reads 0.050-inch off the seat (either opening or closing) and then read the degree wheel.

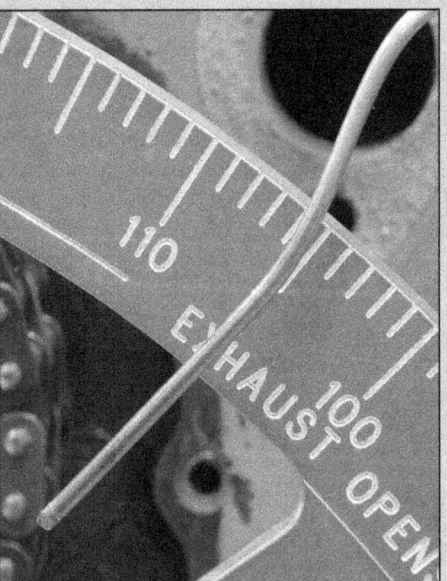

Comp Cams' timing cards don't give you opening and closing points at 0.050-inch tappet lift. Instead, Comp prefers you check the intake centerline. In this case, the intake centerline is within a half-degree of the 106-degree spec.

Some cam companies, like Comp Cams, indicate cam position with intake centerline and only give you opening and closing points at the 0.006-inch checking height. This is subject to significant error, so it's best to use the intake centerline method. Rotate the crank until you find maximum lobe lift. Zero your dial indicator and rotate the crank counterclockwise about 120 degrees before max lift. Now rotate the engine clockwise and sneak up to the 0.050-inch number before max lift and record the degree-wheel number. This may be something like 90 degrees ATDC. Now continue to rotate the engine in the clockwise direction until you achieve 0.050-inch after max lift. This will be a number like 130 degrees ATDC. Add the degree wheel numbers together and divide by two (90 + 130 = 220/2 = 110 degrees). This is the intake centerline.

Once you have established where the camshaft is in relationship to the crank, you can then decide if you wish to change its position. Keep in mind that most cam manufacturers grind their cranks with a few degrees of advance built into the cam. For example, a true straight-up cam with a 110-degree lobe separation angle will also have an intake centerline of 110 degrees. However, many cam companies dial in some advance. In the case of almost all of Comp Cams' street cams, their 110-degree lobe separation angle is followed up with a 106-degree intake centerline. In essence, the cam grinder dialed in 4 degrees of advance. Adding additional advance to this combination is probably not a good idea. At that point, you might be better off to choose a smaller cam that will close the intake valve sooner.

Building and Blueprinting

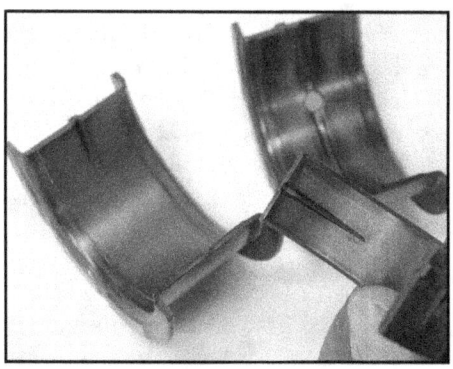

Federal-Mogul has a new 3/4-groove main bearing that extends the oil groove from the upper bearing half into the non-load-bearing portion of the lower bearing half to improve lube to the loaded portion of the bearing.

Crankshaft end play is another critical clearance that entry-level engine builders often miss. The trick is to hand-tighten the main cap bolts on the number 5 main cap, then solidly smack the crank on the nose with a plastic or rubber hammer and then on the flywheel end of the crank. This aligns the pair of thrust bearings, creating a more accurate thrust clearance.

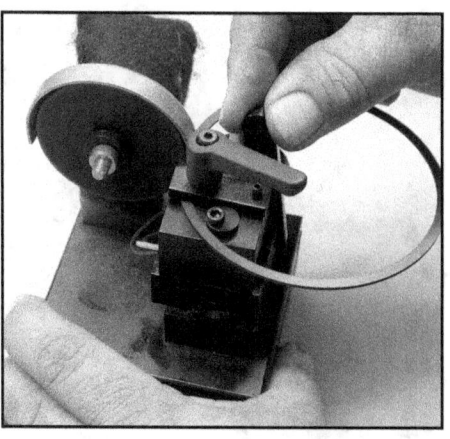

If you plan on building multiple performance engines, there are several companies that offer electric ring grinders that can perform this task very quickly.

Always test-fit the crank, rod, and piston combination in the block, especially if this is a stroker application. This is also a great time to ensure adequate rod-to-camshaft clearance.

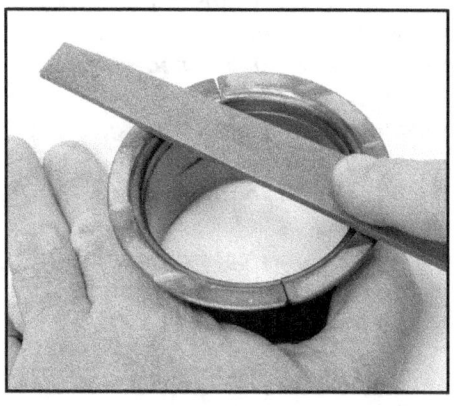

If the thrust clearance is too tight, you may have to lightly file the thrust bearing and then smooth it with 1000-grit wet/dry sandpaper to obtain your clearance.

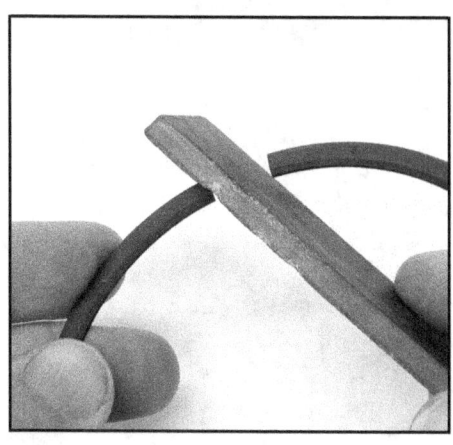

Always chamfer the end of the rings to eliminate any burrs that may remain after ring grinding. Use a whetstone on all four corners. On the cylinder-wall face, always work inward to prevent chipping the moly face.

designed to protect you as well as the engine. We've spent some time on this because failed engines just past startup are a common problem. Sometimes it is the result of a failed component. Much more often, however, an engine that eats the bearings just after break-in either wasn't machined correctly, was poorly assembled, or both. Either way, it's the engine builder's responsibility, and either way, any failure is guaranteed to cost you grief, time, and money.

This may begin to sound like a walk through the Engine Builder's 10 Commandments, but next in line is the simple concept of cleanliness. The days of building an engine on a dirt floor or rolling the engine around on a wooden bench while you assemble it are long gone. Today, if you don't have the rudimentary tools like a clean place to assemble the engine, an engine stand, and most of the specialty tools, then you're better off paying someone else to do it for you. Engine assembly work is not difficult, but it does require a regiment that includes several layers of cleaning before the engine is finally ready for assembly.

The good news is that cleaning doesn't require a ton of expensive tools, but you will need plenty of hot soapy water and a collection of engine brushes that will allow you to access the entire length of the main oil galleys, as well as all those tiny machine crevices where dirt, sand, and metal shavings like to live. This job may in fact involve several shots at cleaning. The block needs to be machined and hot tanked or cooked before you start the pre-assembly

How To Build Big-Inch Chevy Small-Blocks

Chapter 13

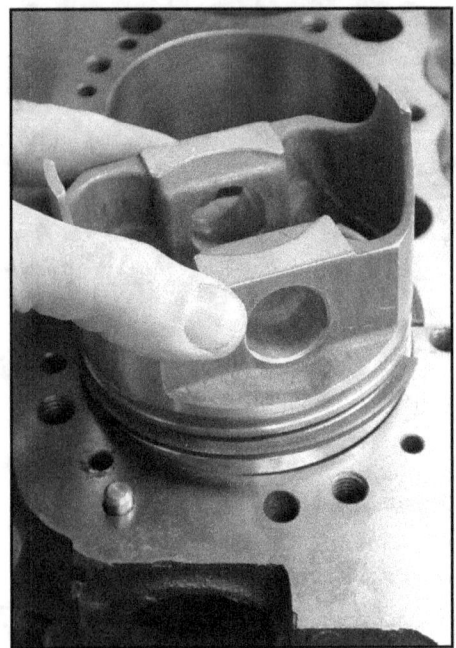

You can buy an aftermarket ring-squaring tool, but an old piston with an old ring installed in the second ring land works just as well.

The best way to check piston deck height is to place the dial indicator in line with the wrist pin. You may still encounter piston rock that will vary the clearance. Rock the piston in the bore and record both readings, then average the two for the clearance.

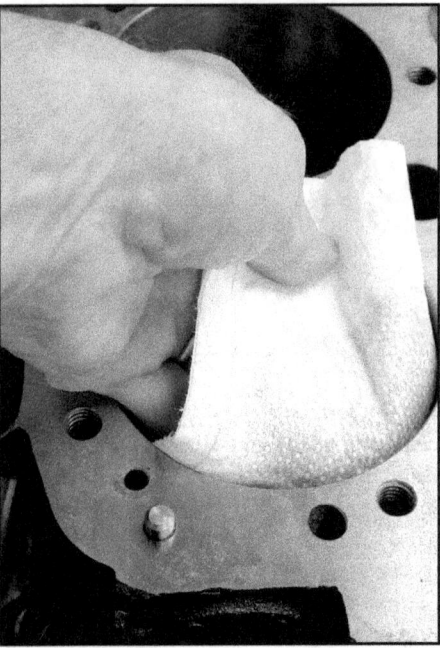

Total Seal recommends using alcohol or some kind of serious petroleum-based cleaner like non-chlorinated Brake Klean to obtain the cleanest cylinder walls possible before assembling the engine. Total Seal does not recommend using automatic transmission fluid as a cleaner since they claim it leaves a residue that may prevent the rings from seating fully. Marvel Mystery oil will work since it does not leave a residue.

process, and then you will need to thoroughly clean the block at least once more before the engine is finally assembled. The minimum equipment needed will be hot soapy water, brushes, and an air compressor with a blow nozzle.

Measuring Tools

Besides the knowledge to do the job correctly, it is impossible to assemble an engine without the right tools. This will involve not only the specialty tools used to assemble this cast iron and aluminum puzzle, but also several invaluable specialty measurement tools. We'll spend a few paragraphs on these instruments because they are so important to doing the job correctly. As dangerous as it may be, we're going to assume that you are serious about building engines and intend on assembling several, if not dozens over a long period of time. This means you will need the best equipment. We'll stick with measurement and assembly tools and leave the machine tools for some other time.

Micrometers should be one of your first purchases on the way to becoming a famous engine builder. The best plan, and generally the least expensive one in the end, is to purchase an entire set of micrometers rather than individual units, since you can then get the very handy wooden box that will protect them while they spend time in your tool box. There are several companies that make high-quality tools, and you can expect to pay anywhere from $700 to $1000 for a complete set of five mics. Also, look for micrometers that are accurate down to 0.0001-inch. You will need this kind of accuracy to set bearing clearances. There are two styles of mics. The classic outside mic measures the outside diameters, like a rod or main journal. There are also inside mics that measure, as you might have guessed by now, the inside diameters of bores, like a main or rod bearing.

Inside mics can be somewhat slow and cumbersome to use, which leads us to dial bore gauges. These handy tools combine a dial indicator with a long handle and a three-point foot at the other end. The foot uses an adjustable pointer that can measure between 2 and 6-inch inside diameters. After selecting the proper diameter foot extension, zeroing the dial bore gauge requires a micrometer. Set a micrometer to the diameter you wish to measure. Zero the dial bore gauge to that diameter and then merely slip the foot of the tool in the bore you wish to measure. This tool can also be used to measure bore taper and out-of-round. This tool is most generally used for rod and main bores and cylinder bores.

Snap gauges can also be used to measure the inside dimensions of many components that may not work with a dial bore gauge. For example, we used several sizes of snap gauges to measure the cross-sectional areas of the heads listed in this book. Since this was not an ultra-critical dimension, we measured the length of the snap gauges with a dial caliper rather than with a micrometer.

Building and Blueprinting

ARP sells thread-chasing taps that clean head-bolt holes but do not remove material from the threads. This allows maximum thread overlap for head bolts or studs. This will prevent pulling threads, especially from used production blocks.

If you really want to blueprint a set of heads, ensure that all the intake and exhaust valves are installed at the same height. This is a bit more difficult than it sounds. You may want to have your local machine shop help with this.

Blueprinting Specs

Any chart listing engine clearances or specs attempting to cover the diverse world of high-performance small-block Chevys is a dangerous prospect. As a result, this chart must be accompanied with an equally appropriate disclaimer. Please don't just blindly accept each of these specs without due consideration of how your engine will be used. This chart is intended strictly for large displacement small-block Chevy engines that operate on pump gasoline, use steel connecting rods, and spend all of their time below 7,000 rpm. Some may scoff at some of these specs as being conservative or excessive, but these are safe numbers that will certainly not get you into trouble. But the line that any good disclaimer hangs on is — enter at your own risk.

Component	Clearance (in inches)
Main bearing	0.0022 - 0.0028
Rod bearing	0.0022 - 0.0026
Connecting rod side	0.010-0.015
Connecting rod bolt stretch	See manufacturer spec
Crankshaft end play	0.005-0.008
Crankshaft to block	0.050
Connecting rod to camshaft	0.060
Oil pump pickup to oil pan	1/4 to 3/8
Piston to bore	Piston specific — see manufacturer spec
Top ring end gap	Piston specific — see manufacturer spec
Second ring end gap	Piston specific — see manufacturer spec
Top and second ring vertical gap	0.001-0.002
Piston-to-head	0.037 min. (more for wider piston-to-wall clearance)
Roller lifter to bore	0.0012 - 0.0015
Roller camshaft end play	0.005-0.010
Piston to valve, Intake	0.070-0.080
Piston to valve, Exhaust	0.100-0.110
Retainer to seal	0.050
Valvespring coil bind	0.060
Rocker arm to retainer	0.050

You may think that you could substitute a snap gauge for a dial bore gauge to measure inside diameters and that will work in some cases. But for bearing clearances, these tools are generally not accurate enough to do the job. Of course, a dial caliper is useful for so many things, that it might well be your first purchase just because you'll use it almost every day.

A good engine builder will own several dial indicators, usually with each one assigned to a specific task. For example, he may have one set up on a magnetic base that can be used to measure valve lift and help with degreeing cams and checking crank and cam end play. He will no doubt have one set up on a deck bridge to quickly establish both piston TDC as well as deck height.

He might have a third, small-diameter dial indicator set up for checking bellhousing alignment to crank centerline. As you can see, there are several uses for a dial indicator and a magnetic base that are essential to engine building.

In order to degree a cam, the minimum tools needed are a dial indicator, some type of mount for the indicator, a degree wheel, some type of mount for

Chapter 13

Tapered ring compressors are the best way to slide the pistons and rings into the bores. One downside to this is that each bore size requires its own ring compressor.

It's also a good idea to double-check that your timing indicator is actually at TDC. With the damper and indicator installed, use a piston stop, turn the engine over in both directions until it hits the stop, and mark the damper. The two marks should be equal distance from the TDC mark on the damper.

Always carefully clean new roller lifters when they come from the factory. These lifters are shipped in packing grease that must be fully removed. Then immerse the lifters totally in 30w engine oil for at least 30 minutes before using.

When using a roller cam in an early block, you must also limit camshaft end play. The best choice is a rollerized cam button that prevents wear. Also, make sure that the timing cover doesn't deflect. A cast aluminum cover might be a better choice here.

the degree wheel, a piston stop (usually two different ones — one to be used with the cylinder head on, and one for when the is head off), and a simple pointer that can be made out of a bolt and a length of coat hanger wire. One point worth making here is that the larger the degree wheel, the more accurate your results. A quick test of the accuracy of your degree wheel is to lay it on a large piece of cardboard and mark the paper with the four 90-degree points on the wheel. Then rotate the wheel and see if all four points still agree. For example, rotate the wheel 23 degrees and then do the math to see if each of our four scribed marks still line up 23 degrees from 90. Smaller degree wheels offer less distance between each degree, creating a greater opportunity for error. The large diameter pro wheels offered by Powerhouse or Comp Cams are expensive, but much more accurate.

The other part of this effort is a seemingly simple one, but one that can easily be overlooked. Do the right thing and buy a wheel that works with one of the professional-style wheel mounts. This mount slides over the crank snout which means you'll have to buy both a small and big-block mount, if you're building engines with rat snout cranks. This mount is then secured with a locking Allen bolt to the snout. On the front is a large, threaded, male stud that mounts the degree wheel and is locked

Computing Piston Volume

There are times when you will use a piston that has been modified. This will have changed the volume that the piston displaces. In order to compute an accurate compression ratio, you will need to know exactly how much volume the piston displaces. There is an easy way to determine this. All you need is a 6x6-inch square piece of 1/4-inch thick clear plastic with a 1/4-inch counter bored hole and a 100cc or larger graduated burette. Place the piston 1/2-inch down in the bore with white grease around the edge to seal the piston to the bore. Then place a flat piece of clear plastic with the hole over the bore. Tilt the block and position the plate so that the fill hole is near the top of the cylinder where all the air will be displaced. Fill the cylinder with liquid (denatured alcohol with food coloring works well) and write down the volume of liquid in cc's required to fill the cylinder. What you have measured is the volume of your irregular-shaped cylinder.

Now will need paper, a pencil, and a simple calculator. In order to know how much volume your piston actually displaces, you need to compare your measured volume to that of a perfect cylinder with the same diameter and depth but with a flat floor and roof. If you remember from Chapter 6, the volume of a pure cylinder is: Bore x Bore x Stroke x 0.7854, which will produce displacement in cubic inches. Remember also from Chapter 6 we mentioned that you can convert cubic-inches (ci) to cubic-centimeters (cc) by multiplying by 16.41. Let's run through an example.

Let's say we've modified a dished piston for more valve-to-piston clearance on our 4.155-inch bore small block and we've measured the volume of the cylinder with a piston 1/2-inch down the bore at 133cc's. Computing the volume of a pure cylinder with a bore of 4.155-inches and a stroke of 0.500-inch (4.155 x 4.155 x 0.500 x 0.7854), we come up with 6.78ci. Now we multiply 6.78 x 16.41 to get 111.25 cubic centimeters. Now when we compare our measured volume of 133cc's to the calculated volume of 111cc's, we see a difference of 22cc's. This is the volume of the piston dish. Had we been measuring a slightly domed piston, the measured volume would have been less than the calculated volume. Either way, this is an easy way to determine piston head volume so that you can accurately calculate true static compression ratio.

If you really want to get serious about accuracy, the only problem with this effort is that it ignores the crevice volume or the area between the top ring and the top of the piston. Measuring the piston volume as described above usually fills this crevice area with white grease to seal the piston. Since measuring this volume would be difficult, let's calculate it instead. As an example, let's say we have a 4.155-inch bore and a piston with a ring land height of 0.250-inch. We also need to know the outside diameter of the piston at the top of the ring land. Typically, this will be around 0.050-inch smaller than the bore diameter, which makes the piston diameter 4.105 inches.

To compute this volume, we'll refer again to our favorite volume formula: bore x bore x stroke x 0.7854 = volume of the cylinder. In this case, we're using the distance from the top of the ring land to the piston top as our stroke. We'll skip the math and tell you that the volume difference in this case is 0.07ci. Since we deal with cubic centimeters with compression ratio calculations, multiply this by 16.41 and we come up with a massive figure of a crevice volume of 1.15cc's that we will add to the above 22cc dish volume. Now our compression ratio calculation is as accurate as we can make it.

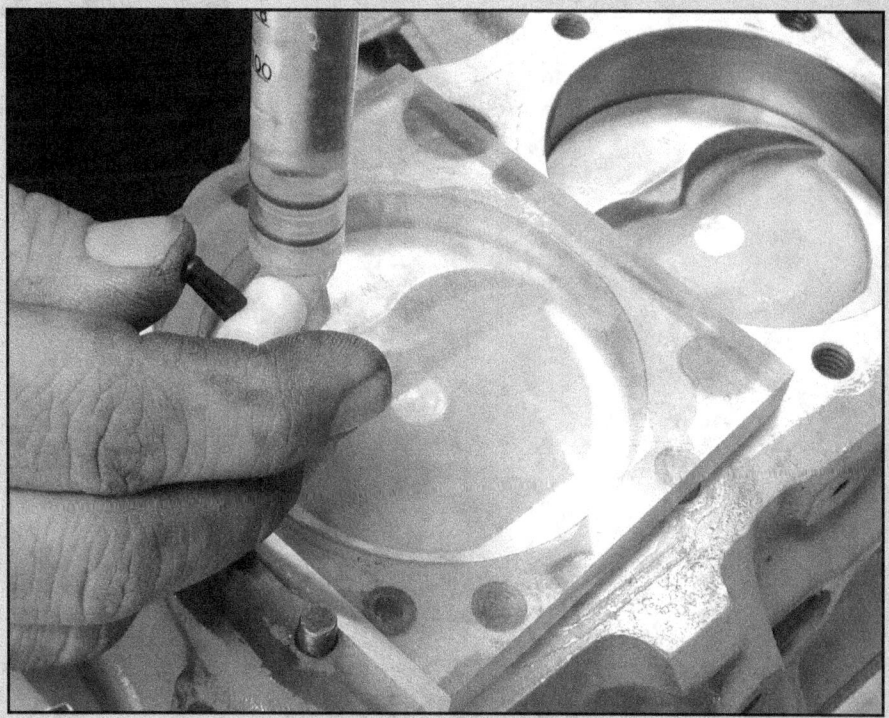

Measuring true piston volume will give you a very accurate volume number to use when calculating static compression ratio.

Chapter 13

Mains and Rods

As popular as the small-block Chevy is, you have to really look to find the specs you need when it comes to specific housing bore diameters like rod and main bores. Remember it is the inside diameter of a main bore or big end of a connecting rod that is one of the major contributors to the inside diameter of a rod or main bearing. In order to determine the proper housing bore diameter, it helps to have the specs. We've assembled this sometimes difficult to find specs for you here to use as reference. The specs listed below are the inside diameters of the main and the big end of the connecting rod without the bearings. All figures are in inches.

	Main Bearing Housing Bore	Crankshaft Main Journal Diameter
Small Journal	2.49100	2.2985
Medium Journal	2.64105	2.4485
Large Journal	2.84110	2.6500

	Connecting Rod Housing Bore	Crankshaft Rod Journal Diameter
Small Journal	2.1250	2.0000
Large Journal	2.2250	2.4485

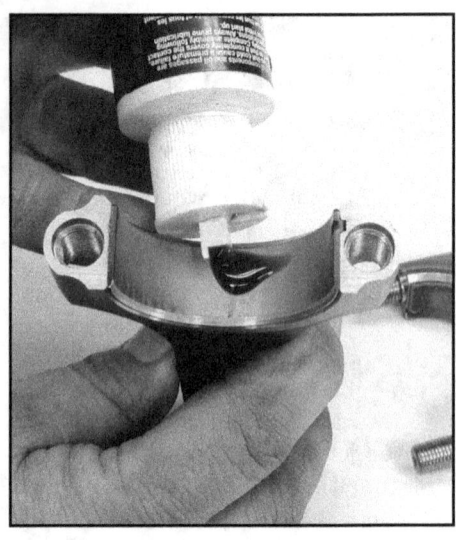

Most engine builders we spoke to prefer to use either the thick red or green assembly lube on bearings and lifter sides to ensure the lube does not drip off before the engine is fired. This is the Federal-Mogul lube that is green.

Do not use moly lube on pushrod ends at the lifter or the rocker arm. Use the heavy green lube instead, since the moly paste can plug the pushrod hole and prevent oil from getting to the rocker arm.

in place with a large knurled nut. In the center of this mount is a 1/2-inch square drive for a ratchet or breaker bar that will turn the crank without disturbing the position of the degree wheel. This mount design requires a large hole in the degree wheel and not all degree wheels use this larger hole.

If you already have a degree wheel with the smaller mounting hole, you can purchase a crank nut that slips over the crank snout. Then the degree wheel can be bolted directly to the snout, using the crank nut to turn the engine over. This also requires a very large wrench (we use a large, adjustable wrench). You may be tempted to turn the engine with the crank bolt that also mounts the degree wheel. This won't work because the risk is that you will move the degree wheel after setting TDC, which will add an error into all your subsequent measurements. There are also times when you must turn the engine backwards, which will loosen the bolt, move the degree wheel, and then you will have to start all over. Trust us on this one; it's not worth the hassle.

You will also need some kind of graduated cylinder for testing combustion chamber volume. The most popular style is a graduated burette with a small

Building and Blueprinting

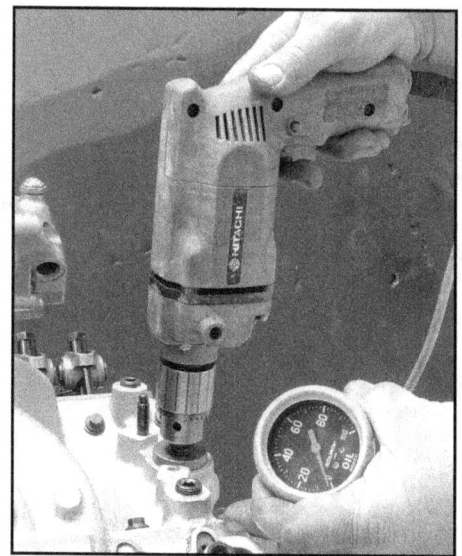

Pressure lubing the engine immediately before firing the engine is absolutely necessary and should never be overlooked. Make sure oil pushes out of each pushrod. This may require turning the engine over one or two revolutions.

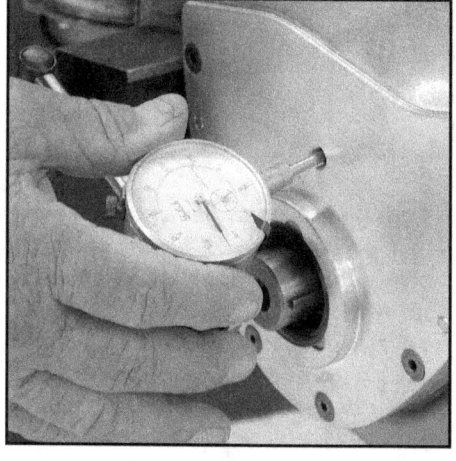

Most big-inch small blocks will employ a roller cam in an aftermarket block. One area you must not overlook is roller cam end play. Too much end play will allow the cam to move, retarding the ignition timing based on the angle cut of the gear teeth on the end of the cam.

Assembly Tools

Let's start with the simplest tool — those little plastic rubber boots that slip over the rod bolts to protect the crank. Never install a piston without these. They're simple, inexpensive, and necessary. Next is another ingeniously simple tool, the tapered ring compressor. This device forever eliminates the hassle of broken rings when installing pistons in the bore. Yes, you do have to buy a separate compressor for each bore diameter, but these simple tools are worth the money in eliminated aggravation.

Staying with pistons for a moment, you will also need some kind of ring filer to set ring end gaps. The simple hand-cranked models work fine and are inexpensive, but they are also slow. There are electric models now that are much faster and you might want to consider the investment in time. A rod vise is another useful tool that we can't imagine doing engine assembly without. It allows you to torque without worrying about twisting the rod and the vise is also an excellent tool for removing stubborn rod caps.

A deck bridge is a simple device that mounts a dial indicator to quickly determine piston-to-deck clearance. This is much easier than using a magnetic base and an indicator. Some of the better bridges also come with magnetic feet to hold the bridge in place. Another useful tool is a cam handle. Yes, you can use a length of 5/16-inch threaded rod, but the cam handles are just so much easier to use.

Finally, you will also need a dampener puller and installer. These tools can be purchased separately as a puller and installer and work well. The latest tool is a heavy-duty universal combination tool that uses Torrington bearings that use the same tool to pull and install the damper. As we said, many of these tools are more money than you care to spend, but once you use them, you'll realize their value and, if you're not too ham-fisted, they will deliver a lifetime of humble service.

We've also included a multitude of photos that deal with specific tasks, blueprinting operations, and ideas that

valve at the bottom mounted on a metal stand. The original ones were made of glass and very fragile. We bought our first one from a chemistry supply house. But now you can purchase plastic versions that are more durable from several companies like Powerhouse. This tool is also useful for measuring piston volume.

The best place to find more information on engine assembly is Rick Voegelin's book, **The Step-by-Step Guide to Engine Blueprinting.** *This S-A Design book offers 130 pages of inside information on modifying and assembling engines and using precision tools.*

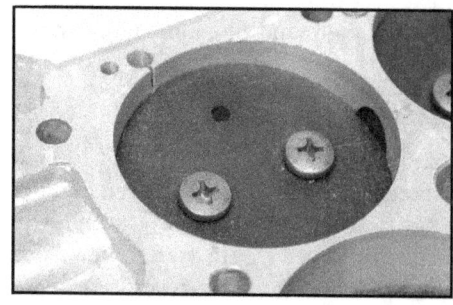

For engines with larger camshafts, it may be necessary to drill small holes in the primary throttle blades to help idealize the position of the throttle blades at idle. The holes allow the tuner to place the throttle blades with transition slot just barely open.

might help you with assembling that street-nasty small block. But the most important tool is the one between your ears, using your head and paying attention to what the engine is telling you. If you work slowly and dedicate your full attention to assembling that engine, it will reward you with outstanding power and reliability. The best part is you'll have the satisfaction of telling your friends — "I built the engine."

Chapter 14

Power Packages

Now comes the fun part. You sweated over selecting the parts, built the rotating assembly, and bolted the heads and intake in place. Now you get to fire that jewel and see what kind of power it makes. Most enthusiasts never test their engines until it's in the car. But since we can't plug each reader behind the wheel of a 10-second street car, the next best thing we can do is at least test some engines and put some numbers on paper that will illustrate the kind of power we're talking about.

This chapter will deliver a broad range of different engines from a mild street 383 and 406 to hard-core, thumper engines that run on race gas and will probably never see the street. We've also rated these engines in terms of horsepower-per-cubic-inch and torque-per-cubic-inch, but these numbers can be deceiving. Generally speaking, as displacement increases, engine efficiency in terms of power per cubic-inch decreases, since internal friction, especially for long stroke engines, has a tendency to cost horsepower. The advantage is that the added displacement still manages to make serous horsepower.

There are a couple engines in this chapter that are serious, high-RPM engines. It may be tempting to move in that direction because of the impressive horsepower that these engines make. As we mentioned in Chapter 2, this siren song of horsepower can be misleading. The reality check that should accompany these numbers are items like how the engine you plan to build will be used. If

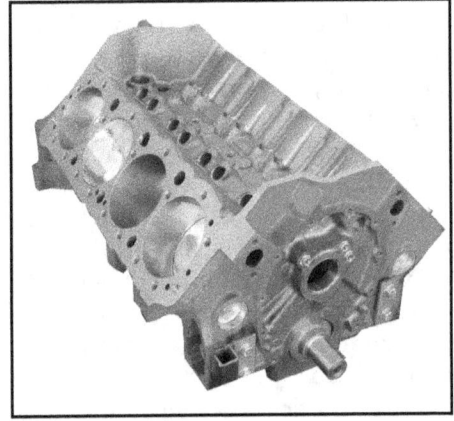

If you choose not to build your own short block, there are literally dozens of engine companies that can. Just add your own heads, cam, intake, and exhaust to complete the engine. This is a World Products 427ci short block that is more than capable of over 500 lb-ft of torque and 500 hp with the right breathing apparatus.

If your goal is great horsepower with a 415ci or larger small-block, a single-plane intake is probably a good idea. This will sacrifice a small amount of torque in favor of a excellent balance between torque and horsepower. This particular intake is Edelbrock's Super Victor 2925.

you just want to run with your pals and impress the drive-in crowd, then a high-torque engine will deliver on the fun factor without costing big dollars down the road in terms of maintenance.

The high-horsepower engines require race gas to keep the engine out of detonation and usually also demand serious valvespring pressure necessary to control the mechanical roller camshaft at high RPM. While you can certainly run these engines on the street, a few thousand miles will also abuse those springs, eventually leading to valvespring breakage, roller-lifter wear, bent pushrods, and an overall abuse of

the valvetrain. If you went further by opting for a set of 0.043-inch gas-ported rings, you can expect to have them live about 2,500 miles before cylinder leakage past the rings becomes a big problem. Frankly, we don't see the fun in replacing rings every 3,000 miles, unless you like spending your weekends swapping engines and replacing rings. Leave that to the Top Fuel guys.

Favorites

If we had to choose a few favorites out of this bunch of engines, there are three that deserve a little additional cov-

Power Packages

Unless your goal is a very mild street small block, roller rockers are an excellent idea. These rockers generally offer a better rocker ratio along with greater durability. These stainless steel Comp Cams roller rockers are also rebuildable.

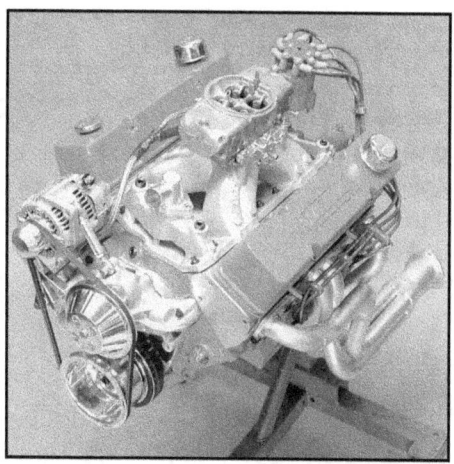

The cool thing about a big-inch small block is that you can build a seemingly tame looking engine with cast aluminum intake, a single four-barrel carburetor, and typical production headers and make over 600 hp and 550 lb-ft of torque. Those are low 11-second quarter-mile numbers for a 3400-pound street car.

Don't assume that just because you've bought all the right parts, that you won't need to tune your combination. Jet changes, timing changes, and experimenting with rocker ratios and lash (if you have a mechanical camshaft) can fine-tune your combination and pick up significant power.

If you get a chance to look at your engine after a few runs on the dyno, you can learn much about what's going on inside the combustion space by looking at the burn pattern on the top of the piston and in the chamber. This particular engine seems to be experiencing some difficulty with the burn, since the top of the pistons appear dark and oily. There appears to be fuel and air separation occurring here, which indicates that the engine requires more fuel to make decent power. This engine also exhibited rather high BSFC numbers.

erage. We'll take them in ascending order with the mildest first — the very streetable 406 in Test 1. This engine would be a ton of fun in a first or second generation Camaro, Chevelle, or even a pickup. With 470 ft-lb of torque at 2,400 rpm, there's only one engine in this assemblage that makes more torque and that's the much larger 454ci small-block. For its size, this engine makes amazing torque, which is what pushes you firmly back in the seat when you jump on the throttle. This engine has excellent throttle characteristics due to its relatively short cam, dual-plane intake, and reasonably-sized carburetor. Because of its strong torque, you would not need to put a deep gear behind this engine. In fact, anything deeper than a 3.73 gear would probably slow the car down in the quarter mile. This is one of those engines where you allow the torque to do the work for you.

The second engine has to be Test 4's 383. This is a understated compromise between horsepower and torque with an excellent set of heads and a decently sized camshaft. Peak horsepower is under 6,000 rpm, which makes things easier on the valvetrain, while peak toque is 506 ft-lb at a slightly elevated 4,900 rpm. This is due to the short-runner Super Victor intake manifold that pushes the torque peak up. With a dual-plane intake, this engine would lose some peak horsepower but gain torque that would help accelerate a medium-weight street machine somewhat quicker because of the torque increase, even with the reduced horsepower. This is a difficult concept for many street machiners to grasp since horsepower has been the gospel for so long. There's sufficient power in this small block to push a 3,500-pound street car with good traction well into the 11s. The beauty is that this engine could perform that kind of service all day long with relatively no maintenance, using pump gas. Pretty impressive for a "small" mouse motor!

Our third selection has to be the biggest engine in the bunch, the World Products 454ci mega-mouse. What's not to love about this engine? It makes as astounding 610 hp at 6,400 rpm with a massive 584 ft-lb of torque at a reasonable 4,500 rpm. The test only started at 4,000 rpm and it's cranking 559 ft-lb even at this low RPM. This engine is probably capable of 500 ft-lb even at under 3,000 rpm, which is awesome torque. But then, it should be for a 454ci engine! The interesting thing with this engine is the amazing power it makes with some relatively small 220cc heads. This pumps the velocity way up with these heads and must be the reason for its incredible power. There are few 454ci rat motors that we've seen that come anywhere close to this kind of power, even with oval port heads. What this points to is the concept that even 260cc oval port rat heads are too big for a 454ci rat motor and that with the right flow potential, it's possible to make better power with a rat motor with very small heads — a concept that is not very popular with most rat motor fans!

Chapter 14

Brake Specific

Included with each dyno chart is a third column with numbers designated BSFC. This stands for brake specific fuel consumption, a rating system used by engine tuners and builders to evaluate how well an engine converts fuel into power. The rating is expressed in pounds of fuel per horsepower per hour, or lbs/hp-hr. What this means is that while all engines convert fuel into power, some perform this task more efficiently than others. An engine will convert one pound of fuel into a given amount of horsepower in a given time period. The rating system assume that if engine ran for one hour, it would consume something like 120 pounds of fuel in that hour at one given speed, let's say 5,000 rpm. If you divide the observed horsepower by the number of pounds per hour of fuel consumed, you will create a fraction like 0.500. That means that roughly one-half pound of fuel is required for that engine to create one horsepower for one hour.

Let's create an example. During a dyno test, we are spinning a 415ci small-block Chevy. It is making an observed (not corrected) 523 hp at 5,800 rpm and our fuel flow meter reports that the engine is consuming 222.8 pounds of fuel per hour. To determine the BSFC number, we divide 222.8 by 523 observed hp to come up with a fraction of 0.426. This is the brake specific fuel consumption number for that engine at that RPM. In this particular case, the number is less than 0.500, which has, for many years, been an unofficial break point as a judge of engine efficiency. The important point to remember is that as the BSFC number gets smaller, the efficiency increases, because the engine is using less fuel to make the same power.

So what is a good number? As we mentioned, anything below 0.500 was once considered excellent, but as research has continued to improve the combustion process, the good BSFC number has continued to drop. It's not unusual now to see BSFC numbers in the low 0.420s. There are high 0.370 numbers in this chapter, and these numbers could be accurate. But the numbers could also be suspect based on incorrect measurement of the fuel flow. Fuel counters on many dynos are notoriously slow, which would contribute to low BSFC numbers. For a street engine, numbers in the low 0.400s would be considered excellent. Generally, the lowest BSFC number will occur around peak torque, since that is when the engine is operating at maximum volumetric efficiency. If the peak BSFC numbers fall outside peak torque, it indicates a potential problem either with the carburetor or some other component that is skewing the data.

This is an important point to discuss because the BSFC number has very little to do with just rich or lean jetting. It is possible to reduce the jetting of an engine to simultaneously improve power and reduce fuel flow. This will dramatically reduce the BSFC number. This could, and often does, create the mistaken impression that the BSFC number directly relates to carburetor jetting. The reality is that BSFC goes far deeper than just carb jetting. Remember, we are talking about how efficiently the engine converts fuel into power. So variables like compression ratio, cylinder pressure, combustion chamber shape, piston-to-head clearance, cylinder head material (iron vs. aluminum), camshaft valve timing, ignition timing, intake manifold air/fuel distribution, carburetor booster efficiency, intake port swirl and tumble flow characteristics, exhaust port efficiency, exhaust system back-pressure, and about a thousand other variables all contribute to the BSFC efficiency rating.

How serious is this number in terms of engine tuning? This little fraction tells a big story. This rating number is used on dyno testing for wide open throttle power generation, so for a drag racer, it's an interesting number that gives him a general indication of combustion efficiency, but it doesn't seriously impact the ultimate performance of his engine in competition, since the amount of fuel used on one pass down the drag strip is inconsequential. However, a NASCAR engine builder who is designing and building a restrictor plate engine for competition at Daytona or Talladega will be highly interested in the BSFC number. If he can find a way to increase power while simultaneously reducing fuel usage, he will have a race-winning engine on his hands, he'll probably get a raise, and his crew chief or owner might mention his name on national television.

The engineers at GM, for example, spend years developing engine packages at part throttle to improve the BSFC numbers at cruise engine speeds so that they can pull down decent fuel mileage. So as you can see, BSFC numbers are important numbers to watch when evaluating an engine's true performance. And now that you know what those numbers mean, you can amaze and astound your friends with your new-found technical knowledge.

Power Packages

This brings up an interesting question concerning the relative size of even small-block heads. If you look back at our first selection of the 406 that makes 525 ft-lb of torque, this is an engine with downright tiny intake ports of only 170ccs. Many might claim that these heads are way too small for decent power. That may be true, but what if you could increase airflow with a similar set of heads by really working on the bowl area and perhaps increasing valve size while working towards a smallest cross-sectional area only slightly larger than these stock Vortec heads. This would increase mixture velocity while keeping things strong enough in the flow department to deliver enough air to make respectable horsepower. This is an interesting concept that deserves more attention and more dyno testing. If a 454ci small-block can make 610 hp from a set of 220cc intake port heads along with outstanding torque, perhaps there is some paradigm shifts that need to occur with respect to smaller displacement small blocks as well. If nothing else, this should spark some rather interesting debate for the next engine-building bench racing session when someone says, "I'm thinking of building a small-block Chevy..."

One last point that is important to note is that the following combinations are proven to make the power as indicated by the dyno curves. These power curves can be duplicated only if the entire engine package is duplicated. The crucial point here is that all the parts must be duplicated. Deviate from any component, even a carburetor, and the power will probably change. Substitute a different cylinder head, intake manifold, or camshaft, and we can guarantee that the power will not be the same. If you have significant experience in building engines, then you may decide to deviate from these combinations and perhaps even improve the power. But if this is your first foray into the world of small-block performance and much of the information presented in this book is new, then we'd suggest choosing a combination and duplicating it.

Having presented this, we should

Dyno testing an engine is an excellent way to know exactly how much power the engine makes, but it can be expensive. $500 a day is the going rate.

Build a 383 with a set of Vortec heads, a great hydraulic roller camshaft, and a decent induction system and you have a 450 hp package that will run strong for years without deflating your wallet.

also mention that these combinations are not the only ones that can make good power. One of the intriguing aspects of performance engine building is that there are dozens, if not hundreds, of ways to get where you want to go.

For each combination presented here, there are easily four or five others that could make similar or even more power. Just keep in mind that if you deviate from what we've presented here, that the power could very well be different.

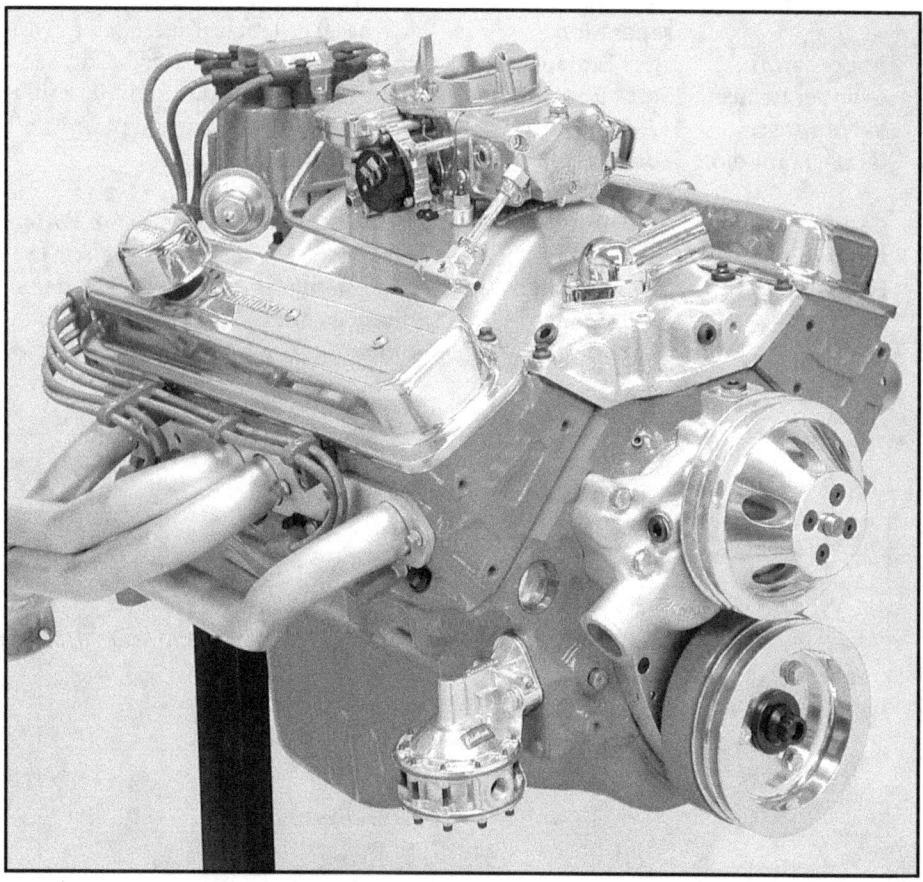

Shorty headers make installation easy, but they tend to lose mid-range torque and don't seem to increase peak horsepower. Longer-tube headers work better and are worth the effort, even if they are a pain to install.

Test 1: 406ci Torque Monster

Engine:	406ci, 4.155x3.75
Power:	427 hp @ 5,100, 1.05 hp/ci
	525 ft-lb @ 3,500, 1.3 ft-lb/ci
Compression:	9.5:1
Ignition timing:	35 degrees
Block:	Factory 400 iron
Crankshaft:	Scat cast iron
Rods:	Scat 4340 I-beam
Piston & rings:	Probe forged dished, Total Seal 1/16-inch
Oil Pan & pump:	Stock 4-quart & stock pump
Camshaft:	Lunati flat tappet hydraulic 230/230 @ 0.050, 0.455/0.455-inch, 114° lobe separation
Rocker arms:	1.5:1 Harlan Sharp
Cylinder heads:	Stock iron Vortec
Valve sizes:	1.94/1.50-inch
Intake manifold:	Edelbrock RPM Air Gap Vortec
Carburetor:	HP 750 cfm Holley
Ignition:	HEI
Headers:	1 5/8-inch Hedman w/ 2 1/2-inch exhaust

This small block was intended as a torque monster from the very beginning, which is why the builder chose the stock Vortec iron heads and the relatively short duration camshaft. This 406 makes an outstanding 525 ft-lb of toque with nothing more than a Performer RPM dual-plane intake and a 750 cfm carburetor. The price for an effort like this is a peak power that's less than what you could generate, but this is also one of the least expensive packages in this chapter. The engine offers an excellent 1,600 rpm power band between peak torque and peak horsepower with a shift point that's well under 6,000 rpm. You could run this engine with a 3.08 gear and give up very little due to the excellent torque. Later, you could add a set of better heads, sacrifice a little torque and probably pickup 40 or 50 hp at the peak.

The 406ci small-block with the Vortec heads looks almost stock, even on the dyno, thanks to its iron heads. But this motor is capable of 525 lb-ft of torque that will shove you back in the seat in a hurry.

Test Results

RPM	TQ	HP
2400	472	216
2500	477	227
2600	483	239
2700	488	251
2800	488	260
2900	490	271
3000	493	281
3100	502	297
3200	511	311
3300	516	324
3400	521	337
3500	525*	350
3600	525	360
3700	524	369
3800	521	377
3900	518	385
4000	515	392
4100	512	400
4200	508	406
4300	504	412
4400	499	418
4500	490	420
4600	480	421
4700	471	421
4800	464	424
4900	457	427
5000	449	427
5100	439	427*
5200	430	426
5300	419	423
5400	410	422
5500	405	421

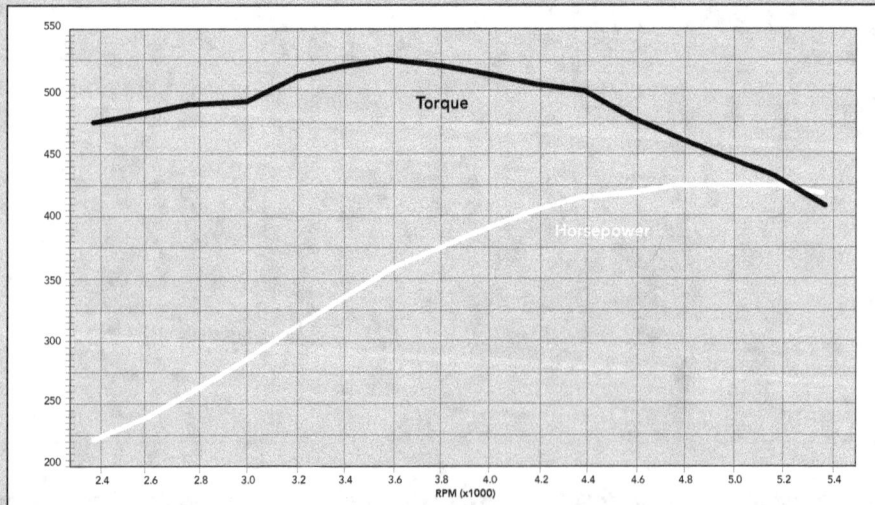

Power Packages

Test 2: 383ci Street Motor

This very streetable 383 small block is evidenced by its relatively mild peak torque point of 4,700 rpm and the fact that it's making over 430 ft-lb of torque at 3,000 rpm. This illustrates the engine's excellent torque and its potential throttle response based on the use of Edelbrock's Pro-Flo single-plane intake and EFI system control. Also note the solid brake specific numbers that dwell in the low 0.430's or lower including some low brake specific numbers around 4500 rpm. The 210cc AFR heads and a good hydraulic roller camshaft are probably the two key power determiners in this engine.

Engine:	383ci, 4.030 x 3.75
Power:	474 hp @ 5,400, 1.23 hp/ci
	486 ft-lb @ 4,600, 1.27 ft-lb/ci
Compression:	10:1 on 91-octane pump gas
Ignition timing:	35 degrees
Block:	Production 350 iron
Crankshaft:	Scat steel 3.75-inch stroke
Rods:	Scat 5.7-inch I-beam
Pistons & Rings:	Federal-Mogul forged, 1/16-inch rings
Oil pan & pump:	Melling standard pump, Milodon 5 qt.
Camshaft:	Comp Cams 280 High Energy hydraulic roller 236/243 duration @ 0.050, 0.552/0.552inch
Rocker arms:	Roller 1.5:1
Cylinder heads:	AFR 210cc heads
Valve sizes:	2.08/1.60-inch
Intake manifold:	Edelbrock Pro-Flo EFI single plane
Carburetor:	1000 cfm throttle body, 36-lb injectors
Ignition:	MSD-6A
Headers:	1 3/4-inch

Test Results

RPM	TQ	HP	BSFC
3000	437	250	0.428
3100	435	257	0.419
3200	436	265	0.414
3300	438	275	0.405
3400	442	286	0.399
3500	450	300	0.396
3600	451	309	0.393
3700	453	319	0.413
3800	453	328	0.414
3900	455	338	0.400
4000	457	348	0.397
4100	461	360	0.389
4200	464	371	0.380
4300	471	386	0.374
4400	481	403	0.374
4500	483	414	0.378
4600	484	424	0.394
4700	486*	435	0.424
4800	486	444	0.433
4900	482	450	0.441
5000	479	456	0.437
5100	476	462	0.436
5200	472	467	0.438
5300	466	470	0.449
5400	461	474*	0.456
5500	453	474	0.451
5600	438	467	0.462
5700	424	460	0.482

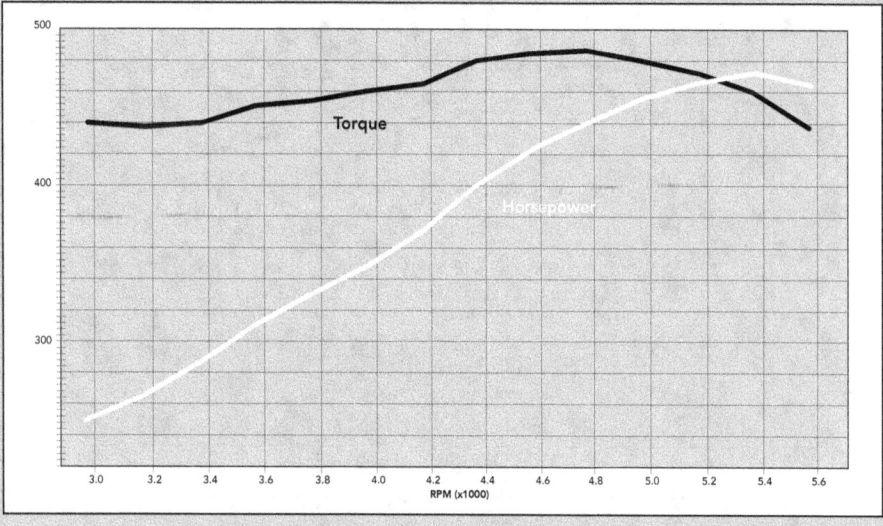

How To Build Big-Inch Chevy Small-Blocks

Test 3: 415ci Street/Strip

Engine:	415ci World Products, 4.125 x 3.875
Power:	482 @ 5,800, 1.16 hp/ci
	545 @ 3,800, 1.42 ft-lb/ci
Compression:	9.0:1
Ignition timing:	36 degrees
Block:	World Motown iron
Crankshaft:	4130 steel forged
Rods:	Manley 4340 H-beam, 6.0-inches
Pistons & Rings:	Forged JE/Weisco
Oil pan:	Milodon
Camshaft:	Crane, mech. flat, 244/252, 0.516/0.525, 106° lobe separation
Rocker arms:	Aluminum roller 1.5
Cylinder heads:	Iron Motown 220cc
Valve sizes:	2.08/1.60-inch
Intake manifold:	World Products dual plane
Carburetor:	870 cfm Bill Mitchell Holley
Ignition:	HEI distributor
Headers:	1 3/4-inch Hooker

This was one of the first World Products engine assemblies offered for sale and uses the Motown iron 220cc intake port heads, a dual-plane intake, and runs on pump gas. This is clearly more of a torque producer than a horsepower animal, since it makes 1.4 ft-lb/ci yet only 1.16 hp/ci. Still, almost 550 ft-lb of torque is amazing power from such a relatively small displacement. In fact, you have to get to 4900 rpm before this engine makes less than 500 ft-lb of torque. This motor's also impressive with a 2,000-RPM power band that's as wide as you'll find anywhere. There are many rat motors that would be envious of this power curve. Throw in 482 hp all below 6000 rpm and you have a thumpin' street engine that in a 3500-pound car would easily run 11s with decent traction.

Test Results

RPM	TQ	HP	BSFC
3000	515	294	.520
3100	523	309	.510
3200	528	322	.510
3300	531	334	.500
3400	535	346	.490
3500	537	358	.490
3600	539	370	.480
3700	542	382	.470
3800	545*	394	.480
3900	544	404	.480
4000	541	412	.450
4100	538	420	.450
4200	534	427	.450
4300	529	432	.440
4400	523	438	.440
4500	519	444	.440
4600	513	449	.430
4700	502	450	.426
4800	502	459	.424*
4900	496	482	.428
5000	484	481	.440
5100	487	453	.453
5200	467	463	.445
5300	486	470	.443
5400	480	473	.448
5500	458	478	.443
5600	452	481	.451
5700	443	481	.454
5800	436	482*	.451
5900	423	475	.452
6000	403	460	.450

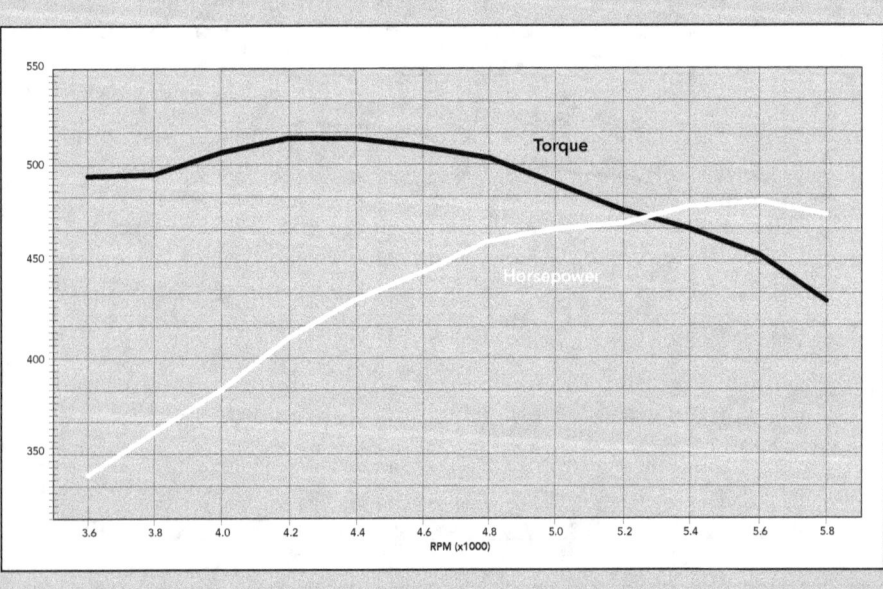

Test 4: 383ci Cruise Night Special

This is an outstanding street engine that again does not have to spin into the stratosphere to make good horsepower. Peak horsepower is achieved at 5,900 rpm, which means the shift point could be around 6,400 rpm, which does not overtly abuse the valvetrain. In addition to the great horsepower, this engine can also crank out 450 ft-lb at 3,000 rpm, which means this engine could accommodate a somewhat tall gear and still accelerate with alacrity. The 240 degrees at 0.050-inch valve lift duration camshaft will give it a definite lope at idle, but that will give this engine some serious authority at the local cruise-in with the muscle to back it up.

Engine:	383ci, 4.030 x 3.75
Power:	530 hp @ 5,900, 1.38hp/ci
	506 ft-lb at 4,900, 1.32 ft-lb/ci
Compression:	10.4:1
Ignition timing:	37 degrees
Block:	Dart Iron Eagle
Crankshaft:	Callies 4340 steel
Rods:	Manley I-beam, 6.0
Pistons & rings:	JE forged, Federal-Mogul
Oil pan & pump:	Moroso pump and pan
Camshaft:	Crane mechanical roller 240/248 @ 0.050, 0.543/0.561, 110° lobe separation
Rocker arms:	Crane Gold Race 1.5
Cylinder heads:	Dart Pro 1 CNC 215cc
Valve sizes:	2.05/1.60-inch
Intake manifold:	Edelbrock Super Victor
Carburetor:	Mighty Demon 750 cfm
Ignition:	MSD 6AL
Headers:	1 3/4-inch Hedman w/ 2 1/2-inch exhaust, Borla Pro XS

Test Results

RPM	TQ	HP
3000	450	257
3100	451	267
3200	454	277
3300	458	288
3400	457	296
3500	456	304
3600	454	311
3700	453	320
3800	455	329
3900	452	336
4000	449	342
4100	450	351
4200	453	363
4300	463	379
4400	475	398
4500	490	420
4600	499	437
4700	502	449
4800	504	461
4900	506*	472
5000	502	478
5100	501	487
5200	498	493
5300	493	497
5400	491	505
5500	490	513
5600	486	519
5700	480	522
5800	477	527
5900	472	530*
6000	462	527
6100	452	525
6200	447	528
6300	441	528

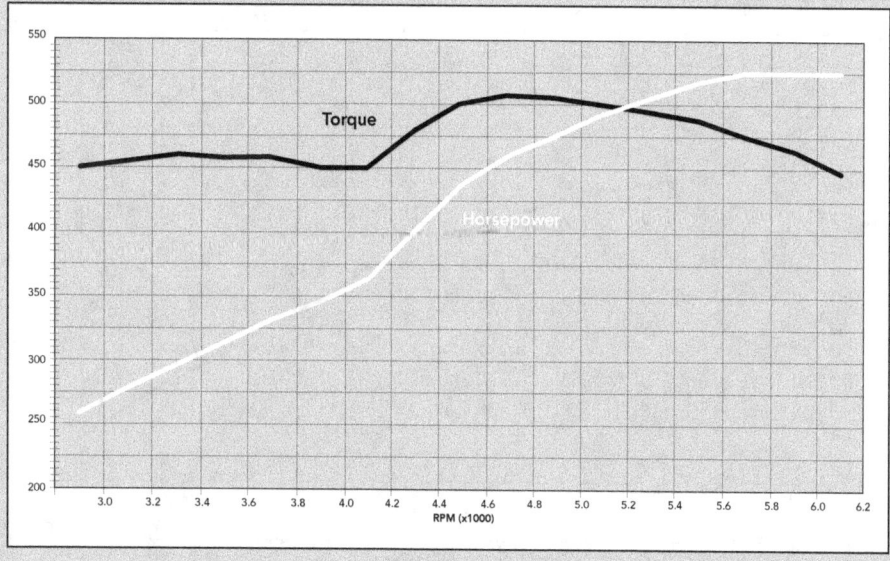

Test 5: 406ci High-Horsepower

Engine:	406ci, 4.155 x 3.75
Power:	581 @ 6,300, 1.43 hp/ci
	554 @ 4,500, 1.36 ft-lb/ci
Compression:	11.5:1, 91 octane fuel
Ignition timing:	36 degrees
Block:	Production iron
Crankshaft:	Callies 4340
Rods:	Eagle 6.0
Pistons & Rings:	JE forged
Oil pan & pump:	Moroso 5-quart
Camshaft:	Isky mechanical roller, 264/274 degrees duration, 0.588/0.588-inch lift, 106° lobe separation
Rocker arms:	1.5:1, 0.020-inch lash
Cylinder heads:	AFR 220cc heads w/ full CNC porting
Valve sizes:	2.06/1.60-inch
Intake manifold:	Edelbrock Super Victor PN 2925
Carburetor:	Holley 950 HP
Ignition:	MSD 6AL
Headers:	1 3/4-inch dyno headers

This 406 is built for horsepower. Unfortunately, again this test starts at peak torque at 4500 rpm, producing a 1500-rpm spread between 4500 and 6300 rpm that spreads to as high as 6600 rpm. This is as much as 2100 rpm, which again is an excellent power area, allowing the user to short-shift by as much as 400 rpm if necessary with very little difference in peak power. What's interesting is the rather large camshaft necessary to create this power. Despite the 264 degrees of duration at 0.050-inch tappet lift, the engine still makes great torque at 4500 rpm. For a street engine, it's possible to shorten the camshaft slightly to increase the torque, but this will pull the peak horsepower down as well. This engine was tested on 91-octane pump fuel despite the 11.5:1 static compression ratio. This is due to the late intake closing of the long duration roller cam. This engine offers the best horsepower per cubic inch below 6,500 rpm of all the test engines included in this book. This combination does not need to spin to 7,000 rpm yet still makes almost 600 hp. This would be a tough combination to beat at the same RPM.

Part of this combination's success is certainly the compression. The standard is roughly 3 percent power for every point in compression increase. The difference between 10.5:1 and 11.5:1 compression is approximately 18 hp.

Test Results

RPM	TQ	HP	BSFC
4500	554*	475	0.444
4600	549	481	0.438
4700	548	490	0.434
4800	546	499	0.427
4900	543	507	0.421
5000	542	516	0.414
5100	540	525	0.424
5200	539	534	0.427
5300	536	541	0.425
5400	532	547	0.430
5500	528	553	0.433
5600	524	559	0.438
5700	520	564	0.450
5800	515	570	0.468
5900	506	569	0.476
6000	501	572	0.484
6100	493	573	0.487
6200	488	576	0.476
6300	484	581*	0.474
6400	476	581	0.475
6500	469	581	0.480
6600	461	580	0.476

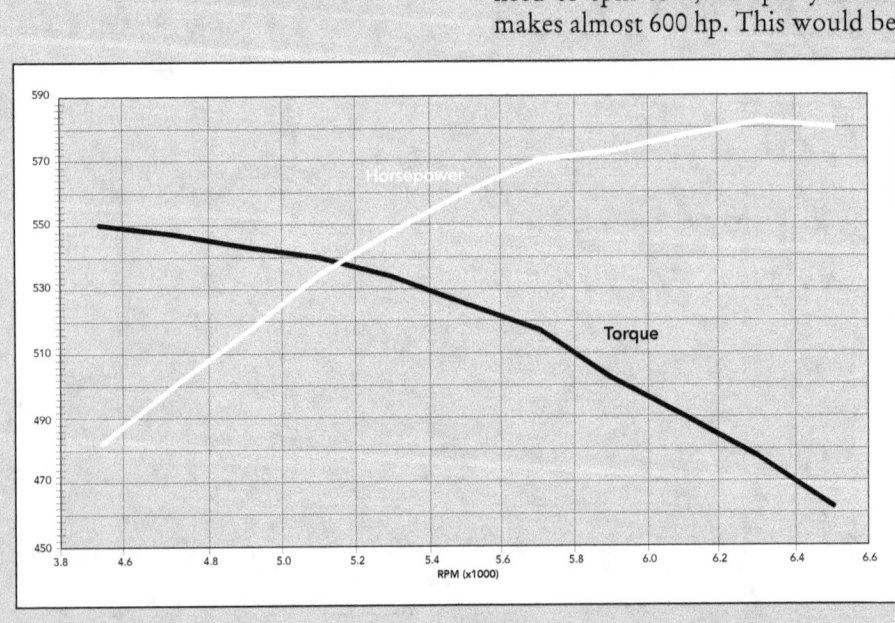

Power Packages

Test 6: 454ci Monster Mouse

This monster 454 runs on pump gas and offers outstanding torque and horsepower throughout its entire RPM curve. The test, unfortunately, didn't start low enough for us at 4,000 rpm. It would have been better to see what kind of torque this big small block could generate at 2200 rpm, but given the fact that it makes an amazing 559 ft-lbs at 4,000, the chances are good that this engine is capable of at least 500 ft-lbs at 3,000 rpm. You won't need a high stall converter with this bruiser! Also note the impressive 1,900 rpm spread between peak torque at 4,500 and peak horsepower at 6,400. Most engines are doing well with a 1,500 rpm-spread. If you pay attention to engines, you should have already picked up on the fact that this 454ci small-block with not-so-large 220cc intake port heads makes more torque and horsepower than a 454ci big-block with much larger heads.

Engine: 454ci World Products, 4.250 x 4.00
Power: 610 @ 6,400, 1.34 hp/ci
584 ft-lb @ 4,500, 1.28 ft-lb/ci
Compression: 9.1:1
Ignition timing: 34 degrees
Block: World Products Motown iron
Crankshaft: 4130 forged steel
Rods: Eagle H-beam
Pistons & Rings: JE forged aluminum
Oil pan & pump: Milodon 6-quart
Camshaft: Crane flat tappet mech., 244/252, 0.516/0.525-inch lift, 106° lobe separation
Rocker arms: 1.5:1 aluminum roller rockers
Cylinder heads: Motown iron 220cc
Valve sizes: 2.135/1.60-inch Manley stainless steel
Intake manifold: World Products dual plane
Carburetor: Bill Mitchell 870 cfm-modified Holley
Ignition: HEI
Headers: Hooker 1 3/4-inch

Test Results

RPM	TQ	HP	BSFC
4000	559	426	.413
4100	565	441	.386
4200	574	459	.378
4300	579	474	.371
4400	582	487	.379
4500	584*	500	.377
4600	582	510	.373
4700	580	520	.378
4800	581	531	.380
4900	579	540	.390
5000	575	547	.388
5100	572	556	.387
5200	572	566	.387
5300	569	575	.395
5400	565	581	.394
5500	555	581	.411
5600	544	580	.419
5700	535	581	.420
5800	527	582	.426
5900	521	586	.433
6000	516	590	.435
6100	511	593	.444
6200	510	602	.439
6300	506	607	.440
6400	501	610*	.438
6500	490	606	.436

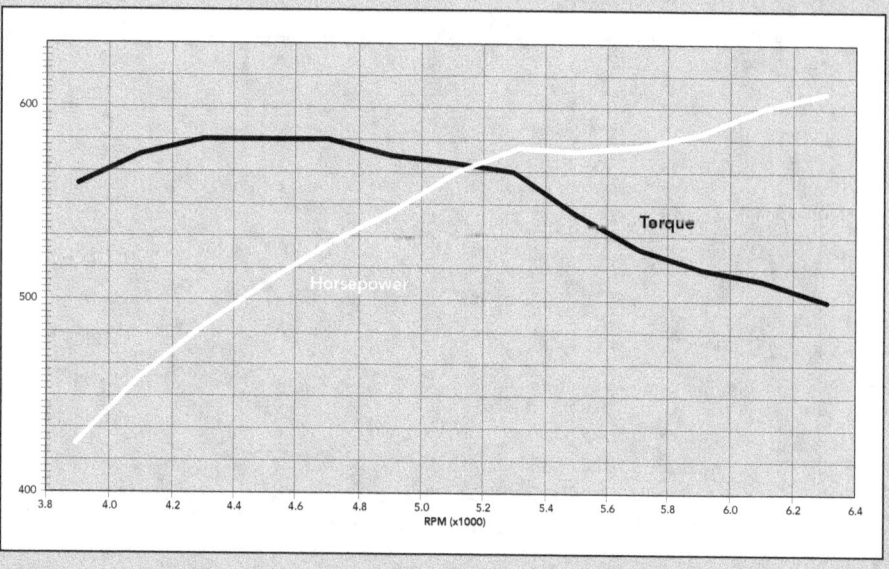

How To Build Big-Inch Chevy Small-Blocks

Test 7: 383ci Quarter Pounder

Engine:	383ci, 4.030 x 3.75
Power:	622 hp @ 7,200,
	1.62 hp/ci
	475 ft-lb @ 6,100,
	1.24 ft-lb/ci
Compression:	13:1
Ignition timing:	37 degrees
Block:	Iron production block
Crankshaft:	4340 steel Crower crank
Rods:	5.7-inch I beam, 4340 Oliver
Pistons & Rings:	JE forged, 1/16-inch rings
Oil pan & pump:	Billet Specialties
Camshaft:	Comp custom mechanical roller 276/288 degrees @ 0.050, 0.660/0.630-inch
Rocker arms:	1.5 Hi-Tech roller
Cylinder heads:	AFR 220cc
Valve sizes:	2.0/1.60-inch stainless steel
Intake manifold:	Edelbrock Super Victor, PN 2925
Carburetor:	Demon 850 cfm w/ 2-inch spacer
Ignition:	MSD-6AL
Headers:	Hooker 1 7/8-inch open exhaust

With a peak torque level at 6,100 rpm, this is a marginal street engine especially with a peak horsepower coming at 7,500 rpm. To maximize acceleration, shift points are generally 500 rpm above the peak horsepower point, which puts this engine at 8,000 rpm. This 383 does offers a fairly wide power band of 1,400 rpm between 6,100 and 7,500 rpm, but this power level almost demands a strong, race oriented manual gear box like a Jerico 4 or 5-speed and a deep rear gear. Neither of these situations lend themselves to street operation. Plus, you'd better be checking those valvesprings on a weekly basis and look at those roller tappets every 100 runs. This engine will demand serious spring pressure, which also abuses the tappets.

Test Results

RPM	TQ	HP	BSFC
4000	421	320	0.484
4100	418	326	0.584
4200	419	335	0.596
4300	424	347	0.614
4400	428	359	0.556
4500	431	369	0.487
4600	433	379	0.454
4700	434	388	0.458
4800	438	400	0.450
4900	445	415	0.436
5000	448	427	0.425
5100	452	439	0.417
5200	455	450	0.416
5300	459	463	0.416
5400	462	475	0.418
5500	465	487	0.423
5600	469	500	0.422
5700	469	509	0.437
5800	472	522	0.444
5900	472	531	0.445
6000	474	542	0.447
6100	475*	552	0.448
6200	475	561	0.448
6300	473	567	0.446
6400	468	570	0.450
6500	465	575	0.448
6600	460	578	0.446
6700	454	579	0.451
6800	449	582	0.451
6900	445	585	0.454
7000	440	587	0.454
7100	441	597	0.478
7200	437	600	0.476
7300	443	616	0.490
7400	436	615	0.493
7500	436	622*	0.471

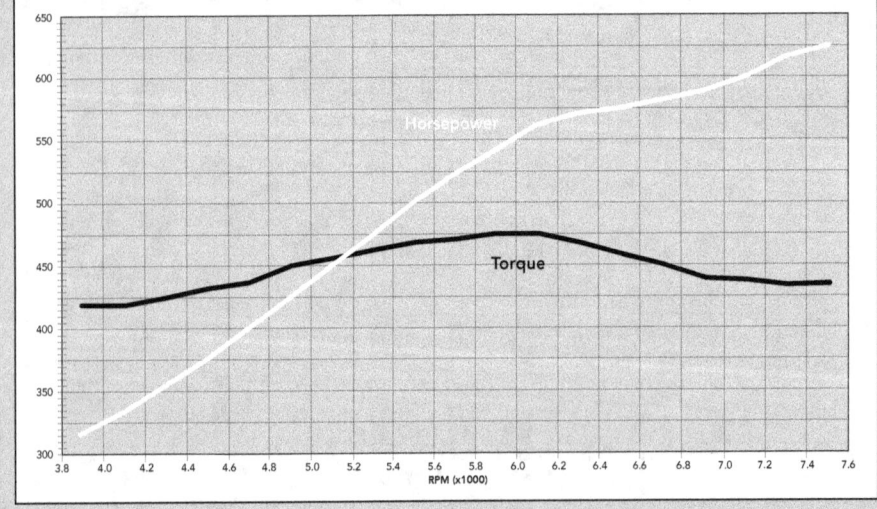

Appendix A

Source Guide

Automotive Racing Products
531 Spectrum Circle
Oxnard, CA 93030
800/826-3045
805/278-RACE (7223)
www.arp-bolts.com

ATI Performance Products
6747 Whitestone Rd.
Baltimore, MD 21207
410/ 298-4343
www.performanceproducts.com

Air Flow Research
10490 Ilex Ave.
Pacoima, CA 91331-3137
www.airflowresearch.com
818/ 890-0616

American Speed Racing Engines
3006 23rd Ave.
Moline, IL 61265
309/ 764-3601

Arias Industries
13420 S. Normandie Ave.
Gardena, CA 90249
310/ 532-9737
www.ariaspistons.com

Aviaid Performance Oiling Systems
10041 Canoga Ave.
Chatsworth, CA 91311
818/ 998-8991
www.aviaid.com

Beck Racing Engines
21616 N. Central Ave.
Suite 1
Phoenix, AZ 85024
623/ 780-1001
www.beckracingengines.com

Demon Carburetion
1450 McDonald Rd.
Dahlonega, GA 30533
706/864-4712
www.demoncarbs.com

Billet Fabrication
649 Easy St., Suite F
Simi Valley, CA 93065
805/ 584-0428
www.billetfab.com

BLP Products
1015 W. Church St.
Orlando, FL 32805
407/ 422-0394
800/ 624-1358
www.blp.com

Borla Performance Industries
5901 Edison Drive
Oxnard, CA 93033
805/ 986-8600
www.borla.com

Brodix, Inc.
P.O. Box D
301 Maple St.
Mena, AR 71953
501/ 394-1075
www.brodix.com

Burns Stainless
1013 West 18th Street
Costa Mesa, CA 92627
714/ 631-5120
www.burnsstainless.com

Callies Performance Products
202 South Main Street
Fostoria, OH 44830
419/ 435-2711
www.callies.com

Canfield Heads
580 W. Main St.
Canfield, OH 44406
330/ 533-7092
www.canfieldheads.com

Canton Racing Products
14 Commerce Drive
North Branford, CT 06471
203/ 481-9460
www.cmfilters.com

Childs & Albert
24849 Anza Drive
Valencia, CA 91355
661/ 295-1900
www.childs-albert.com

Cloyes Gear and Products
P.O. Box 287C
Paris, AR 72855
501/ 963-2105
www.cloyes.com

Cola Cranks
19122 South Santa Fe
Rancho Dominquez, CA 90221
310/537-0506
www.colacranks.com

Comp Cams
3406 Democrat Rd.
Memphis, TN 38118
901/ 795-2400
800/ 999-0853 Cam Help
www.compcams.com

Competition Products
3200 Medalist Dr.
Oshkosh, WI 54901
920/233-2023
800/233-0199 ORDERS
www.competitionproducts.com

How To Build Big-Inch Chevy Small-Blocks

Appendix A

Crane Cams
530 Fentress Blvd.
Daytona Beach, FL 32014
904/ 252-1151
904/ 258-6174 Tech line
www.cranecams.com

Crower Cams & Equipment
3333 Main St.
Chula Vista, CA 91911
619/ 422-1191
www.crower.com

Dart Machinery
353 Oliver Dr.
Troy, MI 48084
248/ 362-1188
www.dartheads.com

Diamond Racing Products
23003 Diamond Drive
Clinton Township, MI 48035
877/552-2112
www.diamondracing.net

Dynatech Competition Exhaust
P.O. Box 608
Boonville, IN 47601
800/ 848-5850
Dynatechheaders.com

Eagle Specialty Products
8530 Aaron Lane
Southaven, MS 38671
662/ 796-7373

Edelbrock
2700 California St.
Torrance, CA 90503
310/ 781-2222
800/ 416-8628 Tech Line
www.edelbrock.com

Electromotive, Inc.
9131 Centreville Road
Manassas, VA 20110-5208
703/ 331-0100
www.directignition.com

Federal-Mogul Corporation
Fel-Pro, Speed-Pro
P.O. Box 1966
Detroit, MI 48235
810/ 354-7700
www.federal-mogul.com

FilterMag
PO Box 2640
2145 McCulloch Blvd.
Lave Havasu City, AZ 86405
800/3345-8376
520/ 505-8108
www.filtermag.com

Flowmaster
100 Stoney Point Rd., #125
Santa Rosa, CA 95401
800/ 544-4761
707/ 544-4761
www.flowmastermufflers.com

Fluidyne Racing Products
2605 E Cedar St.
Ontario, CA 91761
800/fluidyne
800/358-4396
www.fluidyne.com

Mr Gasket Company
ACCEL/DFI, Erson Cams, Mallory
10601 Memphis Ave. #12
Cleveland, OH 44144
216/ 688-8300
216/ 749-0442 FAX
www.mrgasket.com

GM Performance Products
800/ 577-6888 for the nearest GM
Performance Parts dealer

Hedman Hedders
16410 Manning Way
Cerritos, CA 90703
562/ 921-0404
www.hedman.com

High Performance Coatings
550 West 3615 South
Salt Lake City, UT 84115
801/ 262-6807
www.hpcoatings.com

Holley Tech Service
P.O. Box 10360
Bowling Green, KY 42102-7360
270/ 781-9741
800/ HOLLEY-1 For nearest dealer
www.holley.com

Holley Performance Products
Earlís, Hooker, Lunati, NOS,
1801 Russellville Road
P.O. Box 10360
Bowling Green, KY 42102-7360
270/ 782-2900
800/ HOLLEY-1 (465-5391) for dealer
270/ 781-9741 Tech Line
www.holley.com
Lunati Tech 901/ 365-0950
Earl's Tech 310/ 609-1602
NOS Tech 714/545-8319

Iskenderian Racing Cams
16020 S. Broadway St.
Gardena, CA 90248
323/ 770-0930
www.lskycams.com

JE Pistons
15312 Connector Lane
Huntington Beach, CA 92649
714/ 898-9763
www.jepistons.com

K&N Engineering
P.O. Box 1329
Riverside, CA 92502
909/ 684-9762
www.Knfilters.com

L.A. Enterprises
16615 Edwards Dr.
Cerritos, CA 90703
562/ 926-0434
www.crankshaft.com

Lingenfelter Performance
1557 Winchester Rd.
Decatur, IN 46733
260/ 724-2552
www.lingenfelter.com

Manley Performance Products
1960 Swarthmore Ave.
Lakewood, NJ 08701
732/ 905-3366
www.manleyperformance.com

Melling Automotive Products
2620 Saradan Drive
Jackson, MI 49204
517/ 787-8172
www.melling.com

Metallic Ceramic Coatings, Inc.
(Jet-Hot)
55 E. Front St.
Bridgesport, PA 19405
610/ 277-2444
610/277-5646 Tech
www.jet-hot.com

Milodon, Inc.
20716 Plummer Street
Chatsworth, CA 91311
818/ 407-1211
www.milodon.com

Bill Mitchell Products
35 Trade Zone Drive
Ronkonkoma, NY 11779
631/ 737-0372
www.theengineshop.com

Moroso Performance Products
80 Carter Dr.
Guilford, CT 06437
203/ 453-6571
www.moroso.com

Source Guide

Oliver Racing Parts
1025 Clancy Ave. N.E.
Grand Rapids, MI 49503
616/ 451-8333
800/ 253-8108
www.oiliver-rods.com

Performance Trends, Inc.
Box 573
Dearborn Heights, MI 48127
248/ 473-9230
www.performancetrends.com

Powerhouse Products
3402 Democrat Road
Memphis, TN 38118
800/ 872-7223 ORDERS
901/ 795-7600
www.powerhouseproducts.com

Professional Products
12705 S. Van Ness Ave.
Hawthorne, CA 90250
323/ 779-2020
www.professional-products.com

Proform
28314 Hayes Ave.
Roseville, MU 48066
800/ 521-1005
810/ 774-2500
www.proformparts.com

Quick Fuel Technologies
2352 Russellville Road
Bowling Green, KY 42101
270/ 793-0900
www.quickfueltechnology.com

Reher-Morrison Racing Engines
1120 Enterprise Place
Arlington, TX 76017
817/ 467-7171
www.rehermorrison.com

Ross Racing Pistons
625 S. Douglas
El Segundo, CA 90245
310/ 536-0100 (Tech)
800/ 392-7677 (Orders only)
www.rosspistons.com

Scat Enterprises
1400 Kingsdale Ave.
Redondo Beach, CA 90278
310/ 370-5501
www.scatenterprises.com

Setrab U.S.A. Inc.
P.O. Box H
24 South Clayton, OH 43011
614/ 625-6710
www.setrab.com

School of Automotive Machinists
1911 Antoine
Houston, TX 77055
713/ 683-3817

Scoggin-Dickey Performance Center
5901 Spur 327
Lubbock, TX 79424
800/ 456-0211 Parts Center
806/ 798-4106 Tech Line
www.sdpc2000.com

Silv-O-Lite (KB Pistons)
4909 Goni Road
Carson City, NV 89706
702/882-7790
www.kb-silvolite.com

Stef's Fabrication Specialties
699 Cross St.
Lakewood, NJ 08701
908/ 367-8700
www.stefs.com

Summit Racing Equipment
P.O. Box 909
Akron, OH 44309-0909
800/ 230-3030 ORDERS
330/ 630-0230 Customer Service
www.summitracing.com

Sportsman Racing Pistons
15312 Connector Lane
Huntington Beach, CA 92649
714/ 373-5530
www.SRP.com

T&D Machine Products
4859 Convair Drive
Carson City, NV 89706
702/ 884-2292

Tavia Machine Company
12851 Western Ave.
Unit D
Garden Grove, CA 92641
714/ 892-4057
www.tavia.com

Torque Technologies
1826 Woodland Dr.
Valdosta, GA 31601
800/408-0016 Orders
912/ 241-1563 Tech
www.torquetechexh.com

Trick Flow Specialties (TFS)
1248 Southeast Ave.
Tallmadge, OH 44278
330/630-1555
www.trickflow.com

Ultradyne Racing Cams
1881 W. Nail Rd.
Horn Lake, MS 38637
662/ 393-8511
www.ultradyne.com

Venolia
2160 Cherry Industrial Cir
Long Beach, 90805
323/ 636-9329
562/531-8463
www.venoliapistons.com

Victor-Reinz Gaskets
Dana Corp.
PO Box 455
Toledo, OH 43697
419/ 891-1900
708/ 271-4878
www.dana.com

Walker Corp.
DynoMax Performance Exhaust
500 North Field Drive
Lake Forest, IL 60045
847/ 482-5000
800/ 767-DYNO (3966) Nearest Dealer
800/ 594-9815 tech
www.dynomax.com

Westech Performance Group
11098 Venture Drive, Suite C
Mira Loma, CA 91752
909/ 685-4767
www.westechperformance.com

Wilson Manifolds
4700 N.E. 11th Ave
Ft. Lauderdale, FL 33334
954/ 771-6216
www.wilsonmanifolds.com

Wiseco Pistons, Inc.
7201 Industrial Park Blvd.
Mentor, OH 44060
216/ 951-6600
www.wiseco.com

World Products
35330 Stanley
Sterling Heights, MI 48312
810/ 939-9628
www.worldcastings.com

Engine Build Sheet

Photocopy this form and keep it in a file for each engine

Engine Blueprint Record

Engine Type	
Build Date	
Displacement	
Special Notes:	

Block

Material	
Manuf./PN	
Bore Size	
Cam Location	
Main Bearing Dia.	
Special Mods:	

Piston Diameter and Bore Clearance

Cylinder #	1	3	5	7
Bore Dia.				
Piston Dia.				
Clearance				

Cylinder #	2	4	6	8
Bore Dia.				
Piston Dia.				
Clearance				
Width				

Piston

Piston Brand/PN	
Compression Height	
Wrist Pin Brand/PN	
Wrist Pin Dia./Length	
Wrist Pin Clearance	
Wrist Pin Retainer	

Piston Ring

Ring Brand/PN	
Top Ring Type	
Width	
Side Clearance	
End Gap	
2nd Ring Type	
Width	
Side Clearance	
End Gap	
Oil Ring Type	
Side Clearance	
Gap	

Piston Deck Height

Cylinder #	1	3	5	7
Deck Height				

Cylinder #	2	4	6	8
Deck Height				

Notes

Rod and Main Bearings

Main Bearing Brand/PN	
Rod Bearing Brand/PN	
Camshaft Bearing Brand/PN	

Crankshaft

Crankshaft Brand/PN					
Stroke					
End Play					

Main	1	2	3	4	5
Main Bore					
Main Bore w/bearing					
Crank Main Journal					
Main Bearing Clearance					

Conn. Rod	1	3	5	7
Big End Dia.				
Big End Dia. w/bearing				
Crank Journal Dia.				
Rod Bearing Clearance				

Conn. Rod	2	4	6	8
Big End Dia.				
Big End Dia. w/bearing				
Crank Journal Dia.				
Rod Bearing Clearance				

Connecting Rods

Rod Brand/PN				
Length (Center to Center)				
Side Clearance	1-2	3-4	5-6	7-8
Wrist Pin/Piston Clearance				
Wrist Pin/Rod Clearance				
Rod Bolt Brand/PN				
Rod Bolt Torque				
Rod Bolt Stretch				

Valvetrain Data

Rocker Arms:	
Make	
PN	
Material	
Offset	
Rocker Arm Ratio:	
Intake	
Exhaust	
Intake Valve Lift	
Exhaust Valve Lift	
Pushrod:	
Length	
Diameter	
Wall Thickness	
Lifter:	
Make/PN	
Diameter	
Offset	
Rev Kit Make	
PN	

Camshaft

Make of Style/Brand	
Cam PN	
Material	
Intake Duration @.050"	
Exhaust Duration @.050"	
Intake installed at Centerline	
Lobe Separation Angle	
Intake Lobe Lift	
Exhaust Lobe Lift	
Intake Valve to Piston Clearance @ 10° ATDC	
Exhaust Valve to Piston Clearance @ 10° BTDC	
Intake Valve Lash	
Exhaust Valve Lash	

How To Build Big-Inch Chevy Small-Blocks

Cylinder Head

Brand/PN	
Chamber Volume	
Intake Port Volume (cc)	
Intake Valve Type/PN	
Intake Valve Size	
Exhaust Valve Type/PN	
Exhaust Valve Size	
Valvespring Brand/PN	
Valvespring	
Inside Diameter	
Outside Diameter	
Installed Height	
Intake/Exhaust	
Valvespring Seat Pressure	
Valvespring Open Pressure	
Coil Bind Height	
Retainer Make/PN	
Keeper Make/PN	
Head Gasket Thickness	

Engine Balancing

Piston Weight (grams)	
Wrist Pin	
Pin Locks	
Ring Set (1 Piston)	
Rod, Small End	
Total Reciprocating Weight	
Rod, Big End	
Rod Bearing (1 Pair)	
Oil	
Total Rotating Weight	
Balance Percent* 0.50 for V-8 90-degree	
Bob Weight = 2 x (Reciprocating Wt. x .50 + Rotating Weight)	

Cylinder Head Flow

Modifications	
Flow Bench	
Test Pressure	
Bore Fixture Dia.	
Intake Valve Dia.	
Exhaust Valve Dia.	

Intake Flow

Lift	CFM
.100	
.200	
.300	
.400	
.500	
.600	
.700	

Exhaust Flow

Lift	CFM	Exh. to Int. %
.100		
.200		
.300		
.400		
.500		
.600		
.700		

Compression Ratio

Swept Volume*	
Dome (-) or Dish (+) Volume	
Ring Land Volume	
Deck Volume	
Head Gasket Volume	
Chamber Volume	
Total Volume	

$$CR = \frac{\text{Total Volume}}{\text{Total - Swept Volume}}$$

CR = _____ : 1

*Swept Volume (cc) = Bore^2 x Stroke x 12.87

Notes

Notes

www.ingramcontent.com/pod-product-compliance
Lightning Source LLC
Chambersburg PA
CBHW051413070526
44584CB00023B/3413